THE ODYSSEY
OF ECHO COMPANY

THE 1968 TET OFFENSIVE AND THE EPIC BATTLE
TO SURVIVE THE VIETNAM WAR

DOUG STANTON

SCRIBNER

NEW YORK   LONDON   TORONTO   SYDNEY   NEW DELHI

Scribner
An Imprint of Simon & Schuster, Inc.
1230 Avenue of the Americas
New York, NY 10020

First Scribner hardcover edition September 2017

SCRIBNER and design are registered trademarks of The Gale Group, Inc.,
used under license by Simon & Schuster, Inc., the publisher of this work.

For information about special discounts for bulk purchases,
please contact Simon & Schuster Special Sales at 1-866-506-1949
or business@simonandschuster.com.

The Simon & Schuster Speakers Bureau can bring authors to your live event. For more
information or to book an event, contact the Simon & Schuster Speakers Bureau at 1-866-
248-3049 or visit our website at www.simonspeakers.com.

Manufactured in the United States of America

1   3   5   7   9   10   8   6   4   2

Library of Congress Cataloging-in-Publication Data is available.

ISBN 978-1-4767-6191-6
ISBN 978-1-4767-6193-0 (ebook)

Insert photograph credits: 1–5, 7–8, 10, 12–19, 25–40, courtesy of Stan Parker; 6, 11, 22–23,
courtesy of Jerry Austin and Al Dove; 9, courtesy of Maureen Bell; 20–21, 24, courtesy of
Jerry Austin; 41–46, courtesy of Tony Demin. Photograph on p. 290 courtesy of Tony Demin.

For the men and their families of Recon Platoon,
Echo Company, 1st Battalion (Airborne),
501st Infantry Regiment,
2nd Brigade, 101st Airborne Division,
in honor of their service to their families,
neighbors, and country

And for those still coming home,
body and soul

For when the rambler returns from the mountain-slopes into the valley, he brings not a handful of earth, which would explain nothing to anyone, but instead some hard-won word he has gained, pure and simple.
—Rainer Maria Rilke, "The Ninth Elegy"

Some wHere R.U.N
? JAN 68

Dear Maureen,
    I rec. your most welcome
letter yesterday. Man was I glad
to hear from ya and thanks for
that ear picture of you I've got
it with me now, (we're to turn
in any pictures etc before we go
to the boonies, and if we get any
shit in the boonies turn it in
to the supply chopper) But I've
still got you picture. Lets hope
it brings me good luck.
    I've been I in the boonies
for a week now, I sure am
beat. We got 3 ——s (V.C.) last
night on an ambush, it
sure helped my morale.

CONTENTS

AUTHOR'S NOTE

The events recounted in this book are based on dozens of interviews with U.S. soldiers and civilians, as well as those living in Vietnam during the war. These interviews, some of which were in-depth and stretched over a series of days—and, in some cases, years—took place in the United States and Vietnam. Most dwelled on the subjects' firsthand recollections of events related in this book. In addition, the author traveled to the region described in these pages. The author's research also included examination of personal journals, previously published media accounts, contemporaneous photography, and official U.S. military logs and histories.

Many of the events described here transpired under traumatic circumstances. For this reason, and perhaps because memory is often imperfect, the recollections of some of the participants conflicted at times. While the author has made every attempt to present an accurate portrait of the events involved, he has related the version that seemed most consistent with other accounts.

THE RECON PLATOON IN VIETNAM, DECEMBER 1967–DECEMBER 1968

ECHO COMPANY, 1ST BATTALION (AIRBORNE), 501ST INFANTRY REGIMENT, 2ND BRIGADE, 101ST AIRBORNE DIVISION, U.S. ARMY

Of Recon Platoon's original forty-six members—listed in bold— including forward observers in the Mortar Platoon, three were killed in action, twenty-three were wounded in action once, four were wounded twice, and four were wounded three times, totaling a 74 percent casualty rate.

Recon Platoon Headquarters

First Lieutenant John W. Gay, *platoon leader, reassigned to Division LRRPs in late February,* WIA May 23, 1969

Second Lieutenant David Lewis, *platoon leader, assigned late February,* WIA March 20, 1968

Staff Sergeant Freddie E. Westerman, *platoon sergeant,* WIA March 23, 1968

Specialist/4 Timothy R. Anderson, *rifleman/RTO*

SP/4 Thomas A. Soals, *rifleman/RTO,* WIA March 14, 1968

Medics from Headquarters & Headquarters Company 1/501

SP/5 Troy Fulton

SP/5 Paul Sudano, WIA September 17, 1968

SP/4 Daniel Bagley, WIA May 7, 1968

SP/4 Charles Fowler, WIA March 21, 1968

1st Squad

SSG Lee W. Bruce, *squad leader*, WIA March 29, 1968

Sergeant Anthony F. Beke, *rifleman/scout*, WIA March 22 and
29, 1968, and May 17, 1968

SGT Jimmy Benefjedo, *rifleman/scout, March replacement,* WIA
May 6, 1968

SGT Larry Kass, *assistant squad leader,* KIA February 17, 1968

SP/4 Marvin S. Acker, *rifleman/scout,* WIA March 22 and 26,
1968

SP/4 Roy L. Cloer, *M-60/rifleman/scout*

SP/4 Douglas Fleming, *rifleman/scout,* WIA March 29, 1968

SP/4 Dwight D. Lane, *M-60 machine gunner,* WIA April 2,
1968

SP/4 Clifton G. Naylor, *rifleman/scout,* WIA March 7, 1968

SP/4 John W. Payne, *rifleman/scout,* WIA January 15, 1968

SP/4 Charles Pyle, *rifleman/scout,* WIA March 21, 1968, KIA
March 22, 1968

SP/4 Luis Zendejas, *rifleman/scout, February/March replacement,* WIA March 22 and April 2, 1968

Private First Class Phillip Anthony, *rifleman/scout, March
replacement,* WIA April 14, 1968

PFC David Bain, *rifleman/scout, March replacement,* WIA April
9 and 14, 1968

PFC Sam Cooper, *rifleman/scout, late-February replacement,* WIA March 20, 1968

PFC Harold Holt, *rifleman/scout/RTO*

PFC Warren R. Jewell, *rifleman/scout,* WIA March 22, 1968

PFC Eddie Johnson, *rifleman/scout, March replacement,* WIA April 2, 1968

PFC Richard Lapa, *rifleman/scout, February/March replacement,* WIA March 22, 1968

PFC Allen Lawrence, *rifleman/scout, late-February replacement,* WIA March 16, 1968

2nd Squad

SSG Lindsey F. Kinney, *squad leader,* WIA February 18 and March 23, 1968

SGT Ronald W. Kleckler, *assistant squad leader,* WIA February 16, February 18, and July 26, 1968

SGT Michael A. Corcoran, *rifleman/scout,* WIA December 1968

SP/4 Ronald L. Bard, *rifleman/scout, late-February replacement,* WIA March 22 and April 2, 1968

SP/4 Donald F. Curtner, *rifleman/scout,* WIA September 17, 1968

SP/4 Albert W. Dove, *M-60 machine gunner,* WIA February 18, 1968

SP/4 John E. (Mickey) Evans, *rifleman/scout, March replacement,* WIA September 17, 1968

SP/4 Terry G. Hinote, *rifleman/scout,* WIA February 18, 1968

SP/4 Dennis P. Kilbury, *assistant gunner, rifleman/scout,* WIA March 22, 1968

SP/4 Brian H. Lewis, *rifleman/scout,* WIA March 22, 1968

SP/4 John S. (Stan) Parker, *assistant gunner, rifleman/scout,*
WIA February 18, March 14, and April 29, 1968

SP/4 Angel L Rivera, *rifleman/scout,* WIA February 18, 1968

SP/4 Guido D. Russo, *rifleman/RTO,* WIA February 18 and
March 22, 1968

SP/4 Albert L. Smyth, *rifleman/scout, March replacement,* WIA
July 7, 1968

SP/4 Joe Weise, *rifleman/scout, March replacement,* WIA April
20, 1968

SP/4 Francis O. Wongus, *rifleman/scout,* WIA March 22, 1968

PFC Jerry W. Boutwell, *March replacement*

PFC Darryl Lintner, *March 8 replacement,* KIA April 20, 1968

PFC Charles R. Mansell, *rifleman/scout,* WIA June 8, 1968

3rd Squad

SSG Diogenes F. Misola, *squad leader*

SGT James Brown, *assistant squad leader, late-February replacement,* WIA March 20, 1968

SGT Tony Ramirez, *assistant squad leader*

SGT John A. Lucas, *assistant squad leader, ETS early 1968*

SP/4 John H. Arnold, *rifleman/scout/RTO*

SP/4 Jerry R. Austin, *rifleman/scout,* WIA March 29 and July 12,
1968, and May 12, 1969

SP/4 Michael D. Bradshaw, *rifleman/scout*

SP/4 Robert A. Cromer, *rifleman/scout*

SP/4 Ronald Darb, *rifleman/scout, April replacement,* WIA June,
8, 1968

SP/4 Jackie Foster, *rifleman/scout, February/March replacement,*
WIA March 27, 1968

SP/4 Olen R. Queen, *M-60 machine gunner,* WIA March 21, 1968

SP/4 Brian D. Riley, *rifleman/scout*

SP/4 Dennis A. Tinkle, *rifleman/scout,* WIA February 18, 1968

SP/4 David S. Watts Jr., *assistant gunner, rifleman/scout,* WIA October 4, 1968

PFC John Geren, *rifleman/scout, March replacement,* WIA April 29, 1968

PFC Ricky Brooks, *rifleman/scout, March replacement,* WIA May 8, 1968

4.2-Inch Mortar Platoon Forward Observers (FO)
from E Company to Recon Platoon

SGT Andrew M. Obeso, *forward observer*

SP/4 Ronald L. Kuvik, *forward observer,* WIA April 20 and June 8, 1968

SP/4 Marvin Penry, *forward observer,* KIA March 29, 1968

SP/4 David Williams, *forward observer,* WIA June 8, 1968

INVOCATION

January 31, 1968

Landing Zone Jane, Northern I Corps near Hai Lang, South Vietnam

It's 4:00 a.m. when they attack.

Stan lifts himself up from the puddle, whiskered face dripping wet. He's been sleeping in cold water, trying to pull an imaginary blanket over his aching shoulders, water filling his nose, his ears . . . He hears whistles. Shrill whistles, like a referee's, the same sound he'd heard in high school when he was about to pin a wrestling opponent. But now soldiers are running past him. What's happening?

He feels a blow to the head and he's knocked dizzy.

He tries standing, but he can't. He can't move. His cold bed made of muddy water has left him numb. He's scared. He's so utterly embarrassed and ashamed about this. Who's watching? he wonders. Who will know I can't move? He sees an enemy soldier running in his direction. A sweaty face. Lit by flashes as it gallops toward him, coming into focus. Stan freezes. He sees the soldier's silver bayonet riding toward him, the sharp point swinging back and forth in the damp air, hunting him, when the soldier pitches forward and the bayonet falls past Stan's face, just missing. The enemy soldier crashes down on Stan.

He looks up and sees another soldier, an American, an older seasoned trooper, jerking his own bayonet from the attacking soldier's back. The trooper yells, urging him to get up.

The dead soldier is dressed in khaki pants and shirt, the uniform of the North Vietnamese Army. He's young, maybe Stan's age, nineteen or twenty. Stan's never been this close to or touched a dead person before, except when he said good-bye to his mother at her funeral a few months back. He pushes the body away and jumps up.

And he starts running.

He runs toward the concertina wire at the rim of the hill where the landing zone (LZ Jane) is situated. Stan knows the 101st Airborne soldiers have to hold the wire—but how? Artillery is blasting now, long shells crunching over Stan's head, sailing into the dark. The ground is shaking. Illumination flares throw gray shadows against the trees, making enormous apparitions that crawl through the branches, limb to limb.

Stan looks down the hill and sees hundreds of NVA soldiers pouring up the scrubby draw at him. He's afraid of dying. He drops to one knee and starts firing his M-16. And then he sees something even more amazing.

The enemy soldiers start pole-vaulting over the wire.

They run up the hill, bamboo poles bouncing on their shoulders, plant the poles, swing up into the night, illuminated by the flares, hang there, captured at this apex as if in a photograph . . . and fall back to earth on the other side of the wire. Others who leap across the sky disappear in red mist or an expanding cloud of bone as the machine gunners pour fire into them. The heavy rounds eat the men right out of the air.

The surviving pole vaulters run past Stan, headed toward the center of the LZ, clutching canvas pouches.

Stan hears someone yell, "Sappers!"

In the pouches are explosives. The sappers are headed on sui-cide missions to the command bunker.

Everyone in the platoon fires at these running men. When hit, the men detonate with a mighty force. Stan looks up—it's begun to rain. He tastes blood.

It's raining men, exploded men.

And then something flashes in him, some loom is unfolded in him, and the loom's shuttle commences back and forth, across the soft treasure of who he is. Shuttle, whisper, weave; shuttle. Back in high school, he heard stories of nights like these, of U.S. sol-diers overrun in their camp by the North Vietnamese and the Viet Cong soldiers. Around him, the long barrels of machine guns start to glow red. An NVA soldier, ten feet away, raises his rifle to fire— Stan shoots him. He lunges with his bayonet into another man as he rushes past him.

Stan catches a quick movement—something lands on his shoul-der, light as a bird.

He turns and sees two detached fingers perched on his uniform, trembling as he breathes. Pointed upward, they grow still. He lifts his eyes.

The sky, the sky. Who is watching this? Who?

Dear Maureen

Howdy Kid! I rec. your sec. letter to
was glad to hear from you again. I'm back in
base camp (Cu Chi) now, got back Fri night.
made it through that one day and night that
aid was comming up in my last letter.
pe you got it, cause I gave it to a door
gunner on a chopper that brought some suppl
to to us, and ask him to mail it for me. We
e got back Fri night I guess Charlie was
inda mad at us, for he blasted the hell out o
back at base camp with mortar rounds. It
lled three guys and wounded 13. And again
st night more mortar rounds, killing two
nd wounding 11 more guys. The first night I
as taking a shower when it started (our showe
just two big jet fuel tanks on top of a few
y's about 150 yds from our barracks and som
yds from the mortar shelter.) Well there I
s in my birthday suit running like hell
and the shelter along with 3 other guys. Th
t night I was more prepared for the 120 y
h.

PART I

THE GIRL WITH THE PEACHES

April 20, 2005

Kabul, Afghanistan

I first met Stan Parker in May 2005 when I was climbing into a Chinook helicopter on the tarmac at Bagram Air Base in Afghanistan. I was trying to get to a U.S. Army Special Forces camp in Khost, on the Pakistani border. Wearing wraparound shades and a keffiyeh, Stan was older by at least twenty years than many of the soldiers I saw walking around the airstrip. He was in charge of air operations at Bagram Air Base, and this meant that he had charge of me. Unfortunately, the weather was not cooperating, and we weren't flying anywhere. But fortunately for me, Stan Parker started telling stories while we waited.

Short, sandy-haired, broad-chested, Stan had an easy smile and talked a lot like Robert Duvall in *Lonesome Dove*. He was wearing body armor, with an M-4 carbine slung across his chest. I wouldn't want to mess with him. After thirty-five years of military service, he told me, he was finally thinking of "getting ready for retirement."

His had been quite a career. In 1993, he'd been in the Battle of Mogadishu in Somalia. He'd been part of the Special Forces operation in Honduras, the Philippines, Korea, and Eritrea, Africa. He'd been in gun battles in Afghanistan. When I asked Stan how many firefights he'd been in, he could not come up with an answer—hundreds, perhaps. He had achieved the rank of sergeant major and had been assigned to U.S. Special Operations Command, at MacDill Air Force Base, in Tampa, Florida. He was one of the Army's senior elite soldiers, and, on top of this, he was deeply wired into America's counterterrorism fight across the globe. He knew things. He'd seen things, he told me, "beyond a civilized person's comprehension."

Yet when I'd asked him to name the scariest part of his military career, he said, "Coming home from Vietnam."

And on the day we met, that's what Stan Parker really wanted to talk about: what had happened to him thirty-seven years earlier when he was twenty, during the 1968 Tet Offensive.

Vietnam. 1968. January.

Stan had read my book *In Harm's Way*, and this had given him an idea. He'd seen that story about World War II, and the sinking of a Navy ship and the ordeal of its crew, as a survival story.

Stan wanted to know if I would ever write about how he and his buddies had survived the Tet Offensive, when his forty-six-man Reconnaissance Platoon attacked and was attacked by well-trained North Vietnamese Army and Viet Cong fighters. Stan's odyssey had lasted ninety days, until he was wounded for a third time and forced to leave the intense brotherhood of his unit. A soldier awarded three Purple Hearts had no choice but to be shipped home. In order to stay in Vietnam, he'd refused the third award. (He was subsequently assigned to another unit.)

I took Stan's suggestion about writing this story and filed it under "Maybe." I didn't think America was ready to hear that story while in the midst of the wars in Iraq and Afghanistan. Maybe the country never would be ready. Part of this had to do with the age of the men who'd fought in Vietnam. Now in their late fifties and early sixties, they weren't old enough to want to talk, not just yet.

In September 2012, seven years later, I gave a lecture to cadets and command staff at the U.S. Air Force Academy in Colorado Springs, and I remembered that Stan Parker, now retired, lived nearby. We hadn't spoken in several years, and I called him.

"I've been waiting for you," he said, surprising me. "I've told my buddies about you. We're ready. We want to talk about Vietnam."

The truth was that I'd never forgotten meeting Sergeant Major Stan Parker on that helicopter in Afghanistan. I still remembered the sunlight coming in through the green helo's rear ramp as this old soldier asked me to write about something that had happened to him and his Recon buddies years earlier, something that had affected them deeply and that they didn't understand.

Tom Brokaw, he'd said then, was the only civilian who'd ever looked at his Combat Infantryman Badge with star and recognized that he'd served in Vietnam. Stan had met Brokaw a few months earlier on a helicopter in Afghanistan when he was reporting an NBC News special. Stan had been tasked as his bodyguard. He proudly showed me a photo of their meeting. Back in the late 1990s, Brokaw had discovered the willingness of World War II veterans to unpack their secrets about their war as they turned seventy and felt perhaps that it was time to unburden themselves.

Maybe, just maybe, I wondered, the same might now be true of the more than 2.7 million Americans who had deployed in Vietnam, 1.6 million of whom experienced combat or the threat of attack. Their average ages now ranged from sixty-five to sixty-nine.

That's a lot of people, I thought, *a lot of untold stories*. It seemed time for them to come home.

• • •

Even before he retired, Stan wanted to track down his former Recon 1/501 platoon-mates and ask them what they remembered. Some of them he found on the Internet didn't want to be reminded of the past and hung up when we called. He spent a surreal dinner with a former Recon member who made the nervous admission that he'd never told his wife that he'd served in Vietnam. He pulled Stan aside and begged him not to tell his family. Stan made up a fib that they once worked together many years earlier.

This pattern of evasion troubled him. He wondered what it meant when a person couldn't admit that a major chapter of his life, perhaps its most potent and transformative moment, had ever taken place.

And so Stan and I started to talk at great length over a span of several years. As with so many other stories about Vietnam, Stan's would take a long time to tell. As he and I spoke, I occasionally saw a shadow in his eyes—call it memory, call it flashback. Something was there, traveling back and forth through his consciousness, unresolved. *So many things, Doug. If I talk, I might be whole, I'll be unburdened, I'll be heard. I won't be a better person, I know that, but I might be the person I am. Does that make sense?*

It does.

I want to go on.

Go on.

May 20, 1966

Gary, Indiana

Watch him now, in this moment: It's May 20, 1966, a sweltering, blue-sky afternoon in Gary, Indiana, and Stan Parker is crossing the auditorium stage at Calumet High, his tooled cowboy boots peeking and receding beneath the swirl of his maroon graduation robe. He's slightly bow-legged, possessed of a high IQ, and flashes a friendly smile. From an early age, he'd always been ready to defend the bullied and lonely students in exile, the poor kids in class in their ill-fitting clothes ashamed of their uncombed hair. He reaches out now and grasps his high school diploma. *Freeze.* Watch him now as he looks out from the stage for his mother and father, the smiling, raven-haired Helen Laverne, and the tall, quiet John James Parker. He knows his entire life is ahead of him, yet he doesn't know where this will lead. Will he be a good man? Is he brave? To answer these questions, he's decided to enlist in the U.S. Army, a decision he's kept secret from his parents.

Because he has an older brother, Dub, newly married and already a paratrooper (pending assignment to Vietnam), he knows his mother will disapprove of his decision. His father, he's not so sure about. He figures his dad will think it's fine. Whatever their feelings, Stan Parker can't wait to become a paratrooper.

He hopes he's heading to Vietnam, a small, rural country of 38 million people, 8,400 miles away from Calumet High's gymnasium, a country that many of his classmates couldn't find on a map in Mrs. Miller's geography class. An A student, Stan was often bored by school and couldn't wait to graduate and "see more of the world."

Several days after he graduates, he and five buddies pile into a friend's tiny Chevy Corvair and take off at dawn, so anxious are they that they can hardly sleep the night before. They pull up to the recruiting station and go inside.

Stan and his buddy Tom Gervais have decided they will join up using something called the buddy plan. The Army advertised this as a way for high school friends to stay friends even when they entered military service. It sounded like a good idea, kind of like going off on a long camping trip, except with live ammunition.

Stan first asks the Marine recruiter behind the desk, "Are you going to let me jump out of airplanes?"

The recruiter waits a bit and says, "Second hitch."

"That's what I thought. You sure?"

The recruiter says that's the way it is.

Stan walks out of the office and across the hall into the Army recruiter's.

"Can you guarantee me that I can be a paratrooper?"

"I can't guarantee you will be one," says the Army recruiter, "but I can guarantee you the training, if that's what you want. Making the grade is up to you."

"And I get to go to Vietnam?"

"As a paratrooper? Hell, yeah."

"Okay," says Stan. "Sign me up."

Gervais steps forward and says he's going too.

"We want the buddy plan," says Stan.

The recruiter says that will be fine and explains that the plan allows them to go through basic training together. After that, depending on their ability and progress, he can't promise they'll stay together.

"That's okay, Boots," says Gervais. "We'll go as far as we can."

They next board a U.S. government bus to the Army's induction center in Chicago, where they take an aptitude test and a physical, and are officially sworn in as members of the U.S. Armed Forces. Stan makes it home just in time for supper, tired but elated and still guarding his secret. He can hardly believe the adventure that awaits him.

His only disappointment is that the recruiter told him that he can't begin boot camp, several hundred miles away in Fort Leonard Wood, Missouri, until August. He will have to wait. During the long, hot, ghastly Gary, Indiana, summer, he and his buddies broil in their impatience. To kill time, they cruise the streets, ogling girls, listening to the news on the radio in Gervais's Camaro about a massive buildup of troops in Vietnam. There are 385,300 men already in the country. Stan can't wait to join them.

When the day of departure arrives, August 8, 1966, Stan Parker silently stands in the bedroom doorway in his parents' tidy mobile home, scanning his freshman football trophies (he was a decent running back), his junior and senior wrestling awards (he loved the desperate, solitary nature of the sport), and he wonders if he'll ever return to this room. He knows he could be killed, but he also knows this won't happen to him.

At the end of the bed sit his cowboy boots. He'd worn them so often during high school that he picked up the nickname "Boots." On Friday nights, he and Gervais would pull into the Blue Top Drive-In for a milkshake with their girlfriends. Stan had believed his cowboy get-up let people know that he was his own man. He wants to take the boots with him to Vietnam. Out in the driveway, his father honks the car horn.

He closes the bedroom door and walks past his mother's just-washed breakfast dishes, now in their drying rack, past the neat pile of his father's magazines by his chair, as if seeing these details for the first time in his life. His mom is standing at the door, waiting for him. She's crying. She says, "I know you are doing what you want to do. But please take care of yourself, Troop."

Troop. That's her nickname for him since he enlisted. She kisses his cheek. He promises her that he'll be careful.

Stan opens the door for his mother and they descend the wooden steps and climb into the family's Chrysler New Yorker. Stan slides in beside his high school girlfriend, Maureen, and his younger brothers, Bruce, sixteen, and Joe, six. Maureen lays her head on his shoulder and is quiet. They pull away from the house.

At the Greyhound station in downtown Gary, Stan spots Gervais right away.

"Boots!" yells Gervais.

The two boys run up to each other and hug.

"We're doing it, Boots."

"This is what we've been waiting for," says Stan.

Stan thinks he catches a smile creasing his father's solemn face. Stan knows his father is proud of him—proud and terrified, all at once. His father had been a decorated Army Air Corps and Air Force gunner aboard a World War II bomber, just twenty-three years earlier, which doesn't seem all that long ago to Stan. How different can this new war be? John Parker had often described to his son the family's history of military service, even in America's Civil War. "If you get called and you don't answer," he told young Stan, "don't come back home." At the same time, he warns him to be careful what he wishes for, because combat does not resemble anything he's seen in Gary's downtown air-conditioned movie palace. Hearing this, Stan had told his father, "Yes, sir, I understand," though he knew that he really didn't understand.

As far as he can figure out, his father seems to be saying that a man is obligated to die for his country, yet he should hope that he will never have to fight in a war.

Over the summer, he and Gervais had agreed that joining the elite 101st Airborne Division was their best chance for survival. On D-Day 1944, the Screaming Eagles of the 101st had, among many feats of bravery, jumped out of airplanes into combat, fought at the Battle of the Bulge, and finally battled their way to victory in Hitler's Germany. Stan and Tom want to be Screaming Eagles more than anything else on earth.

"Good-bye, Dad," he says. "This is so long for now." And then, seeing the worried look on his dad's face, he says, "I'll make it back, I promise."

His relationship with his father is a potent mix of fierce love and mutual respect. They shake hands, then hug. He hugs his mother and tells her he loves her. He is grateful for their unconditional love of him. Stan understands that his father has taught him how to be a man, while his mother is a mirror in which he can see what it looks like to be that man.

Helen Laverne Parker tells him, "You stay safe, Troop." Stan feels a lump in his throat. He knows his mother opposes his enlistment, especially with Dub serving as a paratrooper too. He kisses Maureen, studies her face, her straight blond hair, and tells her that just the thought of seeing her again is going to keep him alive. She manages a smile and nods through her tears. Stan snatches his luggage and bounds up the bus steps.

Plopping down next to Gervais, he looks out the window as Maureen blows him a kiss. Grinning, he reaches up and snatches it from the air, and, with a flourish, drops it in his shirt pocket. His father and mother are waving at him. He knows that neither of them is able to tell him anything more about the world to come.

In this new world, he knows that he's going to be fighting something called communism, and he knows he's going to be fighting people called the Viet Cong and the NVA. President Lyndon Johnson and Secretary of Defense Robert McNamara have called this a "war of attrition," meaning, as far as Stan can tell, that his job will be to kill as many of these people as possible. The idea is to hurt the enemy so badly that they'll give up. Stan knows this war is different from his father's war. His father flew bombing missions across Europe in order to destroy and capture enemy territory. Stan will be fighting to kill for killing's sake, all by way of winning the war.

Most of what he knows about Vietnam he's absorbed by watching TV. After supper he'd plop down in the stuffed chair and watch Chet Huntley and David Brinkley, their smooth voices brewing within the TV's wooden cabinet, filling the living room with bad news and good news about the war, and with numbers—the "body count." By the end of 1966, 6,350 Americans had been killed, and more than a few of them were from Indiana. The TV flickered with images: destroyed buildings; torn bodies; Vietnamese women in conical hats with children huddled at their feet, ducking and looking scared, as if birds of prey were descending. Through the winter of Stan's senior year, President Johnson, the hickory curl of his voice filling the room, told him, "Yet, finally, war is always the same. It is young men dying in the fullness of their promise. It is trying to kill a man that you do not even know well enough to hate . . . therefore, to know war is to know there is still madness in the world."

16

Stan thought about this: He felt that his world was not filled with madness. He did not know hate. He felt he was the kind of person his parents had taught him to be: someone who loved others and tried to serve them. He wondered how this war would change him.

As a student of military history, Stan also knew that during World War II, after France's armistice with Germany on June 22, 1940, France was forced to surrender its Southeast Asian colony to Germany, which provided European markets with coffee, silk, and rubber. By an agreement with the Germans, the Japanese Army would occupy Vietnam during the war.

But with the war's end in 1945, a question arose: Who would control Vietnam now? France wanted its colony back, but there were forces in Vietnam fighting for independence. A revolutionary poet named Ho Chi Minh, born in 1890 at the height of France's presence, had been organizing the cause of his country's independence ever since leaving his homeland in 1911 aboard a steamer ship for France, where he joined the Communist Party.

Tireless and pragmatic, Ho had traveled through Europe and the Soviet Union, and during World War II, he had assisted the Office of Strategic Services on the side of the Allies against the Japanese. Ho believed that there might be a place for Vietnamese independence in a postwar world led by the United States and Europe, even referring to America's Declaration of Independence as his inspiration. At an international conference in 1946, he asked world leaders to let the Vietnamese people govern Vietnam, but his pleas for self-governance fell on deaf Western ears.

The United States, eager to extend influence in Asia in the face of tightening Soviet tensions, instead ceded control to the French, sparking a nine-year civil war between Ho and his guerrilla forces, called Vietminh, or the League for the Independence of Vietnam, and French forces. The fighting began in December 1946.

This new aggression heightened U.S. Cold War anxieties, which worsened in 1949 when a Chinese revolutionary named Mao Tse-tung captured China and declared it a Communist state. The following year, the Korean War ensued, involving Chinese and Korean troops. Increasingly, the United States saw France's colonial rule as a hedge against communism's spread, particularly after China began providing Ho with weapons to fight the French.

In assessing the situation in 1953, newly elected President Dwight Eisenhower feared what he would come to call the "domino theory," which posited that one nation after another would fall in a line to communism. Ensuring Vietnam's success as a non-Communist state became an obsession of the United States. The following year, when Ho Chi Minh, alongside a military genius named General Vo Nguyen Giap, defeated the French, it seemed the United States would eventually be involved.

Ho Chi Minh and Giap had beaten well-equipped French troops at Dien Bien Phu, in northwest Vietnam. The French, sorely miscalculating the reach of the Vietminh guns, found themselves under siege and were overrun and either killed or rounded up by the thousands as prisoners. They agreed to leave the country in a crushing defeat.

In 1954, both sides signed a peace accord in Geneva, Switzerland, guaranteeing the Vietnamese the opportunity to elect a government. Ho's decades of struggle looked to be over. It was agreed that until elections took place, Vietnam would be partitioned at the 17th parallel, about 100 miles south of Hanoi, into two countries. South Vietnam would be governed by Ngo Dinh Diem, a French-educated Catholic bureaucrat whom many Vietnamese (and U.S. leaders) believed had manipulated a 1955 referendum to wrest leadership from the country's emperor at the time, Bao Dai. Diem had promptly named himself president of the newly minted Republic of Vietnam, commencing an eight-year autocratic rule. The modern political state of Vietnam, which Stan Parker would helicopter into thirteen years later, was born.

Diem would rule in the South, and Ho Chi Minh, or "Uncle Ho" as his followers called him, would govern the North. His ancestral homeland and its capital, Hanoi, would remain a hotbed of revolutionary activity, increasingly Communist inspired.

President Eisenhower opposed the upcoming Vietnamese elections. He feared that the immensely unpopular Diem would not win and that Ho Chi Minh, supported by the Soviet Union and China, would gain control of a unified Vietnam. Diem in fact did not support the elections, claiming they had not been sanctioned by his new South Vietnam government. The tragic result was that the elections of 1956 were never held.

Consolidating power, Diem enacted laws banning dissident activity, executing or jailing as many as forty thousand agitators, Communists, and Buddhists, whose persecution the Buddhists blamed on Diem's Catholicism. Ho Chi Minh's soldiers intensified guerrilla attacks on civilian and military targets, many of them carried out by the newly organized National Liberation Front—peasants, farmers, teachers, and workers drawn from the North and South, successors to the Vietminh who'd beaten the French. The South Vietnamese and U.S. governments called these guerrillas "Viet Cong," which, loosely translated, means "Vietnamese Communist," or, more pejoratively, "Communist traitor to Vietnam." American soldiers would call them "VC," "Victor Charlie," or "Charlie."

In 1961, President John Kennedy, worried that Diem would fail, sent the first of what would be hundreds of "advisors," including specially trained U.S. Army Special Forces Green

Berets, to prop up the regime. On November 2, 1963, President Diem, failing to control the unrest, was overthrown in a coup by some of his own generals. (Two previous coup attempts had been made in 1960 and 1962.) Diem was arrested and, with his brother, Nhu, handcuffed and shot dead in the back of a military vehicle at Saigon's Tan Son Nhut Air Base.

President Kennedy and his administration had been looking for a way out of the worsening situation with the unpopular Diem, but when he heard news of his death, he was shocked. Informed of the impending coup, he'd been under the impression that Diem would be arrested and escorted into exile in France. Diem's death forced Kennedy to consider sending more U.S. military support to an ever-faltering South Vietnam. Three weeks later, on November 22, 1963, however, Kennedy himself was assassinated, and the question of what the country should do fell to his vice president, Lyndon Johnson. The U.S. relationship with Vietnam was conflicted, ill defined, and in flux.

Because conventional wars, often involving thousands, even millions, of troops, are expensive and because North Vietnam's allies, the Soviet Union and China, possessed nuclear warheads, Kennedy had envisioned a less risky, and less expensive, projection of power as a series of small wars, by first deploying U.S. Army Green Berets.

President Johnson, who was most interested in enacting the domestic programs of his Great Society, resisted escalating U.S. involvement. Running for reelection in 1964, he declared, "We are not about to send American boys nine or ten thousand miles away from home to do what Asian boys ought to be doing for themselves."

Yet Johnson also feared being remembered as "the first American president who lost a war." When he received a report that North Vietnamese boats patrolling the Gulf of Tonkin had fired without provocation on a Navy destroyer, the USS *Maddox*, and when this was followed by a report (later discredited) of a second attack on the *Maddox* and another destroyer, USS *Turner Joy*, Johnson ordered the bombing of targets in North Vietnam.

Along with most other Americans, Stan and his family supported Johnson's decision, as well as the passage that week of the Gulf of Tonkin Resolution, giving Johnson the almost unlimited power to fight a war in Vietnam without formal declaration. As 1964 ended, 23,000 American "advisors" had landed in-country, and Ho Chi Minh more than matched the U.S. effort, maneuvering approximately 170,000 Viet Cong and North Vietnamese Army troops into South Vietnam. Bombings, ambushes, and coordinated attacks were a weekly occurrence in Saigon and rural parts of the country.

In response, Johnson dug in. The first deployment of conventional U.S. soldiers landed in Da Nang on March 8, 1965. Thirty-five hundred Marines waded ashore from landing craft, ready for battle, and instead were met by local women who placed flowers around their helmeted heads. This anticlimactic landing, however, was followed by increasingly bloody combat.

On November 14, during Stan's senior high school year, U.S. troops of the 1st Air Cavalry Division were caught in a battle at a place called Ia Drang. The division's 7th Cavalry Regiment fought a thoroughly prepared North Vietnamese Army (NVA) and suffered deep losses. Ia Drang, the NVA would say years later, was its test of America's capability to fight in Vietnam.

In the battle, the 7th Cavalry had brought to bear a new idea in fighting: using helicopters to insert men into combat, by which troops could arrive on the battlefield at any place of their choosing. The use of helicopters would change the war that Stan was about to fight. Helicopters made it possible to reach numerous front lines in a single day, perfect for a guerrilla war in which identifying a symmetric front line was impossible.

This air capability made it possible to fight without the need to declare that territory had been captured from the enemy. It was perfect for a war that counted dead bodies as a means of keeping score.

Yet it had its drawbacks. When the first cavalry soldiers landed at Ia Drang, they found themselves in an enormous ambush. Some 250 U.S. soldiers were killed; the American command claimed that at least a thousand NVA had been killed. Stan had read about the Ia Drang in the newspapers and, instead of being scared, the apparent adventure of combat had made him want to go to Vietnam even more.

As Stan made his way to basic training, more than 30,000 U.S. soldiers had been wounded and 5,008 had died in Vietnam. Each day, nearly 390,000 soldiers like him woke under the emerald glow of jungle canopy or beside the trembling mirrors of rice paddies to fight another day.

He and Gervais shuffle into a barracks at Fort Leonard Wood, Missouri, packed with hundreds of other recruits, many of them looking scared and unsure of what they'd signed up for. Angry drill sergeants patrol the floor, barking, "You, on this side! You, to the other side!"

Half of the crowd will be shipped several thousand miles away to Fort Lewis, Washington, for basic training there; the remaining recruits will train at Fort Leonard Wood. Stan and Gervais stick close together. A sergeant points to Gervais, motioning him to a different side of the barracks.

Stan protests, "Hey, Tom, get back over here."

Stan explains to the sergeant, "We joined up the Army on the buddy plan."

This seems to amuse the sergeant. "Really?" he says. "The *buddy plan?*"

"Yeah," says Stan, "the buddy plan's where you join with a good buddy and go through basic together."

"So," says the sergeant, "what you're saying is, you're queer?"

Stan, confused, says, "What I mean is . . ."

He sees Gervais making a motion with his hands: *Drop this, Boots.*

The sergeant says, "So where's your buddy at?"

"He's over there," says Stan.

The sergeant asks Gervais, "Here's your buddy, huh?"

Gervais nods.

"All right, you two, get in the middle."

Stan and Gervais step forward.

The sergeant, addressing the crowd, says, "You want to hold hands or anything? Something you want to tell us to get out of the Army?"

Stan can't believe he's been so naive. *The buddy plan?* Right.

"No, sir," he says, "we've got nothing to say, except we both have beautiful girlfriends."

The sergeant isn't amused. "You want to go to Fort Lewis or stay here?"

"I'll stay here," says Gervais.

Stan says, "Me too."

That's how they end up going through basic training together. The bullying infuriates Stan, but he keeps quiet. He's an Army man now, hoping to be a Screaming Eagle. He doesn't want to do anything that will ruin this chance. He writes home to some high school buddies, warning them, "Do not, whatever you do, join up on the 'buddy plan.' *It will not go well.*"

Stan discovers that he enjoys the misery of basic training a great deal. The challenges of running, marching, and especially shooting, coupled with the psychological question of whether he can prevail with excellent marks, excites a part of him he never experienced in high school athletics. He graduates basic training with honors and scores at the very top of his proficiency test. (He will find even greater pleasure in the new hardships of Advanced Individual Training at Fort Huachuca in Arizona, practicing map reading and survival skills and how to stay alive in close combat. At Fort Huachuca, however, he and Gervais will be forced to split up. The buddy plan is not to be, just as Stan suspected.) He already feels wiser than the naive kid who'd left Indiana just weeks earlier.

In early September, while in basic training, his father writes to tell him that something is wrong with his mother. She's been having bad stomach pains. The doctor thinks she probably has a case of gallstones. She's young, just thirty-nine, and in otherwise good health, his father assures him. She'll be fine.

A few weeks later, his father writes again. His mother has seen another doctor. It's not gallstones, his father tells him. It's cancer.

He tells Stan that he'd better be prepared to come home on emergency leave. Stan finishes the letter, stunned. He's also worried. The Army, preparing to send more troops to Vietnam, is speeding up its training schedule and all two-week leaves, usually granted to basic training graduates, have been canceled. Stan knows he must find a way to see his mother.

His Basic Combat Training graduation day is October 14. The next day, he's supposed to take two flights and a bus ride to Fort Huachuca. Stan notices that he'll have a five-hour delay in Chicago, where his mother is being hospitalized. That should be long enough to pay her a visit.

He calls his dad to ask him if he can meet him at O'Hare Airport the next day, but he can't reach him. He then calls Maureen, his girlfriend, and asks if she and her mom might be able to help. Her mom, listening in on the other line, readily agrees.

They meet Stan at O'Hare and quickly drive him to Chicago Hospital/Medical Center. Stan and Maureen find his mother alone in her room, asleep. He approaches the bed and leans close, kissing her cheek.

She opens her eyes and looks at him. After a moment, she says, "Troop. Is that really you?"

She gives Stan a long hug. She asks him how in the world he's been able to visit. Stan is shocked that she looks so sick. They talk for several hours until, finally, a doctor pulls Stan aside and delivers some news. He doesn't think his mom will survive until Christmas. Stan has to compose himself, then turns back to his mother.

She is smiling, looking so happy. She tells him that his father won't believe that he's stopped to see her! She says that he'll think she's only been dreaming again!

Stan thinks a moment, then tells her that he's come prepared. He pulls one of his Army trophies from his bag. He'd like to leave a part of himself that would stay with her forever but this shiny piece of plastic will have to suffice. He places the trophy in her hands. His mother looks at it and starts to cry. She says she has something to tell him. She wants him to know that she's no longer mad at him, that she's forgiven him for joining the Army. Stan leans down and kisses his mother good-bye.

Less than a month later, on November 12, he is standing in morning formation at Fort Huachuca when he's told to immediately report to his company commander. He's informed that his mother is desperately ill, and that he's been granted emergency leave. Eight hours later, he's landing at O'Hare and a family friend drives him to Gary. It's cold and raining as he stares out the car window, the rambling buildings and smokestacks of Bethlehem Steel sliding past. His mind drifts, and he wonders how long he and Maureen will last as a couple. Before he left for basic training, she started talking about how maybe they should date other people. Stan doesn't want to date anyone else. He feels that as long as people like Mo exist in the world, the world has to be an okay place.

He pulls up outside their mobile home and Stan thanks the family friend and steps out into the rain. So many times as a boy, he'd come home after school to see his mother at the kitchen table, ready with a piece of pie and a glass of milk. She wrote him often at boot camp, letters he loved reading. She'd sign off, "Well, Troop, there's chores to do. I'll close now. Make us proud."

Stan walks inside and sees his younger brother Bruce reading at the kitchen table. They greet each other and Bruce explains that their dad has left to pick up more pain medication for their mom. He nods toward their parents' bedroom door.

Stan pushes it open and finds her in bed, her dark hair fanned on the pillow. Stan looks back at Bruce, who walks up and starts to cry. He mumbles that she's been unconscious for two days, and Stan drops to one knee, taking hold of her limp hand. He's holding it when their dad walks into the room. He and Stan embrace and stand beside her bed in silence, searching for any sign of renewed strength. The vigil will last four days.

On November 15, Stan is sitting by his mother's bed while Bruce and Joe are still asleep. His dad has gone out for coffee. His brother Dub is due to arrive from Fort Bragg later in the day. Stan is holding his mom's hand and she takes a deep breath. Silence, and then another breath. Now she isn't breathing at all.

She's quiet for a few minutes, but Stan can't be sure for how long. He's so distraught, he can't keep track of time. He feels for her pulse and then for a heartbeat. Nothing.

He looks up as his father enters the bedroom and their eyes meet.

"She doesn't look too good," his dad says. "How is she?"

"Well, Dad," Stan says, after a moment, "I think she's gone."

Stan watches as his father opens both hands and the white Styrofoam cups of coffee drop to the floor. He runs to the bed and puts his head to her chest.

"She's not breathing," he says and starts crying.

Stan has never seen his father cry. He's always told Stan to fight any hardship, no matter how difficult. Stan feels a hole open within himself, which he decides, without really being aware of it, that he will fill by going to war.

That night, his father gathers the four Parker boys and tells them that their mother is going home to Texas. Stan's dad will accompany the body by commercial airline with Stan's youngest brother, Joe.

Stan, along with Dub, his wife, Shelia, and younger brother Bruce, will drive the family car on the 813-mile cross-country trek to Queen City, Texas, in the state's hilly northeast corner. Stan's father grew up in Queen City, population eighteen hundred people, and Helen Laverne had lived in the west Texas town of Muleshoe, near the New Mexico state line. She'll be buried in the Parker family cemetery.

Arriving in Queen City, they encamp at his grandparents' farmhouse, where Stan and Dub spent some of their childhood summers. His grandfather W. O. (William Owen) Parker had paid them a nickel for every melon they brought in from the fields. W.O. always seemed to know just how many melons were still unpicked, telling Stan and Dub they'd left one or two behind. He said this even when he knew there wasn't a stray melon in the field. None the wiser, Stan and Dub always resumed their hunt, always coming back empty-handed. Whether it was cruelty, or perhaps a macabre sense of humor, his grandfather taught Stan to have patience and forbearance and not to complain about situations he hadn't created or couldn't control, a lesson that would serve him well in Vietnam.

When his father explains that their mother will be buried on November 20, Stan realizes he has a problem. He's supposed to return to Fort Huachuca that very day. In order to attend the funeral, he'll need to extend his leave. He phones his company commanding officer in Arizona, expecting to fix this problem quickly.

The CO doesn't take long to think it over: No, he says, most emphatically. "And if you're not back here, Parker, you're AWOL. So your ass will be grass! And I'll be the lawnmower!"

Well, that's clever, Stan thinks. He pleads for more time, believing that reason will win here. But it's no use. His request is denied.

He tries thinking the problem through, believing that no matter the circumstance, there's a solution. He walks into the living room, its oak floor covered with a braided rug, its walls bearing pictures of generations of Parkers, and sits down next to his father, who, Stan thinks, has suddenly begun to look older.

A news story on TV catches Stan's eye. The report is that President Lyndon Johnson will be at his Texas ranch for the Thanksgiving holiday. Stan has an idea—a crazy one, he thinks. But what does he have to lose?

He picks up the phone in the hallway and dials the operator on the local party line. The operator's name is Sarah, and the

Parker family has known her as long as Stan can remember. The party line connects the Parker household to all other houses in Queen City and to the rest of the world.

"Why, Stan Parker," says Sarah, hearing Stan's voice. "How are you?"

"I'm fine, Sarah. I'm in Queen City."

"I was sorry to hear about your mother."

"That's kind of why I'm calling."

Sarah asks him what he means.

"Well, I have a strange request. My company commander won't let me stay in Texas for the funeral. And I need to be here for my dad."

"You're kidding me. They won't let you stay?"

"No, ma'am. And I saw on TV news that the president's in Texas, and I'm in Texas, and, well, I thought I might talk to him."

The LBJ ranch in Johnson City sits about four hundred miles southwest, near Austin. Sarah says she doesn't see why she can't at least try to connect him.

"You don't go anywhere. I'll call you right back."

Several minutes later, the phone rings.

"Stan," Sarah says, "you're on with the LBJ ranch in Johnson City."

Stan pauses. Is this really working? A man on the other end asks him what he can do for him.

Stan stumbles a bit, then says, "Hi. Yes, this is Private Stan Parker, of the U.S. Army. May I please speak with the president?"

The voice at the other end seems amused. Stan will later discover he's a military aide. "Perhaps I can help. Tell me what you'd like to discuss."

Stan explains how his mother has died and that he'd broken her heart when, he, Stan, had signed up for the Army after high school graduation. And now he wants to give her a proper funeral. But his company commander back at Fort Huachuca has forbidden him the time he needs.

There's silence on the other end of the phone. Stan figures the person is absorbing this news.

"And everything you're telling me is true. Is that correct?"

"Yes, sir. It is."

"Okay, you stay on this line. Sarah," the aide says, "I'm going to give you a number, it's unlisted, and I want you to tell them that this call has been directed from the LBJ ranch."

"Yes, sir, thank you."

"Now, Private Parker, don't hang up."

"No sir, I won't."

The aide hangs up, and Sarah dials the number, saying, "Stanley, I'm connecting you now."

After a few rings, a woman's voice is on the line. Sarah says, "Yes, this call has been referred to you by the LBJ ranch in Johnson City, Texas."

Almost immediately, a male voice picks up. "This is Robert McNamara speaking. How can I help you?"

Stan is floored. He's talking with the secretary of defense of the United States of America! He presses on with his story about his mother's funeral. Mr. McNamara listens and seems to express shock at the company commander's refusal to extend Stan's leave. He tells Stan that he'll take care of things. As unexpectedly as it began, the phone call ends.

The secretary remains true to his promise. The following day, when Stan calls Fort Huachuca again, he learns his leave has been extended. He also learns that the U.S. military will pay for his return flight and even provide a military escort from Chicago to Fort Huachuca in Arizona.

Upon arriving at base, his escort, an Army colonel, strides crisply into the CO's office. The CO looks up in surprise.

"I've been sent by the secretary of defense to bring Private Stan Parker back to your command. He's been at his mother's funeral. And he is, I repeat, *not* AWOL."

The CO turns completely white. Stan thinks the man is going to have a stroke. The colonel says good-bye and strides out the door.

Stan considers saying something clever, but thinks better. He simply salutes and hustles from the office. *This*, he thinks, *is how you survive in the Army: be bold, act swiftly, and keep moving.*

Fort Benning, Georgia, to Fort Campbell, Kentucky

On February 1, 1967, Stan Parker completed jump school and received his "blood wings." It had been two months since he triumphantly walked out of the CO's office at Fort Huachuca. He was a paratrooper now.

His training over the past seven months had changed him in ways he hadn't anticipated. First, he realized that surviving anguish and physical suffering was often a mental game. He also realized he was capable of making grave mistakes, especially when it came to knowing how to defend himself in close-quarters combat. At Fort Leonard Wood, his platoon drill sergeant had pulled him aside and told him, "Private Parker, I know that you joined the Army to be airborne and go to Vietnam, and you're going to need this knowledge on the battlefield."

The man, a Korean War veteran, then demonstrated how to thrust his bayonet into a man's chest without flinching. Stan repeated this over and over on a practice dummy filled with straw, and then learned how to deflect the drill sergeant's actual attacks. His fatigues were slashed, his arms bloodied. When Stan wanted to rest, the sergeant refused. He told him he was going to instill in him "the Spirit of the Bayonet Fighter, which is to kill or be killed." As he fought, Stan felt a sense of pride at being able to defend himself. He wondered if he'd get to use this stuff in real life.

In jump school, however, he sometimes felt just plain incompetent. On his second jump, his main chute failed to fully open and he forgot to open his reserve chute as he'd been instructed in case of emergency. He looked up and saw a half-dozen lines tangled and didn't give this much thought. He was floating along just fine, enjoying the view.

Over a bullhorn from the ground, though, he heard an urgent voice: "Would the trooper with the malfunction now activate his reserve! All other jumpers, slip away from the trooper in distress!"

He tried spotting the jumper in trouble, then realized that the others had drifted away from him and he was descending faster than anyone else. He looked up at the parachute and understood he was in trouble. He pulled the cord to deploy the reserve chute but still hit the ground at dizzying speed. He couldn't move and lay croaking and groaning as his parachute drifted over him and then covered him completely.

He lay under the silk, gasping for breath, pretty sure that he would be drummed out of training for this mistake, when he saw a shadow pass over the billowing fabric. For a moment, he thought he might be dead and he'd just seen an angel. Then the angel yelled at him.

"Airborne, are you okay? Answer me, Airborne! ARE YOU OKAY UNDER THERE?"

It was Sergeant Gorilla, his jump instructor. All the instructors had nicknames—Sergeant Daddy Rabbit, Sergeant Shithead, Sergeant You-Bet-Your-Boots. These men, towering figures who'd jumped and fought in Korea and World War II, were to be feared. They went by the more official Army name of "Black Hats," for the wide-brimmed head gear they wore on the training field.

Stan gasped, "I think so. I *think* I'm okay."

"Trooper, You *THINK* so? Or you *KNOW* so?"

Stan then heard a Jeep pull up and skid to a stop. Whoever was driving was certainly in a hurry to get here.

"You better decide quick, Trooper, as someone more powerful than me is here to check this out."

Stan guessed that Sergeant Gorilla was referring to Colonel Lamar Welch, commander of the Airborne School and a famed combat veteran in World War II, during which he'd jumped with the 101st at D-Day and fought in Korea and Vietnam.

Stan was sure his dream of being a paratrooper was finished. To earn his jump wings, a student had to make five successful jumps from a low-flying C-119 or C-130 transport plane, and land on target in a designated landing zone. A lot of guys, for whatever reason, seemed to wash out on the second jump. These guys were known as "two jump chumps."

Sergeant Gorilla told him to get up and out of the way before Colonel Welch could see what happened. He told Stan to double-time it back to the recovery area.

Stan quickly gathered his chute and left. At the recovery area, he turned and stood at attention, staring out at the drop zone, and waited for the colonel to arrive and decide his fate. He thought back to the other time he'd really screwed up in jump school. He'd been on Kitchen Police (KP) in the dining area when several officers entered and Stan called out, as he was required to do, "Attention, officers present!" As everyone snapped to attention, including himself, one of the instructors yelled in his ear.

"Private, are your feet nailed to the floor? Get six cups of *hot, black* coffee and an *assortment* of pastries."

That task was part of Stan's duty as a member of the Kitchen Police, but he'd forgotten.

Still at attention and without thinking, Stan replied, "Okey-dokey, sir."

"Okey-dokey?" snarled the officer.

"I mean, 'Yes, sir'—Sir."

The officer yelled again, when a colonel, the ranking officer, interrupted.

"Step over here a minute, son," the colonel said. "Where you from?"

Stan, out of the corner of his eye, could see that this was Colonel Welch, and he was tongue-tied.

"Are you deaf? Answer Colonel Welch!" said the instructor.

"I'm from Arkansas, sir. I mean—Indiana."

Colonel Welch laughed and put his arm around Stan.

"Okey-dokey," he said, chuckling. "Why, I haven't heard someone say 'okey-dokey' since I was a boy. So, are you a Razorback or a Hoosier?"

"Both, sir," said Stan, nervously. "Born in Arkansas, joined the Army in Indiana."

"That's good, son. A well-rounded soldier is what we need here at Airborne."

He patted Stan and said, "You know, coffee and pastries are just *okey-dokey* with me."

He thought a moment and added, "While you're at it, bring a cup for yourself and sit down so we can talk about home."

Stan was still standing at attention at the recovery area when Colonel Welch pulled up. Stan's knees were shaking, and he couldn't make them stop. He was so disappointed in himself that he thought he was going to throw up.

Colonel Welch approached and looked him over, as if trying to place Stan's face. And then a smile spread across his face.

"Private Okey-dokey!" he said. "Well, well."

Stan let out a smile too and relaxed—just a little.

Welch sternly lectured him about his mistake and explained nonetheless that he had earlier appreciated his inadvertent humor when they'd met at breakfast. He told Stan that he'd blurted out something from the heart and that this probably meant that he was an honest person. The colonel said that he also appreciated the way he hadn't shown fear when faced with the prospect of being punished for his protocol lapse.

"That can be useful on the battlefield," said Welch. "Just what a paratrooper needs to perform when fright is about to overtake him. *Calmness.* Now fall in line with the other students."

Stan saluted smartly and walked back to the others, who were standing openmouthed over what had just transpired.

Right then and there, Stan knew that nothing would ever prevent him from becoming a paratrooper.

Later, at his graduation, Stan and the other students nervously waited in formation to receive their "blood wings," repeating a tradition dating to World War II.

Colonel Welch appeared and approached Stan, holding the much-treasured metal parachute-shaped badge. He placed it against Stan's fatigue blouse and gently pushed the two metal pins through the fabric. But instead of affixing the badge with the customary metal clasp, he reared back with an open hand and struck Stan with a hard, decisive blow, driving the badge's metal pins into his chest.

Stan winced, his body aflame, feeling a terrible but sweet stinging as blood trickled down his chest.

Colonel Welch stepped back and saluted, and Stan smartly returned the same.

"Make me proud, son," said Welch.

"All the way, and then some, sir." Stan smiled.

Newly minted as a paratrooper, Stan Parker stood at the Fort Benning depot, waiting for his bus ride to the Atlanta, Georgia, airfield and a flight home for a thirty-day leave before deploying to Vietnam.

As he stood in line, he heard the name of every soldier but his own called out. He approached a clerk with a clipboard and waved his set of orders. Now that he'd passed jump school, Stan was to become part of the 173rd Airborne Brigade, aka the Herd. In May 1965, the 173rd had been the first major U.S. Army ground combat unit deployed to Vietnam. The other major unit, the 1st Brigade of the 101st Airborne Division, had arrived in July.

The clerk studied his clipboard. "Your name Parker? Says here you've been scratched. You ain't going to the Herd."

Stan thought there must be some mistake. "So where am I going to?"

"Don't know. But you ain't going nowhere in Vietnam. You're on hold."

"*Hold?* Why?"

"Don't know, but you can go to the Head Shed and ask." He pointed over to a set of buildings.

Stan walked up to the personnel office and explained his problem.

A secretary checked her paperwork. "Oh," she said, "there's a congressional against you."

"What do you mean, 'congressional'?"

"Evidently your daddy says you're not going to Vietnam, and

he got your congressman involved. He's not having two sons in combat at the same time."

"My dad's involved?"

The clerk shrugged and pointed to a pay phone.

He dialed and when his dad answered, Stan didn't even give him time to say hello.

"Hey, Dad," he said, "we got a problem here in Fort Benning, Georgia. I ain't going to Vietnam."

Stan could hear his father sigh. Finally, he replied, "I know it."

"You do?"

"You're not going at the same time as your brother," his dad said. "One or the other."

"I'm going. I got my orders."

He cut him off. "Your brother's already got his orders. He's going."

"But he's married and I'm single."

"He beat you to the punch. You've been reassigned." And then he explained what he'd done.

Shortly after his wife's death, he had called his congressman and asked him to notify Stan's Army superiors that by no means was Stanley Parker to be sent to the front lines in Vietnam. He told the congressman that one son in combat was enough for any family. The congressman agreed.

"So where am I going then?"

His father told him that he was going to Germany.

"*Europe!*" Stan protested. "I don't want to go to *Europe!*"

His father explained that he'd serve his time as part of the U.S. Army's Long-Range Reconnaissance Patrol or LRRP (pronounced "lurps"). It would be honorable service with a venerable unit, his father told him.

"But I want to go to Vietnam!" Stan shouted, and hung up the phone.

• • •

He went to Europe.

Shortly after he arrived in Germany in March 1967, he got a letter from Tom Gervais, who had gotten to Vietnam first. *"Boots,"* he wrote, *"do not come* over here. If you need to, fine. But if you don't, *do not come.* People are getting shot and *killed."* Another high school buddy wrote, "I'm not even in the infantry, I'm a *dental assistant.* I have a cot, a place to sleep, and I hate it here. Stay in Germany!"

What could his friends possibly mean? Then came a letter from Dub, also in Vietnam, who warned him to stay where he was. Stan looked at the letters, disbelieving, and decided to ignore the advice.

Thinking he still might avoid LRRP duty, Stan pointed out to his new commanding officer that he had not received the proper training and wasn't qualified. *Don't worry*, he was told, *we'll train you.* Having just finished jump school, he was in excellent shape, and after a series of punishing running, marching, and shooting exercises, which he passed easily, Stan was now a qualified LRRP soldier. He wasn't happy.

As a member of Company C, 58th Airborne Infantry, Long-Range Reconnaissance Patrol, he was part of a storied tradition of reconnaissance soldiers dating to America's French and Indian and Revolutionary Wars. A LRRP soldier is trained to raid in enemy territory and to be the eyes and ears of a larger fighting force. In Germany, Stan's LRRP company had the job of standing eye-to-eye at the Czech border with the Soviet Union soldiers. Should the Soviets go to war with Europe, Stan and his 208 fellow LRRP scouts would parachute behind enemy lines and report their positions so that artillery and firepower could be brought to bear.

One day, a Soviet soldier from the Czech side of the border

walked up and offered Stan a cigarette, as if they had nothing better to do than have a friendly conversation. *This isn't war,* Stan thought. *I'm babysitting a piece of ground.* He pulled out a laminated card his company had printed as a joke: It read, in sum: "In case of invasion, call HQ, tell them World War Three has started, bend over, and kiss your butt good-bye. It's over." After seven months of guarding the border from Soviet attack, he couldn't stand any more boredom.

He approached his company commander and told him he wanted a transfer.

The officer asked him where he wanted to go.

"Vietnam," said Stan.

The officer was dumbfounded. "You're kidding. I have people who'd die to be assigned to this LRRP company."

"Well," said Stan, "I'll switch with one of them."

The officer brought up the fact that he already had a brother in Vietnam. He refused to let Stan leave the unit.

Nonetheless, every Monday morning, Stan showed up at the commander's office and asked for a transfer. He knew that the Army couldn't deny his effort even if it could deny what he was asking for. And every week his request was denied.

Then Stan saw that his fortunes might change. The Army was planning to increase its presence in Vietnam, which meant it would need more soldiers like him, and it enacted something called a levy. Stan wanted to be on the levy list of guys headed to the 101st Airborne Division who would get shipped from Germany to Fort Campbell, Kentucky, the 101st's home, and then to Vietnam.

He pulled the company clerk aside and asked, "Any way you can get me on that levy?"

"Not with your brother over there—unless you sign a waiver."

Stan had never heard of such a document. He asked the clerk when he could sign it.

"I can't talk about it now," said the clerk. He told him to meet him after hours.

That night, the clerk produced a piece of paper and told Stan that if he signed it, releasing the U.S. Army from any responsibility should anything happen to him while he was in Vietnam, he could get him orders to leave Germany. Stan signed the document.

"But this'll never work," Stan realized, "unless the commanding officer signs it too."

"You let me worry about that," said the clerk.

The next day, the clerk walked into the commander's office with a stack of papers. "These all need your signature, sir. Just standard paperwork."

The commander signed Stan's waiver.

As the clerk handed the paper to Stan, he said, "Now get the hell out of here before anyone finds out what I've done. There's a truck leaving at dark. You get in the back and *hide*. It'll take you to the air base in Frankfurt. A lot of guys are already there, waiting to fly to Fort Campbell."

In the dark of night, Stan snuck into a supply truck, curled up, and covered himself with a canvas. He had no idea what would happen if he got caught—he'd probably be court-martialed. Who would believe him when he explained that he was trying to sneak *into* the war?

The three-hour truck ride was bumpy and miserable. Stan banged up and down on the metal bed, trying to lie still and not make any noise. When the truck arrived at the airport, he peeked out of the back, slipped to the ground, straightened his uniform, and looked around for other paratroopers headed to Fort Campbell.

He finally spotted the group and recognized a few guys he knew from the LRRPs who'd also gotten on the levy list. Two of them he'd become good friends with: Dwight Lane, from rural Indiana, and Brian Riley, from Maryland. Stan was glad to see them. They were always good company, ready with a joke, and always ready for adventure. Riley had a wicked tattoo of an eagle across his broad shoulders. Stan was hopeful they'd have even bigger adventures in Vietnam.

On September 18, 1967, a little over a year after he joined the Army to become an airborne soldier, Stan Parker walked off the plane at Fort Campbell, into the sunshine of a Kentucky autumn as a member of the 101st Airborne Division. When his other friends from the LRRP saw him, they were shocked. They had known about his father's decision that he shouldn't be allowed to fight in Vietnam.

"Jesus, Parker," they said. "How'd you get here?"

Stan flashed his smile. "By hook and crook, fellas," he said. "By hook and crook."

His journey had begun.

September 18, 1967–January 30, 1968

Fort Campbell, Kentucky, to LZ Jane, South Vietnam

After Stan got off the plane, he and hundreds of others were loaded onto buses and trucked to their barracks at Fort Campbell. As they got off the buses, they were met by platoon sergeants shouting at them, "Who's a medic?" "We need radio men!" And, "Where are the LRRP soldiers?"

Stan had entered the 101st just as it was undertaking the biggest airlift of troops and matériel in U.S. history, code-named Operation Eagle Thrust. The 101st's 1st Brigade had already been in Vietnam for two years, slugging it out in some of the earliest fighting Stan had seen on TV news back at home. The 2nd and 3rd Brigades were part of this massive airlift and would comprise its main force. The 101st would be the largest ground unit fighting in Vietnam. Over the next four weeks, 10,024 men and 5,357 tons of equipment were shipped overseas in preparation for the war's biggest buildup at the end of the fourth year of fighting. By December 1967, some 500,000 men and women would be serving in the country.

As Stan stepped down off the bus, a gruff-looking first sergeant bearing a clipboard in massive hands approached. The sarge had the crisp manner of a professional lifer who had seen serious battle and for whom garrison life was a bore he would quietly endure.

He was Echo Company's First Sergeant Lawrence Koontz, a thirty-three-year-old West Virginian and veteran of the Korean War. Koontz had already seen extensive combat in Vietnam with the 1st Brigade, 101st Airborne. At Fort Campbell, he'd been put in charge of standing up Echo Company's Reconnaissance Platoon, of the 1st Battalion (Airborne), 501st Infantry Regiment, 2nd Brigade. He was joined in this task by Staff Sergeant Freddie Westerman, from Missouri.

"You a LRRP from Germany?" Koontz asked Parker.

"I was," said Stan, "but I want—"

"This way, step forward."

Private First Class Stan Parker stepped forward and waited as Koontz continued through the crowd, calling out more soldiers. Sergeant Westerman approached a lanky fellow named Private First Class Al Dove, whom he found goofing off around the bus door, with a buddy.

Westerman asked them, "You want to volunteer for dangerous duty?" Always calm, possessed of a lively sense of humor sharpened by hard battle, Westerman, age twenty-eight, was already on his second tour. He was all business as he addressed Dove.

Dove said that he sure would like to volunteer. His friend wasn't so certain. "You're going to get me killed!" he half joked to Dove, who nonetheless yanked him into the volunteers' line.

Dove had been happily drafted into the Army, which had allowed him to escape a home life in Hawaii dominated by an alcoholic father. Dove had dropped out of school in the eighth grade and cruised the beaches, surfing, and occasionally stole food to help keep his family fed. He couldn't read and signed his enlistment by placing an X on the paper, his illiteracy being a secret he kept hidden from all others, and which fueled, along with his dislike of his father, a fierce temper. Street smart, mechanically minded, he knew that if he stayed in school he'd continue fooling everyone but himself, and that he'd graduate unable to read his own high school diploma. He was glad to be volunteering for the dangerous mission of the platoon.

After an hour of this recruiting, Koontz and Westerman had assembled some twenty-eight young men, including Stan's buddies Dwight Lane, Brian Riley, and several other LRRPs he'd met in Germany. From places as varied as Texas, Georgia, New Jersey, Ohio, Connecticut, the Michigan farm, the Chicago street, and the California beach, they had entered the army out of a combined sense of duty, adventure, and family tradition. In varying ways, they understood they were being sent to fight something called communism. Many were following their father's or grandfather's example of military service, and some assumed—and their perceptions would dramatically change when the fighting started—that their combat experience in Vietnam would resemble their fathers' in World War II.

Specialist Michael Bradshaw, tall and deep-voiced, from the central valley of California, had left Fresno to escape a suffocating home in which he couldn't listen to rock music and was lorded over by parents who were social workers and college teachers. His senior year, he'd moved to a ranch to earn his room and board, reveling in a newfound adult freedom to listen to the Beatles and come and go as he pleased. During his airborne training, he conjured up a name for a confederation of his trainees—Jerry Austin, Tim Anderson, Tom Soals, Al Dove, Dennis Tinkle—which he felt communicated the mystique of their new Army life. They would be known as Los Recondeleros.

Medic Paul Sudano, from Oregon, had entered the war to try to make his father proud, a man he worshipped for his bravery in charging Iwo Jima's beaches in World War II. When Sudano met a U.S. Army Special Forces soldier in his senior year, he decided he wanted to be a Green Beret. He was crushed when he learned that at age nineteen, he was two years too young to enter the training. When he joined the Recon Platoon, he felt he was sure to be tested to his limits and then some.

Growing up in suburban New Jersey, Tony Beke, one of four sons of working parents in an extended family of veterans, ran a neighborhood paper route and a morning trapline in nearby woods and streams. After high school, he'd begun work at U.S. Steel, which afforded him a much-coveted draft deferment. Beke, however, felt he hadn't a right to sit out a war while others were fighting, and quit his job to enlist in the Army, following the example of his father, who'd enlisted during World War II.

Tim Anderson's classmates in Tacoma, Washington, had signed his senior yearbook, "Never lose your sense of humor, man!" Tall, blond, the proverbial class clown, Anderson had run track and played football and gone to work after graduation making manhole covers in a local foundry. He had not been unhappy when his draft notice arrived. *Escape*, he thought. *I'm getting out of Tacoma!* He volunteered to be a paratrooper to earn an extra $55 per month in jump pay, to be added to his monthly $87 paycheck (he'd also collect a whopping $65 in monthly combat pay). By joining Recon, Anderson figured he'd have it made. He'd be with the best troops, and enjoy the best chance of survival.

He'd completed basic training with a like-minded and athleti-cally gifted Californian, Tom Soals, the son of a much-respected Navy submariner. Soals, upon graduation, had dreamed of either being a mountaineer or scientist. As a Boy Scout, he'd begun climbing peaks and glaciers in the West, but he now chose to study science in college. After a year, though, he made the deci-sion to quit and relinquish his draft deferment. Like Beke, and others in the platoon, Soals didn't like feeling he was sitting on a sideline while others his age were fighting in Vietnam. He wanted to take part in something *out there*. When he heard Ser-geant Koontz's pitch to join Recon, he welcomed the idea that he was entering an elite brotherhood.

Koontz explained to his gathered volunteers that they were now members of Recon Platoon, belonging to Echo Company, 1st Battalion, 501st Airborne Infantry Regiment. He told them that Echo Company, in addition to Recon, also consisted of a Mor-tar Platoon and a Radar Surveillance Platoon, and that it would support four companies of infantry soldiers.

Koontz told them not to let this "support role" fool them. A Recon soldier, he said, is a seeker of violence in a violent world, operating behind enemy lines, ambushing and attacking, shoot-ing, and surviving. The platoon's job would be to move from hot zone to hot zone, acting as the roving eyes and ears of the bat-talion's four line companies, offering fire support and intel on enemy movements. A Recon soldier's home is what he carries in his rucksack. His platoon is his world; his squad is his closest family. His Huey helicopter is his ride into battle and back to life in the relative safety of camp. He might land on two to five dif-ferent LZs in one day, most of them "hot," under fire. The pace would be dizzying, sleepless. Among soldiers in Vietnam and in a war known for its surreal qualities, men in Recon were to be feared and held in awe. The young men of Recon, he told them, were hunters who might become the hunted at the snap of a twig.

Since this sounded something like what he'd trained to do with the LRRP in Germany, Stan was pretty sure that this new life was the job for him. Except in this new life, he figured he'd actually get to do some real fighting.

Each of the battalion's four line companies, Alpha through Delta, had its own platoons and squads and served as the battalion's main force infantry on the front line. These soldiers called themselves "Line Doggies." Stan and his group called themselves simply "Recon."

The Recon Platoon would be divided into three squads, with the headquarters section commanded by First Lieutenant John Gay, a handsome blond West Point graduate. Staff Sergeant Freddie Westerman, as the platoon's sergeant, would act as its train conductor and martinet. Specialists Thomas Soals and Tim Anderson were the platoon's RTOs, or radio/telephone operators, and would follow Lieutenant Gay wherever he went. All orders for the platoon would come from him, handed down from the battalion level. Echo Company was commanded by Captain Donald R. Taylor and run by First Sergeant Koontz.

The headquarters' medics were Specialists Troy Fulton, from Pennsylvania; Paul Sudano; Daniel Bagley; and Charlie Fowler, from California. Fulton was a survivor of the 1st Calvary's 1965 battle in the Ia Drang Valley and looked like a throwback to old GIs in black-and-white photos of World War II. Charlie Fowler, nineteen, was a happy-go-lucky kid from Napa who liked reading science fiction and mystery novels. His mother had been working as a waitress when she met his father, a Greyhound bus driver, and Charlie had had little contact with his father as a young man and had struggled in school. He'd excelled at sports, especially football, and joined the Army thinking that he might, as his mother's seven brothers had told him, "become a man."

Over the next week, as the platoon's original ranks filled, 1st Squad would be commanded by Staff Sergeant Lee Bruce, from Massachusetts, assisted by Sergeant Larry Kass, from Ohio, and M-60 machine gunner Specialist Dwight Lane.

The squad's remaining nine members were Sergeant Tony Beke, New Jersey; Specialist Marvin Acker, Wisconsin; Specialist Roy Cloer, Georgia; Private First Class Harold Holt, Maryland; Specialist Douglas Fleming, Mississippi; Private First Class Warren Jewell, Indiana; Specialist Clifton Naylor, Georgia; Specialist John Payne, Illinois; Specialist Charlie Pyle, Texas.

Second Squad was led by Staff Sergeant Lindsey Kinney from Hawaii and Sergeant Ronald Kleckler from Maryland, with Al Dove as the squad M-60 machine gunner. The other nine platoon members were Sergeant Michael Corcoran; Specialist Donald Curtner, Texas; Specialist Terry Hinote, Florida; Specialist Dennis Kilbury, Washington; Specialist Brian Lewis, Arizona; Private First Class Charles Mansell; Specialist Stanley Parker; Specialist Angel Rivera, New York; Specialist Guido Russo, Illinois; Specialist Francis Wongus, Connecticut.

Third Squad was led by Staff Sergeant Diogenes Misola, from the Philippines; assistant squad leaders Sergeant Tony Ramirez and Sergeant John Lucas, from Michigan (who would leave the platoon in early 1968); and machine gunner Specialist Olen Queen, from West Virginia. The remaining six squad members were Specialist John Arnold; Specialist Jerry Austin, California; Specialist Michael Bradshaw; Specialist Robert Cromer, Georgia; Specialist Brian Riley, Maryland; Specialist Dennis Tinkle, Arkansas; Specialist David Watts Jr., Indiana.

The Recon Platoon was accompanied by forward observers from Echo Company's Mortar Platoon: Sergeant Andrew Obeso,

California; Specialist Ron Kuvik, Missouri; Specialist David Williams, Michigan; and Specialist Marvin Penry, Indiana.

Forty-six young men in total, all of them white, except for four African American troopers, Arnold, Holt, Jewell, and Wongus.

Their four months of training had made them expert at land navigation, fire and maneuver, hand-to-hand combat, night ambushes, helicopter assaults, and airborne jumps. Living so closely together, they had no choice but to grow close. Stan, Francis Wongus, Guido Russo, and Californian Jerry Austin shared cramped quarters with four metal bunk beds; the barrack's roof was made of tin that drummed in the heavy autumn rains. Stan felt that Wongus knew he'd have his back in any fight, including with white troopers who might not be used to living alongside an African American.

They blew off steam by sitting on their footlockers, listening to records—Eric Burdon, the Stones, and the Mamas & the Papas were favorites—smoking cigarettes, and playing air guitar using their M-16s as instruments. As Christmas approached, Stan dressed up as Santa Claus—they called him "Stan-ta Claus"—and reached into a laundry bag and pulled out a new rucksack for Al Dove, who received it with his hat cocked sideways, and a wide, aw-shucks-you-shouldn't-have grin. When Jerry Austin sat on Stan's lap and asked what Santa had brought, Stan handed him a rifle and said that this year he was getting an all-expense paid vacation to a far-off country, compliments of Uncle Sam. They were excited about their coming deployment, and the word going around was that they'd be leaving sometime just before Christmas, just several weeks away.

When they had permission to leave the post, they piled into a cab and drank in the bars in nearby Clarksville, Tennessee, or in the strip clubs and bars outside the guard gates. They often wound up in fights, usually with regular soldiers whom the Airborne troopers called, dismissively, "legs." They were proud of the Screaming Eagle patch they wore on the shoulder of their uniforms, which, by tradition, they had sewn on their combat uniforms themselves.

One of the platoon's senior noncommissioned officers, who was an excellent boxer, got drunk one night in a bar and beat up three soldiers, then offered to take on anyone else willing to step up. When he saw someone run out of the bar, he took after him. The fleeing man managed to get to a car, and as he tried to speed away, the Recon NCO jumped on the hood and hung on with his left hand while he reared back and punched through the windshield and hit the soldier in the face, knocking him out. His foot came off the gas and the car came to a stop as the attacking soldier tried to pull his hand back through the hole he'd made. His arm was stuck and horribly lacerated. Stan ran up and had to crush the glass so that his platoon-mate could escape. They limped back up the street and caught a car back to the post. Stan thought that this guy had to be one of the toughest soldiers he'd ever met and made a note to stay close to him once they got to Vietnam.

Always hovering around the edge of their consciousness was the wider world and its own conflagrations, the growing civil unrest in their own home states.

During the summer of 1967, not only was war brewing in Southeast Asia; America was erupting as well. Riots and civil unrest seemed to be everywhere, largely because the fight for civil rights was everywhere, and Martin Luther King Jr. had begun speaking out against the Vietnam War.

That summer, President Johnson had ordered five thousand federal troops to Detroit, including members of the 101st and 82nd Airborne, after the city erupted in a race riot. (Also deployed were eight thousand Michigan National Guardsmen and thousands of local and state police officers.) On July 22, Detroit cops had busted into an illegal drinking establishment and discovered eighty-two African Americans celebrating the return home from Vietnam of two soldiers. The arrest of dozens of bar patrons flipped a switch, and long-simmering tensions burst into the open. Fires were burning throughout the city, and people could be seen driving up and down Woodward Avenue, a main thoroughfare, with rifles sticking out their car windows. The 101st Airborne had arrived to restore order, Sergeant Tony Beke among them. Beke was quickly uncomfortable with the idea that he'd been sent to Detroit "to settle things down" during the city's riots. He found the experience of pointing weapons at fellow citizens disturbing—"an ugly scene all the way around," he would later say. In a very real way, and to many men in the platoon, America seemed to be at war both in the United States and in Vietnam.

In October, Norman Mailer and other writers, alongside thousands of protesters, had staged an "exorcism" of the Pentagon, led by poet Allen Ginsberg, yippie leader Abbie Hoffman, and Fugs band member Ed Sanders. First, the protesters declared they were going to levitate the Pentagon in a display of "mass mental unity." The building's exorcism went like this, in a text written by Sanders: "In the name of the amulets of touching, seeing, groping, hearing and loving, we call upon the powers of the cosmos to protect our ceremonies in the name of Zeus . . . in the name of all those killed because they do not comprehend, in the name of the lives of the soldiers in Vietnam who were killed because of a bad karma."

Stan found newspaper stories about the war protests confusing. He knew what he should think about the protests—to his thinking, these were the efforts of unpatriotic Americans. But still he was aware that this war, and perhaps any war, was not a clear-cut event like a high school football game.

Americans were simultaneously confused, angered, and emboldened when boxer Muhammad Ali, a man who beat people unconscious for a living, refused to register for the draft and faced a five-year prison sentence (which he avoided). He defiantly told America, "I ain't got no quarrel with them Viet Cong." This prompted Stan to wonder what beef *he* had with the VC. He was unsure, except he did know that he felt a duty to answer his country's call.

On December 13, 1967, after three months of training, sixteen days before Stan Parker's twentieth birthday, the men of Recon Platoon along with 10,500 other paratroopers leave for Vietnam.

On their way, they fly from Fort Campbell to Travis Air Force Base, northeast of San Francisco, and refuel again at Wake Island, a remote Air Force base 3,867 miles east of Vietnam in the Pacific Ocean. Landing on this famous World War II battlefield feels like a pilgrimage for many of the 101st Airborne soldiers, whose fathers had fought the Japanese here twenty-six years earlier.

Tom Soals gets off the plane and stretches his legs by walking down to the beach and diving into its emerald water. Paul Sudano, who'd marveled at his father's stories about Pacific warfare, is shocked at the island's size, measuring just less than three square miles. As they walk around the island, Stan, an avid reader of military history, provides a running commentary for the platoon about World War II Marines defending the beach under Japanese fire. The reality is that the Wake Island beachhead looks small and placid. How could so many people have died here, Stan wonders, in such a peaceful place? After several

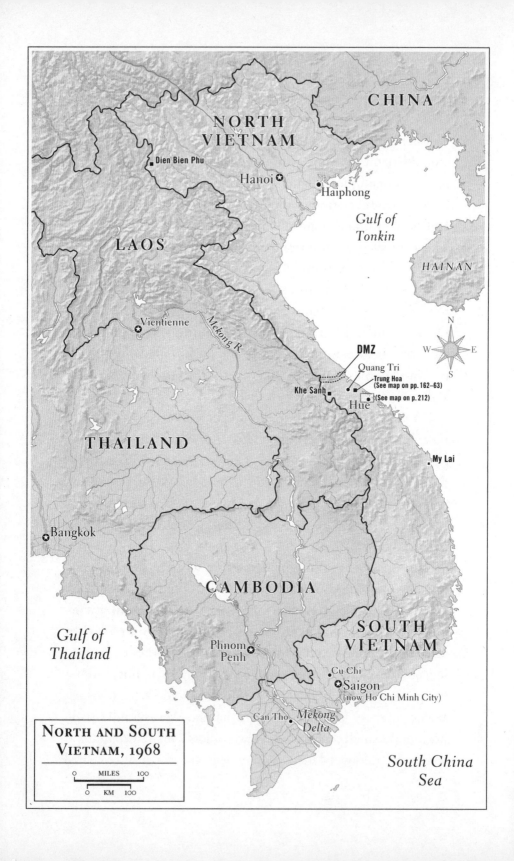

NORTH AND SOUTH
VIETNAM, 1968

CHINA

NORTH
VIETNAM

Dien Bien Phu

Hanoi

Haiphong

Gulf of
Tonkin

LAOS

HAINAN

Vientienne

Mekong R.

DMZ

Quang Tri

Trung Hoa
(See map on pp. 162–63)

Khe Sanh

(See map on p. 212)

Hue

THAILAND

My Lai

Bangkok

CAMBODIA

SOUTH
VIETNAM

Gulf of
Thailand

Phnom
Penh

Cu Chi

Saigon
(now Ho Chi Minh City)

Can Tho

Mekong
Delta

South China
Sea

N
W   E
S

MILES   100

KM   100

hours, they leave Wake and refuel in the Philippine Islands, at Clark Air Base, and touch down in Vietnam.

They land at Bien Hoa Air Base, about sixteen miles northeast of Saigon, a spinning hive of thousands of Army troops, F-4 fighter bombers, Huey and Chinook helicopters, Jeeps, tanks, and a constant stream of incoming and outgoing men. It's the heartbeat of America's war in the country.

The ramp of the enormous C-141 Starlifter drops to the tarmac, and waves of humid heat rush into the plane's interior, nearly flattening the tired soldiers inside. Stan smells sweet wood smoke, jet exhaust, cooking oil. His first look at Vietnam is intoxicating. Looking out the back of the plane, he sees a woman standing knee-deep in a rice paddy, her hands plunged to the elbows as she tucks new plants into the rich soil.

The 1st Brigade of the 101st Airborne has been fighting in Vietnam since 1965, and now, with the addition of the 2nd and 3rd Brigades, these ten thousand paratroopers are to help clear parts of the country's northern highlands and arid plateaus, areas infiltrated by NVA and VC fighters. Operation Eagle Thrust is to be quick and decisive.

Stan and the rest of his platoon file into the hangar past a thicket of microphones during a news conference, where the 101st Airborne's commander, Major General Olinto Mark Barsanti, is holding court with reporters. A military band strikes up, and Barsanti presents the famous Screaming Eagles to General William Westmoreland, Commander, MACV (Military Assistance Command, Vietnam). "The 101st is ready for combat," Barsanti tells Westmoreland, a prior commander of the 101st Airborne Division and Fort Campbell, from 1956 to 1960. (Westmoreland also served in World War II and Korea.)

A few months earlier, Westmoreland, whom *Time* magazine had named its 1965 "Man of the Year," had assured the public that America was winning in Vietnam. Stan guesses that by the end of his yearlong tour, he and his platoon-mates will prove Westmoreland correct.

The newly arrived soldiers celebrate their first night in-country by filling sandbags and fall asleep on cement floors under canvas roofs stretched over makeshift wooden walls. Stan drifts off thinking of home, of nights back home when he pulled into the Blue Top Drive-In with Tom Gervais, without much of a care in the world. He wonders about Gervais's warning: *Stay away, Boots.* Why would he write such a thing? He thinks of his mother and wishes he could speak to her, ask her if she is proud of him yet. He wonders when he'll discover just what Gervais meant.

The next morning, December 14, Echo Company is transported northwest, through Saigon, to a place called Cu Chi, located in a thirty-square-kilometer region of expansive enemy fortifications that U.S. commanders call the Iron Triangle.

Since the end of World War II, the Cu Chi area has been a haven for guerrilla fighters. Recon's job, Stan learns, will be to hunt and engage these fighters.

When he looks around Cu Chi, he sees acres of forest braided with creeks, a shaded, pleasant place. A year earlier, the U.S. Army's 25th Division set up their base, completely unaware of the danger living below them, literally under their feet.

They had located atop a nerve center of the North Vietnamese Army and its guerrilla cadre, the Viet Cong. Miles of tunnels snake underground all the way to the city limits of Saigon. As the war has grown in intensity, the guerrillas have built hospitals and kitchens underground and devised an ingenious system that pipes the cooking smoke aboveground. The hidden piping might extend fifty feet on a horizontal plane and finally emerge on the forest floor, with the chimney opening screened by woven leaves. To anyone passing by, the emerging mist looks not like smoke but resembles a marvel of morning sunlight. The tunnels' interior doors lead farther down into protected dwelling spaces. Some of the tunnels lead to a river, where, by a clever feat of engineering, a soldier can enter and exit the complex through an underwater opening. The tunnels are part of a large underground city with infirmaries, dormitories, and armories.

Dotted around the Cu Chi area are dozens of "spider holes," fighting positions dug by the Viet Cong close to the myriad tunnel entrances. A fighter can hide in a spider hole and wait in ambush, fire off a few rounds, and slip undetected through the tunnel's camouflaged entrance.

You could crawl through these tunnels—measuring maybe three feet high and two feet wide—and eventually pop out of a trapdoor in sight of a busy street in Saigon, pull yourself up through the hole, replace the camouflaged lid capped with leaves and twigs, tamp it back in place, brush off your clothes, and walk into town into the flow of traffic and become one of millions of South Vietnamese living in Saigon. That, in fact, is precisely how the North Vietnamese Army has been moving into position to attack the Americans in a planned early-winter operation, scheduled for the Tet New Year.

Chiefly, the NVA are using the six-hundred-mile-long Ho Chi Minh Trail that snakes through Laos and Cambodia; once they get close to the cities in South Vietnam, they hide in places like the tunnels at Cu Chi, which had been built under the command of Ho Chi Minh in the late 1940s. This means that by the time Stan Parker and the Recon Platoon arrive, the Viet Cong know these Cu Chi woods as intimately as Tom Sawyer knew the caves of Hannibal, Missouri.

By December 15, Stan and his fellow soldiers settle into new quarters, struggling to acclimate to the tropical climate. They have been warned about the dangers of sun exposure and instructed to acclimate by getting a "suntan" (read, "sunburn"). After a week of filling sandbags, Stan longs to go on a patrol. He expresses some of his frustration of garrison life in letters to his high school girlfriend, Maureen.

"I have a few extra minutes," he writes, "so I thought I would drop you a few lines. A lot has happened since I wrote to you last":

> Around the end of the month, we're going to join up with the 101st's 1st Brigade and with 3rd Brigade and the whole 101st Airborne Division is going up on the Cambodian border and kick some ass. We're going to end this war.
>
> General Westmoreland himself said, "Give me the 101st Airborne Division and I'll give you Vietnam." Besides, this is an election year and something has to change about this war.
>
> Have a real good tan now, real nice weather for getting a tan over here, but sure as hell gets cold over here at night. Oh shit does it get cold, oh shit does it get hot. . . .
>
> I never did tell you thank you for going out with me when I was home. . . .
>
> Well, I've got to go now and do what I was sent here to do (get a good suntan). . . . Tell your mom hi for me, love you, Stan.

Finally, after two weeks, they start patrolling and scouting for VC fighters. Stan is surprised by the dryness of the vegetation;

he had expected to be in thick, wet jungle. The dust he kicks is red, like paprika, and tastes oily. He passes straw and bamboo huts and smells what he guesses is fish cooking. He soon comes to learn that the smell is nuoc mam, a fish oil, and an essential flavoring in food. The patrols are an assault on his senses, while his heart hammers in his chest.

They patrol a place they call Hobo Woods and through a French-owned rubber plantation called Filhol. They walk in single file, as trained, separated by about fifteen feet; this way, if they are attacked, they're not bunched in groups and are slightly less vulnerable to mass casualty. The lead soldier is the point man and the guy behind him is called the slack position (as in, he's "walking slack"). The slack guy's job is to keep an eye out for anything the point man might have missed—literally, take up the slack. Most days, a Huey will land and pick them up from their patrol, before dark, and take them back to Cu Chi. One night, Viet Cong soldiers probe the camp's perimeter and in the thirty-minute fight that ensues, thirty Viet Cong soldiers are killed and two taken as prisoners.

Through all of this, Stan still hasn't fired his weapon. "We were itching for something to happen," he writes to his father.

In the minds of the men of the platoon, the Viet Cong and NVA are wily, elusive opponents, quick as wraiths. They view them as able adversaries, but feel they are cowards because they've heard they rarely stand their ground in a fight. Almost as soon as battle begins, they melt back into earth and trees.

They've also heard that the VC and NVA are masters of devising ways to maim, having perfected all manner of booby traps, often made of sharpened bamboo stakes called punji sticks, smeared with human excrement, mounted on swinging boards, and triggered by an unsuspecting footfall on a trip wire. The stakes can come swooping down from a tree branch or fly up from the ground, impaling the soldier in his path.

There are trapdoor booby traps that, when you step on them, flip up and drop you down into a grave-like hole lined with punji sticks. There are spiked booby traps strung in trees designed to drop down and target a man's genitals and puncture arteries. The uses of sharpened bamboo go on and on, the ingenious answer of a poor people to a richer country's superior technology and firepower.

"Come on, do something!" Stan writes to his father. "*Shoot at us!*"

Little does Stan know that beneath them, enemy soldiers are gathering and waiting to do just that.

On Christmas Eve, Stan receives an early present. He's on patrol when he gets word that he is urgently needed at platoon headquarters. He finds First Sergeant Koontz, who looks as if he's going to chew him out.

"Parker, I don't know who you think you are," Koontz begins, "but you must think you're special."

He points at a Huey landing nearby. "But let me tell you, you're not special." And then he smiles, as if to say, *I'm kidding*, and steps aside, revealing Stan's brother Dub on short-leave from the 1st Brigade, 101st combat operations near Phan Rang, where he is fighting in the highlands. Stan is overjoyed as he realizes he'll be spending Christmas with Dub.

They grab each other and hug, and Stan introduces him to the other guys in the platoon. He's seen Dub only twice since the summer of his high school graduation—when he'd joined up for the Army and when they were both on emergency leave for their mother's death and funeral.

Someone in the platoon has gone into the brush and cut something down that kind of looks like a Christmas tree. They decorate the scraggly twigs with hand grenades and machine-gun ammunition and different arm patches guys have taken off their uniforms for the occasion. Stan thinks it looks pretty cool. For Christmas dinner, the cooks serve turkey, cranberry sauce, and mashed potatoes.

On Christmas Day, Colonel John H. Cushman, commander of the 2nd Brigade, which has control of Stan's 1st Battalion Recon Platoon, visits the bunker line and inspects its readiness to repel enemy attack. The word is that the enemy is going to try something soon. Stan certainly hopes so.

Something called the Tet holiday truce is in effect. In October, while Stan and the rest of Recon were training at Fort Campbell, the North Vietnamese government had announced hostilities would pause at the end of January, so that the Vietnamese, North and South, could return to their villages and cities. During the Tet truce, they would eat and drink and pay homage to ancestors, as part of the liturgy of the country's Confucian, Buddhist, and animist theology.

That night Stan has perimeter guard duty. He is standing in the bunker with Al Dove, Brian Riley, and Dub. As Stan looks out of the bunker slit, he sees phantom shapes hovering in the dark night, like cutouts from black cloth. It dawns on him: it's happening! And then the firing starts.

Stan and the guys alongside him start shooting back, and the noise and the sight of the tracers is spectacular. Beside him, Al Dove racks the big M-60 machine gun, swinging the barrel around in the direction of the firing, the darkness pricked by the enemy's muzzle flashes. The shooting, to Stan's ears, is *Duh duh duh*. This first exchange of enemy fire for the platoon lasts just three minutes. After about half an hour, the firing begins again and continues intermittently for several hours. The night turns into dawn, December 27, and it's Stan's birthday. He is twenty years old.

He does feel different, but not because he is officially a year older. He'd felt a special bond with Al in the bunker, as Al banged away with the machine gun and he with his M-16. He and Al are growing tight. Al, he thinks, is a magician with the .60.

Dub, Stan's brother, tells him that in Vietnam you learn to mark time, and cherish life, by your brushes with death. Stan thinks of this realization as a kind of birthday present.

The excitement of the firefight is followed on December 28 by the much-anticipated appearance of Raquel Welch in camp, alongside Bob Hope, as part of Hope's USO tour. Her presence is felt among the men as a kind of hormonal tremor. The year before, 1966, Welch starred in two movies, appearing in an animal-hide bikini in *One Million Years B.C.*, whose promotional poster showed her in wide-legged stance, arms out at her sides, as if prepared to leap from the poster itself. The other movie, *Fantastic Voyage*, was about a submarine filled with intrepid scientists who are shrunk and inserted into a scientist's bloodstream in order to repair his health. When these movies came out, Raquel Welch was perhaps the world's number one sex symbol, and her appearance at the Cu Chi base camp seems as otherworldly and improbable as a story line from one of her movies. The guys dream of getting laid by Raquel Welch.

Before the show, Colonel Cushman comes around again to inspect the battalion's line of defense, which faces outward in a 360-degree perimeter. He is not happy that his troops will be sitting around staring at Raquel Welch while the North Vietnamese and Viet Cong prowl around them.

When she walks onstage wearing a white miniskirt and a blue blouse drawn tight across her bosom, the men go nuts.

Stan is sitting too far back to see much of Raquel and he must peer at her through his binoculars. He and Jerry Austin go one step further: they start taking pictures of her by placing their binoculars to the lens of their cameras, so that Welch's fulsome image is magnified in both their amazed eyeballs and on the Kodachrome film inside the camera. They click away as she high-steps across the stage. All the while, Bob Hope prances and vamps as he did in the old Bing Crosby Road Show pictures, his trousers slipping down and his shirt hiked up to expose a pale belly.

After the show, Stan and a group of the platoon make their way to the stage. When Stan's turn comes, Raquel Welch turns her wattage in his direction and asks in the sweetest voice Stan has ever heard, "Would you boys like a picture?" And Stan stammers, "Uh, yeah." Before he can say more, she hands him a black-and-white eight-by-ten of herself. He is about to ask her to sign it when a military policeman sees the Screaming Eagles patch on his uniform and tells him to move along. He learns that this VIP area belongs to the boys of Tropic Lightning, the 25th Infantry Division, and Airborne soldiers are not welcome. Stan is too happy gazing at the photo to be annoyed. He walks away gingerly holding it before him.

When he gets to his hooch, he rolls it up, sticks it inside a cardboard tube, and ships it home. He will later get a letter from his dad, kidding him, "What's this picture all about? I thought you were there fighting a war, son . . . Love, Dad."

On December 30, Stan goes on a patrol that teaches him a painful lesson about how the war is to be fought. He and Guido Russo walk up to a thatched hooch and stand looking at it, their rifles pointing at the front door. Suddenly, out steps a Vietnamese man dressed in loose black pants and shirt with an American-made M-1 carbine, which is odd. Most VC and NVA soldiers carry AK-47s. He is standing just ten feet away.

The Vietnamese guy is shocked, points his rifle at Stan and Russo, who stand frozen, their guns pointed at him.

"Who is he?" Russo says out of the side of his mouth.

"I don't know," replies Stan. "He's carrying an M-1 carbine. Could be a good guy. But he's dressed in black pajamas. Could be a bad guy. Not sure."

"What do we do?" asks Russo. The soldier is definitely Vietnamese, but Stan and Russo have never seen an enemy soldier up close and never actually shot anyone. And Stan doesn't know *how*, exactly, you decide to shoot someone as you stand staring them right in the eyes.

Then another man, similarly dressed, steps from the building, looks up in surprise, and he too raises his rifle and points it at the two Americans.

"Do we shoot?" whispers Stan.

The first enemy soldier starts inching sideways along the building, and then, when he gets to the corner, he gives a little bow to Stan and Russo and suddenly vanishes around it. Immediately, another surprised Vietnamese soldier walks out of the house, only he is dressed in a khaki uniform with an AK-47. He joins the second one, who by now is inching along the wall, until he too gives a bow at the corner and disappears. In total, five North Vietnamese soldiers exit the building and flee, all without a shot being fired. Stan and Russo look at each other shaking their heads, and breathe a sigh of relief. They have miraculously escaped death.

A few moments later, First Sergeant Koontz, who has witnessed part of the standoff from a distance, rushes up to them. Without warning, he punches Stan, knocking him off his feet.

"What are you doing!" he bellows. "Don't you know who these guys were?"

"Well, we couldn't tell at first—"

"Didn't you see the red star on his helmet? He was NVA, the enemy. Your job is to *kill* bad guys! Do you understand?"

"Well, yes, but . . ." Stan says.

Koontz interrupts. "Do you understand? You kill bad guys, period!"

"I understand," says Stan, rubbing his jaw. "I understand. *Kill or be killed.* I understand."

Koontz tells the platoon: "There are two types of people in Vietnam. The quick and the dead." He asks them, "Which are you going to be?"

Every day after that, Stan reminds himself what his job is: *Kill the enemy. Kill the enemy.*

Kill them.

That night, Stan goes on ambush with Al Dove and Francis Wongus.

Wongus takes the rear position, and Stan the twelve o'clock, facing down the trail. Al Dove is next to him with the M-60 machine gun. Stan sets up some Claymore mines, each about the size and thickness of a paperback book and slightly concave. He runs the wires with the clacker handles back to their ambush position, tucking the wires along the way under leaf matter. He sets the clackers up on a little berm. They look like those exercise handles you buy off late-night TV, meant to strengthen the hand.

Each Claymore, named by its inventor, Scotsman Norman MacLeod, has on its front the odd but necessary wording: "Front

Toward Enemy." It's packed with C-4 explosive and 700 steel balls that spray out in a killing pattern highly effective at fifty-five yards but still lethal at a hundred yards. When the clackers are squeezed, they send an electric charge down the wire and explode the mine.

Next to the clackers Stan also sets two grenades with the pins straightened for easier pulling. The only thing to do now is to sit and wait for the enemy to walk by.

Soon they hear footsteps in the night, the rustle of plants underfoot. Stan, Al, and Wongus open fire and see out in the darkness the flashes of the enemy's gun. Soon the unseen enemy begin dropping mortars around them, and it's terrifying to lie in the dark as the sky explodes. When the explosions stop, Stan is exhilarated and scared, all at once.

The next morning, he is sure there will be a lot of dead VC strewn about them, but when they check, they find only thick blood trails on the grass and jungle floor. The living have dragged the dead and dying away. He follows the tracks and soon they simply disappear. As a boy, living along the edge of Lake Michigan, he and his brothers had followed trails in the beach sand and imagined that they belonged to German soldiers; these tracks in Vietnam end in human-sized blossoms of blood, glistening under a tropic sun. How far has he traveled, he wonders, from that time when he played war as a boy? He also knows that part of him is still that boy along the lake. He can feel the change. He knows they killed some of the soldiers in the ambush, and this makes him feel good. Nor is he filled with reflection about what it means to end someone's life. He's happy that he is still alive. He's happy that he's no longer a combat virgin—or "cherry."

Something fateful happens on January 15, 1968, after a month at Cu Chi. Stan thinks that perhaps this fateful thing is not fateful at all, but only random, the result of inexperience among the platoon. After all, how can a thing be fated and random at the same time? The platoon is restless because it's wondering how it will act when it meets its first large firefight. Every day in Cu Chi, the momentous event seems around the corner. Yet the fight has not yet arrived.

It's about 2:20 p.m., and what happens involves Sergeant Larry Kass, who isn't popular with some men in the platoon, and Specialist John Payne from Illinois. Once, during a training exercise in the States, Kass had charged a position and accidentally knocked a fellow soldier unconscious with the butt of his rifle. In response, realizing he'd screwed up, he went running off into the woods. Al Dove, who has had lifelong problems with braggarts on account of his difficult father back in Hawaii, thinks Kass is egotistical, always declaring himself to be a tough soldier. When Al Dove met him the first time, he punched Kass in the nose. They avoided each other after that. Stan Parker finds Kass to be a bully. He'll say to Kass, "Why can't you *not* be a jerk?" And Kass will answer, "Because I outrank you." That is true, but barely. They're both enlisted, but Kass does outrank him. Stan is a PFC/E-3 and Kass is presently a Sgt./E-5. Stan tells him, "If you think that's going to stop me from fighting you, you are sadly mistaken."

What happened next tells itself a couple of different ways, depending on with whom you speak. Jerry Austin hears that John Payne is asleep, leaning against a tree, with his hand on the trigger of an M-79 grenade launcher. It looks like a shotgun, with a wide-mouth barrel that shoots a three-inch, 40mm grenade—lobs it, really—much farther than anyone can throw such a thing, which is the whole point of the weapon.

Kass walks over and kicks Payne with his boot, trying to wake him, frogging around, the way Kass will do. *Oh, fercrissakes,* thinks Al Dove, and then Payne, startled, sits up, depresses the trigger, and the launcher fires.

The wide-mouthed barrel of the weapon is aimed straight up at his face. The grenade races from the barrel (its terminal velocity is two hundred fifty feet per second) and travels the several feet to Payne's chin, and smashes his lower jaw, removing his teeth and lips and rendering him unconscious. Somebody immediately calls for a medevac. Within minutes, they hear a Huey coming in for a landing. Payne lays motionless and silent on the ground, bleeding from the place that had been his jaw, while Kass runs off again, as if to escape his stupidity, where he might get shot (and mercifully so, think some of the guys) by a VC. They can hear Kass out in the boonies muttering to himself, half-yelling, half-crying, as if to say "Oh, what have I done!"

Later, Al Dove remembers it differently. He and Stan and Guido Russo are sitting together, laughing and joking, when this noise happens. They're about seventy-five feet away, far enough to be aware of Kass and Payne moving around in a general way, but not close enough to pay attention to details—except Al, who for some reason is watching. He sees Kass walk over to Payne, pick up the grenade launcher like he doesn't care about much and isn't paying attention to anything, and in this mood, he does not see that the launcher is loaded, points it at Payne, and fires. Al swears to this day that he watched this happen. Either way, Payne is nearly dead, shot right in the face. And in the end the details don't matter, do they? This story, like all of these stories, is about, what? Forgiveness? Making peace?

When the shooting happens, Al Dove and Stan and another soldier have just cranked open several cans of C-rations, ham and lima beans, and are eating over the tops of their knees, Al sitting behind them a little ways, up a slight incline, with the machine gun lying on the ground beside him, quiet as a dog.

Then they hear this noise. Stan thinks the sound is the *whoosh* of an incoming mortar round, and he ducks down, ready for the explosion. Then he hears hollering and screaming coming from the direction of Kass and Payne. Stan thinks that perhaps a sniper round has come in and found its mark. But he doesn't know who has been shot or how badly. Sergeant Westerman comes running up. He has not seen the incident happen either, but he's heard the sound of a gunshot, or something like it, and he tells Stan and the other soldier to run over to those trees yonder, about seventy-five yards away, and see what the hell is there, if anything. If anyone has taken a shot at them, it would have come from that vantage point. Stan and the soldier take off running.

Just then the situation gets more complicated: a helicopter appears overhead, making passes, surveilling the ground from the air. And then somebody on the ground near the tree line starts shooting at the helicopter, though Stan can't tell where this fire is coming from. But the helo scoots this way and that, evading the firing, and then it tips and starts firing back at the sound, the bullets ripping through the trees around them. Stan and the soldier stop moving, for fear they'll be misidentified as the enemy firing on the helicopter. Because they've been forced to stop, this allows them to look around, and that's when they see the old man standing out in the middle of the rice paddy.

He has something in his hand. A rifle? At first, the soldier with Stan thinks this is a rifle, and he's ready to drop the old man right then. Stan thinks differently: *No, this can't be the work of this old man.* For one, it would have been a helluva shot. And when he gets closer, about thirty yards away, Stan is quite certain that what the man is holding is not a rifle but a farmer's hoe. The old man isn't moving, frozen in place beside the rice paddy, still as an egret. Stan's platoon-mate is still convinced the old man somehow has a weapon on him. He insists, "He's holding a rifle."

"No, he's not."

"I'm going to shoot him."

"Don't you dare shoot this guy."

"We don't know if he's VC or NVA."

"That's right. We don't know anything," says Stan. "If he makes a move, I'll be the first to kill him. But until then, do not shoot him. If you do, I'll shoot you. Do you hear me?"

They look back and see another helicopter land and somebody is loaded aboard and it lifts off and Stan and the soldier walk back to the spot where all the commotion has been. The ground is strewn with tangled, bloody bandages.

Stan still doesn't know what has happened, so he asks Westerman, who tells him that Payne had been shot by one of their own. Kass. Stan asks where Kass is now, and Westerman says he got in the chopper with Payne. The poor bastard, he felt so terrible. He says Kass just stared and stared at Payne as the helo lifted off for the hospital at Cu Chi. Stan feels this thing overcome him, a sickly feeling, maybe it's anger, or fear, or dread, but his reaction, upon hearing this news, is to throw up.

He walks into the bush and bends over with his hands on his knees and keeps throwing up. He decides that it's *anger* that's making him sick. Stan has never lost anyone under these kinds of violent circumstances. This is something he realizes he must learn in this new life. He looks for a place inside himself to hide the pain and reaches up and places the feeling on a shelf in his brain, next to the sad feelings he has for his mother, now that she is dead. He remembers the way she whispered in his ear calling him "Troop" one last time as she lay dying. Lord, he misses her.

Some of the guys in the platoon are plenty mad at Kass for what he's done. Stan is beyond getting mad. What he realizes he feels instead is . . . peace. Maybe forgiveness. At least, call it understanding. He doesn't think that Kass shot Payne on purpose. He doesn't think Kass has committed this terrible deed because he can't help being a jerk. The shooting is something that happened. *It's something that happened.* Who knows why? Who was watching when Kass walked over with the M-79 and fired at Payne? Who? Stan doesn't know. His whole life he's been sure someone has been watching over him—first his parents, then his friends, then God. He still doesn't doubt any of this is true. Not yet.

When Kass returns from the hospital, he seems devastated. He comes back to the platoon a different man, as if coming back from a journey. He won't give orders, doesn't boss people around. He used to give the impression that he'd punch someone if they didn't obey him. Now when he speaks to Stan, he won't look him in the eye. Stan thinks it's sad, how Kass's been wrecked. And when Kass is killed about a month later in a firefight, shot three times in the chest, some of the guys in the platoon will have no remorse over his death, still blaming him for Payne's disfigurement. But what, Stan wonders, could Kass have done differently, except to have decided *not* to walk up to John Payne and *not* pick up the grenade launcher, or reach over with his combat boot and nudge Payne? Somehow, and by someone, the launcher is fired, and from it, the rest of Kass's life and Payne's life follows behind. When Kass returns to the platoon from the hospital, Stan imagines that Kass must feel he'll live forever with this regret, when in fact he'll live with it for just another month. When he's shot and they pick him up from the battlefield, he's still alive—he'll die in a matter of minutes—and in these precious minutes he's still somebody's son, somebody's brother, the kid you see waving as he gets in his car at high school's end, driving away to the rest of his life, and you don't remember him again until his name appears in the news: *KIA Larry Kass.* When Stan learns that Kass has died on the medevac, he's sad and reaches inside and puts this feeling too up on that shelf in his brain. He feels this death diminishes him, diminishes them all.

A few days pass, and Stan and Al Dove and Brian Riley and Dwight Lane feel that they should go and see Payne. His time in the Nam is done, they know that. It has ended before it began, really, before they've even begun to fight. Stan knows that visiting Payne is a way of making peace with the incident, the terrible *pop* and very short *whoosh* of the grenade as it leaves the launcher and heads for his chin.

They catch a chopper ride to the hospital and walk up and down the halls for ten minutes looking for Payne. They can't find him. Stan walks into one room where a couple of guys are camped out in beds, sorry-looking young men all banged up from the war, and he looks right at one of them, and it's John Payne. He doesn't even recognize him and walks out of the room.

He gets halfway down the hall when he thinks, *Wait a minute. That was a Screaming Eagle patch on the foot of that guy's bed*, and turns and walks into the room, and there's Payne looking at him with baleful eyes, which are about all Stan can see because his face is so swollen and bandaged. He just stares and thinks, *Oh, Payne,* and he sits on the bed while every inch of his body says, *Run, leave.* There's a small chalkboard hanging from the edge of the bed and it's covered with white chalk smears and Stan guesses that he's not been the first to visit Payne. Stan picks it up and starts writing, *How are you feeling?*

And he turns it for Payne to see and Payne just looks at him, nineteen years old, and he says nothing, nothing, with his pale eyes.

Payne takes the board from him. Stan thinks how perfect his hands look, in comparison to his ruined face, his hands clean and unscarred, and Payne takes the chalk and writes in cursive, "Parker, I understand that you almost shot the wrong guy." Stan doesn't know what he means at first, and then he figures that Payne must've gotten word somehow that another soldier was hopping mad and had wanted to kill the old man with the hoe. Payne goes on with his chalk, writing, "I'm glad you didn't shoot him. I'm glad you let him live."

This makes Stan feel good because after the shooting, some of the guys yelled at Stan for not wasting the old man.

Payne has tubes running down his nose because his mouth opening is ruined and Stan can see the tube into his arm through which he's being fed. After a short while they feel they've run out of things to say, and Stan erases what he's written on the board and he too leaves a white chalk smear on the black slate and sets the board swinging from the edge of the bed and says good-bye to Payne and gets up and walks out of the room. He never sees him again. He tries calling him once when he gets out of the Army, using the number he's had, but the recording of the operator's voice tells him the number is disconnected. Stan hangs up the phone and walks away, goes back to work, or back into whatever part of his life he is living.

As far as he knows, Payne does get out of the hospital and away from the war, the pain of his wound being the price he pays for that journey back. Stan hopes that he finds happiness and that, somehow, his face has come back, almost like a near-dead plant, or a field of clover, the way the field can grow back overnight, especially after a rain, as if by magic. But Stan knows he's only dreaming and that dreaming in this new life will kill a man.

They count the days until they can get out of Cu Chi.

They count the days until they can get into the war and leave behind this chickenshit, the shooting of John Payne.

At 7:15 in the morning, January 22, 1968, they load up on twenty-two Hueys and head out for a place called Black Virgin Mountain.

This is it: the big move, the big battle.

The five companies of the 1st Battalion, 501st Airborne Infantry Regiment—Alpha, Bravo, Charlie, Delta, and Echo—lift off, the helicopters' windscreens flashing in the sun. The Hueys fly at a thousand feet over rice paddies and hamlets. Soon, up ahead, Stan sees the mountain itself looming, a nearly perfect cone rising from the plain floor. They are going to assault the mountain.

Stan has never before felt such anticipation, such worry, such excitement.

They have flown for about thirty minutes when, suddenly, without any explanation, the long line of Hueys begins a slow arc to the right, as if rounding a bend on the air, and soon the lead Huey is heading past Stan, flying in the opposite direction, all of them headed back to where they'd come from.

Stan does not know where they are going. It isn't evident at first that the mission is off; maybe plans have changed and they are going to assault from another position. But soon the airfield at Cu Chi comes into view and the Hueys are touching down. Immediately Stan and the rest of the soldiers are loaded, one company after another, onto a waiting C-130. They won't be assaulting Black Virgin Mountain.

It's increasingly evident to the platoon that there will be no rhythm to their movement or their days, no sense of forward progression.

They fly north to an airfield four hundred miles away, in the northernmost province in South Vietnam, near a town called Phu Bai, about eight miles southeast of Hue. It takes the U.S. Army twenty-one flights, or sorties, to transfer all of the men and cargo of the 1st and 2nd Battalions, 501st Airborne Infantry Regiment, from Cu Chi to this new northern base. (The 2nd Battalion, 502nd Airborne Infantry Regiment, will follow within a few days.)

Once at Phu Bai, Stan and the platoon load onto two-and-a-half-ton trucks and are driven about four miles west of Phu Bai to a place called Landing Zone El Paso.

The soldiers in Recon are told to cover their Screaming Eagle shoulder patches, clue enough that their presence is supposed to be a secret from the enemy. Stan figures they are probably being watched from some far-off vantage point, likely having spotted the trucks' black clouds of diesel smoke.

So much for secrecy, he thinks.

They roll into LZ El Paso, a bustling new "city" of about five hundred soldiers whose job it is to defend this most northern sector of U.S. interest in Vietnam, called I Corps (pronounced "Eye-Core"). El Paso has previously been called LZ Tombstone, for the Vietnamese graveyard at its entrance, which consists of a large aboveground mound with a cement front and doorways leading to mausoleum-like structures. It's a dusty, treeless place, loomed over by the distant eight-thousand-foot peaks of the Day Truong Song mountain range.

The provincial capital of this area, Quang Tri Province, is the city of Quang Tri itself, located sixteen miles south of the demilitarized zone. The DMZ runs along a river, the Ben Hai, for about fifteen miles, east to west, across a thin waist in the country's topography. The DMZ, which extends about two and a half miles on either side of the river and which also follows the 17th parallel, was established in 1954 when Vietnam was partitioned in the aftermath of the French withdrawal after their defeat at Dien Bien Phu. It is, in essence, the last line of defense, the demarcation between the Communist North and the U.S.-controlled South.

There have been reports that the NVA are going to attack the South, and this means they are going to come pouring across the DMZ. Since November 1967, the North Vietnamese Army has been increasing its presence in Quang Tri Province, and General Westmoreland had been alerted that the enemy might attack this area in northern I Corps.

On January 30, six days after arriving at LZ El Paso, Echo company loads into trucks again. This time, they are headed to an ill-equipped and poorly fortified outpost—LZ Jane—where they will make a stand against the supposed coming attack. They arrive in a cold rain at a forlorn hilltop bulldozed out of dirt and scrub, bounded by dark skies and encircled by tree lines several hundred yards down rocky, root-entangled slopes. The LZ is about the size of a football field and overlooks hill upon green rolling hill. It has been named, as is tradition, after somebody's girlfriend. It sits about twenty-five miles south of the DMZ, and five miles southeast of Quang Tri City, a thirty-minute, double-time march for the boys or a two-minute helicopter ride, low and fast over the treetops. To the southeast, about fifteen miles away, is Hue, the longtime cultural capital of the province. To get any heavy machinery and resupply, such as tanks and artillery pieces, to Quang Tri and Hue, the enemy would have to use Highways 9 and 1. The 101st Airborne's job is to stand in the middle and prevent this movement to these strategic centers.

• • •

Stan drops his rucksack and sets about exploring his new home. He fills sandbags and at about 9:00 p.m., dead-tired, he falls asleep in a puddle of water, hoping the small depression in the ground might provide some small degree of protection from ground fire, should it ever come.

January 31, 1968

LZ Jane

At 4:00 a.m., Stan is awakened by the shrill cry of whistles. At first he thinks he is in Indiana, on the wrestling mat in high school, and that the referee has just given a signal to start the match.

When the whistles don't cease but grow louder, Stan sits up, wiping muddy water from his eyes. Something loud and big is shaking the ground.

When he looks up and sees the waves of attackers heading up the hill, he freezes.

Illumination rounds drift overhead, swinging like lanterns, their light casting shadows across the trees, across Stan's face.

The artillery fire seems to be coming from North Vietnamese guns hidden along the western perimeter of the LZ. And then Stan sees them—hundreds of North Vietnamese soldiers in khaki uniforms, accompanied by Viet Cong fighters in black "pajamas" and sandals, are storming up the hill.

The soldiers are blowing whistles, and some of them are carrying long bamboo poles whose ends bounce ahead of them as they run.

Stan had fallen asleep near Jerry Austin, a machine gunner named Olen Queen, Tony Beke, and Michael Bradshaw, and all of them now fear they are being attacked by an entire battalion of NVA, about five hundred men. They—Stan and the rest of Recon Platoon, Alpha Company, and a 105mm artillery battery—number only about two hundred.

The NVA are hitting the two steepest positions, focusing their massed wave at these parts of the perimeter. The concertina wire at the edge of the LZ stands only about thirty-five feet away from the sandbagged positions. Al Dove sees that the enemy are hitting these positions because the steep grade shields them from a direct angle of fire. Al, manning his M-60 gun, is leaning over the sandbag berm and shooting so much that the barrel of his machine gun begins to glow red in the dark, like the inside of a furnace.

Jerry, Stan, Tony, Michael, and Alpha Company troopers are firing their M-16s and are amazed that the NVA run right past them as if they are invisible. The enemy soldiers, it turns out, are more concerned with capturing the center of the camp, the command-and-control bunker, and the howitzer batteries. These guns are firing from behind and directly over their heads, at the positions from which the NVA are charging the hill. Overhead, green tracer rounds race in from the assaulting enemy while red tracers swim in the outgoing fire of the LZ's U.S. troops.

An NVA soldier suddenly emerges from the dark, raises his rifle, and smashes Stan on the head with his rifle butt. The attacking soldier falls, shot by someone Stan can't see. Next, he's rushed by another NVA fighter. Stan can see his face, his mouth twisted in a scream, but what he sees most is the sharp point of the man's bayonet at the end of his AK-47, aimed at his chest. Stan can almost feel the metal tip, the first hint of pressure against the sweat-damp fabric of his jungle fatigues, like the deliberate touch of a finger atop something baking, *Is it done yet?* and then the entrance, the piercing, the enormously painful entrance of the steel into his chest, through the ribs, so painful that he does not feel it at first, and then the silver point entering his heart.

Stan knows he's supposed to raise his weapon, his M-16, and fire. He knows he's supposed to raise the rifle, with the bayonet fixed to its end, and stab the soldier. But he can't move. He sits there, feeling helpless, still foggy after getting clobbered by the NVA soldier and his rifle.

Off to his right, a burst of gunfire goes off. He can't hear it because the night is already too loud, but he can see the muzzle flashes, and Stan sees a paratrooper with his M-16 firing on the bayonet-wielding NVA soldier. The trooper stabs the soldier in the back and the body falls across Stan, who pushes it away, just as the paratrooper grabs Stan's hand and pulls him to his feet. The paratrooper keeps moving forward, leaving Stan behind.

Just then, another soldier runs up, and he yells above the din, "What are you doing?"

Stan shrugs—he feels stupid and he doesn't know what to say.

"Follow me!" yells the guy.

Out there in the dark, Stan can see the bayonets moving above the ground. Floating, moving forward. Toward him. Something awakens in him. He feels *alive*. Stan knows he's going to attack them.

He turns around and is shocked to see a platoon-mate, Ron Kuvik, "The Kuv," from Missouri, either dead or fast asleep. "Hey, Kuvik, wake up!" Stan yells. Nothing. In truth, Kuvik is exhausted by the day's trip to LZ Jane from the south, and he will even sit up at one point, see all the red dots swarming around him, the tracer rounds, and fall back asleep. Stan jumps up and follows the soldier. They run to the center of the fighting, the point at which the NVA are most intensely attacking.

Stan watches as the men carrying the poles plant them like vaulters and launch themselves over the concertina wire. It is then that Stan sees that some of these men are carrying satchel charges—bombs. Their plan is to run through the camp and into its command bunkers and machine-gun nests and blow them up.

He and Jerry Austin are shooting and loading new magazines as fast as they can. He can't shoot fast enough. When Al and Olen Queen join them at the wire with their M-60 machine guns, the firing is so loud it seems to be held by no sound at all.

Stan tries shooting the pole vaulters out of the air. He will later learn that these approaching sappers, armed with satchel charges, are from the 10th Sapper Battalion, 812th NVA Regiment, 324B NVA Division, and that they were sometimes drugged with opium to induce euphoria.

Some of the pole vaulters don't have enough momentum, and they teeter at the apex of their arc and begin falling back—at which point their comrades rush in, grasp the pole, and begin to push it forward, delivering them to the other side. Stan in his addled state marvels at this and thinks it reminds him of the flag raising at Iwo Jima.

Other NVA soldiers take a more direct route to glory. They run at the wire and leap up, arms spread wide, and do a swan dive right onto its impaling blades. Stan watches as several of the enemy do this, making a soft human carpet on the wire, over which dozens of NVA are scrambling. Stan thinks, *How in the hell are we going to win against men like this?* He's firing so fast and so much that he doesn't know what he is hitting. He spots some of the sappers who have made it inside the camp. Stan aims at them, trying to hit the satchel charge so it will blow up.

Looking over to his left, he watches a rocket-propelled grenade race in and blow up one of the M-60 machine-gun positions. Just then he also sees a lone, tall figure, an American, charge the position, fire, and retake the gun. Even in the dark, amid the explosions, he can recognize the silhouette of the gunner as Michael Bradshaw. Stan is filled with joy that Bradshaw has rushed to the position to counter the enemy's attack; his decision to do this may help save them. Stan knows Bradshaw must be scared, but in the din he can't hear if he's screaming or yelling or swearing; silence. He's a flickering image amid hundreds of explosions.

Looking back to his front, Stan sees one sapper detonate nearly in front of him, just about twenty-five feet away. Stan closes his eyes and hears a sickening rain fall around him. When he opens his eyes, he sees two of the dead soldier's fingers stuck to his shoulder.

And then the combat turns hand to hand. The North Vietnamese and Viet Cong jump into the shallow bunkers, and Stan is fighting them off with the bayonet fixed on the end of his M-16. He remembers what his instructor told him at Fort Leonard Wood—that he would teach what it means to feel the "warrior's spirit." Only now is Stan comprehending what his instructor had meant. Stan shoots two soldiers as they run past, then stabs a third. He is surprised at how hard it is to get a man unstuck from the blade. He has to lift his foot, place it against the dead man's chest, and pull back hard. He has just gotten one of the dead NVA to slide off his bayonet when he's again rifle-butted by some unseen enemy. It knocks him backward, and he clenches, waiting for a next blow. But it doesn't come. He jumps back up and keeps shooting and stabbing.

When the attack is over, the silence of the night is deafening.

In the morning, January 31, the Recon Platoon stares out at dead enemy soldiers piled up along the concertina wire. Severed legs, heads, and arms scattered across the spindly ground. Stan and many of his comrades, covered in blood, pieces of flesh, and bone fragments, break open their C-rations and eat breakfast. For a moment, Stan expects the worst to happen: he expects his fellow soldiers to *know* that the night before he'd momentarily froze in the midst of combat. He wonders who the soldier was who noticed him and got him to his feet. He'd like to thank him for saving his life.

He watches Jerry Austin pick up something from the ground, look at it, and pass it around. Stan thinks it looks like a square piece of a sponge. . . . The object is squishy to the touch. Troy Fulton, the medic, says, "What the hell are you doing? That's a *hand*." In fact, it's a hand with no fingers.

Al Dove rouses from his position and counts twelve feet, detached from the shin down, scattered about. He looks more closely and sees that they were right feet. He figures the blast that had ripped them apart had come from their right side, for how else to explain the inexplicable? He doesn't dwell on this; there are too many macabre sights to take in. Stan looks around the LZ and sees that some of the heads look as if they have been emptied, the faces folded nearly in half. The night's attack had lasted just twenty minutes.

If this is what it's like, Stan thinks, *we are really in for a war.*

The official after-action reports would record that fourteen enemy soldiers had been killed in the night, but when Bradshaw and Austin and Parker and the others start counting, they tally up nearly one hundred dead enemy soldiers. Bradshaw has the unfortunate job of driving a flatbed vehicle called a Mule and picking up their remains. He and a crew throw them onboard, drive them to the pit the engineers had bulldozed that morning, toss the pieces in the hole, and cover them with lime. Bradshaw loads the Mule four or five times with eight to twelve enemy bodies each time. He works for several hours at this job, and as much as he dreads it and is repulsed by the gore, he hates even more the words he hears next: he and Recon will be heading out beyond the wire to take up ambush positions in case the NVA plan another attack.

In those first predawn hours of the Tet Offensive, about 100,000 North Vietnamese regular army soldiers attacked thirty-six cities throughout South Vietnam. Planning for the attack, led by Ho Chi Minh and General Giap, had begun about seven months earlier in Hanoi. Tons of matériel and thousands of fighters had been quietly inserted into South Vietnam by way of the Ho Chi Minh Trail. The swift execution of the countrywide offensive stunned the American military.

Enemy soldiers and guerrillas attacked the radio station and U.S. embassy in Saigon and even attacked Westmoreland's head-quarters at Tan Son Nhut Air Base, outside Saigon, setting it on fire. Westmoreland called the attack "deceitful." He complained that the NVA and VC broke a holiday truce they themselves had agreed to.

The surprise onslaught was meant to shock the American public. At the same time, the attacks were supposed to inspire Vietnamese citizens to rise up and take arms against the American "occupiers" and South Vietnamese "puppet regime" living among them. The hope was that the Vietnamese in Hai

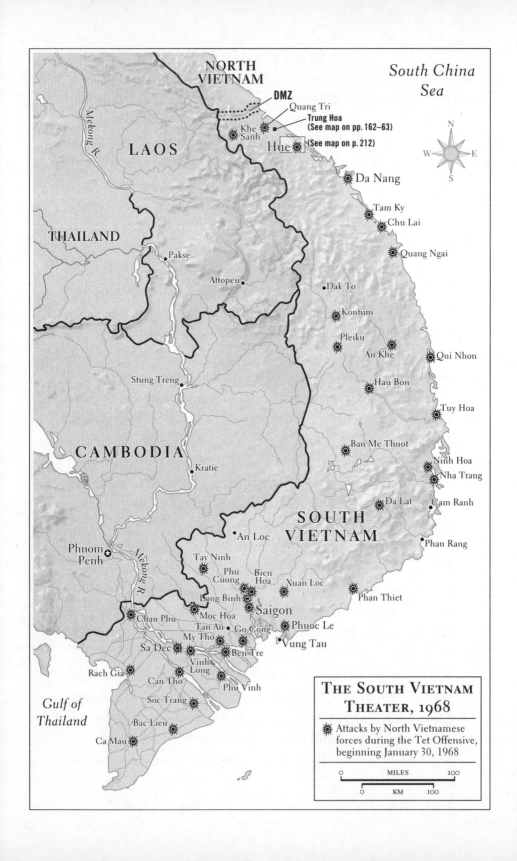

NORTH VIETNAM

DMZ

Quang Tri
Trung Hoa
(See map on pp. 162–63)

Khe
Sanh

(See map on p. 212)

Hue

*South China
Sea*

LAOS

Da Nang

Tam Ky
Chu Lai

THAILAND

Pakse

Quang Ngai

Attopeu

Dak To

Kontum

Pleiku

An Khe

Qui Nhon

Stung Treng

Hau Bon

Tuy Hoa

CAMBODIA

Ban Me Thuot

Ninh Hoa
Nha Trang

Kratie

Da Lat

Cam Ranh

**SOUTH
VIETNAM**

An Loc

Phan Rang

Phnom
Penh

Tay Ninh

Phu
Cuong

Bien
Hoa

Xuan Loc

Long Binh

Phan Thiet

Moc Hoa

Saigon

Chau Phu

Tan An

Go Cong

Phuoc Le

My Tho

Vung Tau

Sa Dec

Ben Tre

Vinh
Long

Rach Gia

Can Tho

Phu Vinh

Soc Trang

*Gulf of
Thailand*

Bac Lieu

Ca Mau

Mekong R.

Mekong R.

THE SOUTH VIETNAM
THEATER, 1968

Attacks by North Vietnamese
forces during the Tet Offensive,
beginning January 30, 1968

MILES

0   100

KM

0   100

N
W   E
S

Lang, in Hue, in Quang Tri City, in Saigon—throughout the entire country—would foment their own insurrection. But the understaffed, ill-equipped, and poorly trained citizen soldiers who might have led a countrywide rebellion did not coalesce as a fighting force.

News and images of these surprise attacks rippled back to the United States in a matter of hours via teletype and the beaming of TV combat footage. Nearly overnight, American perceptions of the war changed. The North Vietnamese Army and Viet Cong would win a victory in the realm of psychological operations, but suffer enormous losses on the ground. By March 4, the end of the Tet Offensive, estimates of enemy dead would number 40,000, and some 14,000 South Vietnamese, including women and children, would die. The combat deaths of Americans would number 4,000. General Westmoreland would put a diplomatic point on the moment: "Although the enemy has achieved some temporary psychological advantage," he remarked, "he suffered a military defeat."

The Tet Offensive would last another thirty-four days.

At about 7:30 on the foggy and cold morning of February 1, with a light rain falling, the men of Recon Platoon load into a three-truck convoy and leave LZ Jane.

The truck Stan is riding in hits a hole in the road, jostling his helmet. Stan doesn't want to wear the "steel pot" (as the soldiers called their metal helmets), so he throws it off and it bounces in the road as the truck continues on. He's glad to be rid of it. It's always knocking around on his head, heavy and hot, and it really doesn't seem it would do a damn bit of good. It hardly seems worth the discomfort. So he's glad he's rid it. But then he's amazed to watch one of the Loach helicopter crew members, flying in a tiny bubble-headed chopper escorting the convoy, lean out of the canopy, reach down, and grab Stan's helmet off the road. The Loach rises and moves up and over the truck where Stan is riding at the tailgate. He then drops down a notch or two in the shimmering air (the rotor wash is tremendous during this entire incident), and the crew member hands Stan his helmet. He looks up, takes it hesitantly, and finally puts it on—to have refused would have seemed an insult. The Loach lifts away and is gone.

Well, I'll be damned, thinks Stan. *Now I've seen it all.*

When they reach the western edge of Hai Lang, they get out of the trucks and walk into town. Along the road, they see piles of bandages and blood-smeared helmets and rifles, but they don't find any wounded or dead.

The houses they pass are empty.

The people of Hai Lang have fled.

On the same day that a helicopter crewman plucked Stan's helmet off the road, South Vietnam's national police chief made history on the streets of Saigon. Nguyen Ngoc Loan raised a .38 pistol and fired point-blank at the head of a Viet Cong fighter turned prisoner, Nguyen Van Lem. Loan made history for two reasons: for the brazen, swift act of killing the prisoner in broad daylight on a busy Saigon street and because it was in full view of AP photographer Eddie Adams, who took a picture at the instant the bullet entered the VC fighter's head and at the same time a cameraman for NBC News was filming the execution.

Loan approached the short, slender man, whose arms were bound behind him, quickly raised his pistol, and fired. The fighter toppled over, dead before he landed on the pavement, with bright blood shooting from the exit wound on the left side of his head onto the pavement. Adams won the 1969 Pulitzer

Prize for the photograph and would later say that two people died in the picture; the VC fighter and Loan. What Adams later explained was that earlier in the day, Nguyen Van Lem had been leading a Viet Cong "revenge squad" and had executed families of Saigon police officers. Lem had been brought to Loan for questioning and Loan, on hearing about the revenge kills, had killed Lem. After the execution, Loan is reported to have said, "These guys kill a lot of our people, and I think Buddha will forgive me."

The movement of his arm was that of a quick rising motion, of a man suddenly raising his arm to light a candle at head height. At the touch of the pistol to his head, the man instantly crumbled. Back in the United States, millions of Americans, gathered around television sets, were horrified by the execution of an unarmed man.

The fallout of the cold-blooded killing followed Loan the rest of his life. After the war, in 1975, he moved to the United States and opened a pizza parlor in a shopping mall in suburban Washington, D.C., but even there he was haunted by his act of revenge. Once when he visited the pizza parlor, Adams, who remained in touch with the outcast general, found graffiti in the pizza shop men's room that read, "We know who you are, fucker." Loan died in 1998, only sixty-seven years old. Cancer.

The U.S. artillery starts dropping on Hai Lang, and the men of Recon begin walking house to house with the intent of clearing the remaining enemy.

As they patrol, an artillery shell lands in a nearby neighborhood.

That's when the wailing starts.

A moaning, a tide of grief—rising.

Stan can only imagine the damage the shelling has done, crumpling tin, smashing mud, burning thatch.

Can imagine the dead persons lying amid the rubble.

Kids.

Women.

And probably the VC, too, which is why the neighborhood has been targeted. The intention had not been to kill civilians, but Stan can hear them wailing. He's beginning to feel that his mind's not right, that he's having trouble thinking.

Things are becoming disconnected, he realizes. There's some relationship between the landing of the artillery shell and the wailing that ensues, but it's harder and harder for him to make this connection.

That night, hunkered in a shallow hole in the yard of an abandoned school, Stan sits and listens to the wailing, wishing with all his might that it would stop. Sitting in the dark, he and Beke, Lane, and Dove also hear a mysterious *thunk* and *swishing* noise at least a dozen times. The morning light reveals a dozen NVA hand grenades scattered about them, within two to five feet of where they were resting—all of them duds, miraculously.

The next morning, they get up and start walking back into the village, but now it's quiet. The wailing has stopped.

In Hai Lang, Stan and the Recon Platoon are battling the 5th Battalion of the 812th NVA Regiment, tough bastards. Stan crouches in the street, watching a column of the 101st Airborne's Alpha Company 1/501 advance up the street. At the same time, he sees a squad or two of NVA soldiers, at least several dozen, sneaking up on Alpha Company by using a building and some abandoned vehicles as cover. He can see the whole thing happening from where he's crouched. Alpha Company is about to be ambushed.

He pulls his M-16 up to his shoulder, takes aim, and fires off two shots—about seventy-five yards away, kind of Hail Mary shots at that.

His aim is good: his shots are headed straight for the RPG gunner in the group of enemy soldiers. Both shots strike the leader and topple him over backward. As he falls back, the RPG tube swings over his shoulder, pointing directly at the line of men behind him. Evidently, in the contraction of death, his finger tightens on the trigger and fires the rocket, which flies out of the launcher and starts tearing through his men, who drop like bowling pins. It travels about thirty feet and explodes. The devastation is nearly total. Stan has taken out a large portion of the assaulting force with two lucky shots. He's thrilled.

Four days after the start of the Tet fighting, February 4, big U.S. guns, firing from a nearby firebase, shoot six hundred high-explosive rounds into Hai Lang for several hours. Stan can feel some of the explosions in his boots, as the sonic rumbles dissipate in the rest of his body. Echo Company's sister company, Bravo Company, has moved into Hai Lang to engage the NVA, and they are under attack. Stan can hear the gunfire and mortars, and as the battle heats up, Bravo Company has to withdraw because the artillery fire is dropping too close to their own positions. In midafternoon, after several hours of this fighting, Charlie Company comes under attack too. The U.S. casualties are enormous: forty-two wounded and six killed, including the company commander and two platoon leaders. For the fourth day in a row, Stan doesn't know if he'll still be alive at sundown.

The platoon is falling now into a rhythm as a unit: walk and patrol during the day and set up ambush at night. Stan begins to feel they exist in a place between waking and sleep, between hyper-alertness and somnolence. The street fighting is relentless. Stan is carrying a canvas pouch over his shoulder, hanging by a strap and made to carry Claymore land mines. The pouch, however, is filled with cans of C-ration peaches he's collected along the way. The cans fit nicely in the hand, are made of heavy tin, painted Army green. They say "Peaches" on the side, in black letters.

Stan now finds the peaches to be a delicacy, a rare thing in an ugly place. He likes carrying the peaches in the pouch and feeling them thump against his chest as he patrols. They reassure him that there is still something beautiful in the world.

They're about a half mile from the village of Hai Lang. Stan is walking point, and Francis Wongus is taking the slack. Wongus's job is to keep an eye on things and spot anything Stan might miss. Stan is moving down the trail, heel-toe, heel-toe, with Wongus about twenty feet behind him, and suddenly an NVA soldier jumps out from a tree, levels his AK at Stan, and fires a quick four-round burst. Stan falls. Wongus wheels around and shoots the NVA soldier. No telling what the soldier was thinking, unless he didn't anticipate Wongus would be walking in the slack position. Francis nearly cuts the guy in half, and he's lying facedown on the ground. Stan's lying on the ground too. He does some self-examination with his hand and fears he's been hit in the spine. He can't move; his legs are numb. He fears not that he may be dying but that he might not walk again.

Bullets pass all around him and overhead. The woods are filled with the hollow banging sound of gunfire. But for this minute, within this chaos, he's worried he's a cripple, worried, maybe, that his peter won't work anymore, that he'll be dead sexually, and he wonders whether this will have any effect on his ability to fight or defend himself during the rest of his life.

Stan reaches around and touches the wet spot on his back,

where he thinks he stops feeling anything from there on down. He rubs his fingers together and brings them up to look: on his fingers is white cream.

Oh, God, he thinks, *that's my bone marrow.*

He stares at the white marrow and smells his fingers. The fragrance is odd and he realizes that for his entire life he had no idea that bone marrow had any smell at all.

He hears somebody crawling up to him. Here comes Troy Fulton, a medic, to save the day. Stan couldn't be happier to see him. There's a photo Stan will look at years from this moment, a picture he will keep in a shoe box in a closet in his otherwise quiet house in Colorado; it's of Troy, in grainy black-and-white, bending down to tie his boot, a white cigarette clenched in his jaw, unlit, while he squints in concentration over the laces. He will think, *God bless, Troy Fulton*, and wonder, *Whatever happened to him?*

Troy says, "Parker, you all right?"

"I'm hit."

"Where?"

"I think my back's broken."

"Can you feel anything?"

"No." And Stan can't. He's numb from the waist down, as if the lower half of his body went to sleep on him. Tingling.

"Let me see," says Fulton, ducking down as more gunfire whizzes overhead. Fulton's touching the wet spot on the back of Stan's fatigue shirt. He has to root around to find the spot and then he pauses as if to say, "Wait a minute," and he starts to rummage through Stan's pack itself.

"That's my bone marrow," Stan says. "Can you feel it?"

"You mean this?" asks Fulton, pulling out a can of Barbasol shaving cream.

It's got two bullet holes in it. Fulton shows him the smear of shaving cream in his own hand. Stan's confused at first, then relieved and smiles.

"You haven't been shot," says Troy. "You're fine."

"Really?"

"You're damn lucky to be alive."

"But what about my legs, the numbness?"

"They'll come back. Don't worry. The nerve's been bruised."

Stan has no idea if nerves can be bruised, and if they can be bruised, if they'll come back. But he trusts Troy Fulton. Even though he's only a few years older than Stan, he seems so much wiser. Stan figures it's due to all the death Troy had seen in Ia Drang. His sole job is to save people, to treat their broken bodies.

Fulton's starting to edge away from Stan to help someone else. "You lay still. Don't shoot back or you'll make yourself a target, and they'll kill you this time," he says. "I'm going to check on you in a little while." He explains he can't call in a medevac right now—too much enemy fire.

Fulton reaches out and squeezes Stan's arm and smiles a big, hundred-watt smile and says, "And when I come back, I'll be sure to bring a big ol' razor so you can finish the shave."

Each day more bombs fall on the village. More wailing commences each nightfall. Each aria of pain, pure, as if an angel is singing with its throat cut, rises and finishes with a crystalline flourish. One night, Troy Fulton creeps up in the dark of an ambush and whispers to Stan that the NVA had come through the neighborhood and killed even more people, including the local South Vietnamese suspected of collaborating with the Americans. The women of the neighborhood had been spared, though. These were the people who were wailing.

• • •

The schoolhouse yard, where they've dug a fighting position and that they have begun to inhabit regularly each night, seems an odd place to make a killing ground. Yet here they are, digging in again with the job of watching the main highway in front of them. They are to kill any VC or NVA they see. Stan is coming to the conclusion that his real and even bigger job is simply to stay alive.

He and the others have passed a line: they've stopped fighting for any ideas and they're certainly not fighting for the Vietnamese. Stan is amazed and angry about the way some of his South Vietnamese soldiers will not stand with him and the other paratroopers and slug it out in a firefight. But he admires their cooking. They catch freshwater shrimp no bigger than a June bug, string them on a skewer, and roast them over a fire—*delicious*. But beyond this, beyond an admiration for the way the South Vietnamese Army may occasionally stand and deliver with a rifle, Stan feels almost nothing for his Vietnamese countrymen. He does feel immense remorse for the U.S. troopers killed in the battles he's fought in, but no remorse for the dead NVA and VC scattered about the village of Hai Lang.

He's fighting in a room overlooking a street in Hai Lang. The street is filled with gunfire. The room, a second-floor bedroom, is filled with smoke and American soldiers who are sticking their M-16s out the windows and shooting at the NVA soldiers down below in the rubble-strewn street, who are firing back up at them. The back wall of the bedroom is popping as the rounds from the street hit it. He looks out of his left eye, at the barrels sticking out of the window next to him, and realizes these are AK-47 barrels, which means that the people next door are North Vietnamese or VC fighters. Holy mackerel, he realizes; they are fighting next door to each other. He does some quick thinking, pulls out a Claymore, and sets it against the wall with the blast radius directed into the adjoining room. He steps out into the hallway and squeezes the clacker handles, setting off the mine. He steps back into the room in time to see the stunned fighters next door stumbling around, covered in dust; a few of them are lying dead on the floor. Stan steps up into the gap in the wall and takes aim and guns down the remaining soldiers. It's like shooting men in a barrel. The stunned enemy soldiers don't put up any resistance, and it's in this kind of moment that he realizes that war is really about elimination—eliminating, erasing, wasting, greasing, making nonexistent. You kill the other guy, until there are more of you than there are of them.

Many mornings, Stan wakes up feeling old. He doesn't feel twenty. He feels like he's fallen into another story about another life he'd never imagined he'd be living, here in Vietnam, living "like an animal," living to kill. He feels there's no story except the one each of the platoon members tell themselves, by each act of staying alive, which means often committing another act of killing more enemy. Each man taps into the story, it hangs down out of the sky in gray shreds, as if torn from the sky.

Stay alive. Walk home. Crawl home. Get home. Journey.
Kill.

Stan and another soldier are walking down a trail and Stan finds a foot. As a matter of course these days, he finds body parts lying to the left and to the right wherever he goes. It seems fitting that he keeps finding feet because so much of his life is about movement now. It's as if the universe is strewing feet in his path to guide him onward.

This foot is lying a distance from the guy it once belonged to and is still strapped inside its sandal. The sandaled foot looks like one of those fake feet/ankle displays that merchants use in department stores and dress with men's dress socks, so you can see what the sock will look like when you slip it on. Sticking out of the top of the foot, cleanly detached from the leg at the middle of the shin bone by an explosion, are the tendons.

The tendons are sticking up like little stiff wires. Stan, half out of his mind, looks at them. He pulls at one of them, and the toes start moving. Then he picks at them and watches as each toe, one by one and then in concert, rises and drops, like fleshy piano keys, or, more accurately, like the hammers of a piano. Stan does this with real fascination. There's a purity to this strange activity, watching the silent tapping of the toes on the air close around his face as he holds the foot and ligaments and understands, as if for the first time, what? That the body is a machine, that it's built of parts, that it can be destroyed.

Finally, still fiddling with the foot, Stan takes the bayonet attached to the barrel of his M-16 and stabs it down into the meat at the top of the foot, so that now, at the end of his bayonet, is a man's foot, looking quite normal, clean. When he holds his rifle up, pointing at the air, the foot is heavy and threatens to tip the rifle one way and another. He holds the rifle at his side, by the stock, and lets the foot rest on the ground, where it leaves a print, and then he takes a step forward and the rifle swings forward like a leg itself and the foot on the end of the bayonet swings forward and lights on the ground and leaves another print. Stan steps forward and, swing, the foot comes forward and lands. Slowly, and then quickly, Stan is mesmerized by this pattern evolving alongside him, as if he's being accompanied by a one-legged man. He knows what he's doing is highly irregular, but it's hypnotic. About five or ten minutes later, the radio cracks to life and Russo answers it and gives the handset to Stan. "It's for you." It's Sergeant Kinney, located behind them on the trail, asking, "Parker, which way did you go?" Stan tells him, and Kinney says, "Okay, you see that one-legged guy hobble by?"

Stan is surprised that his prank has been noticed, but he thinks, *What the hell?* and says, "Yeah, I saw him," and then he says, "We're following him."

"Did you find him?"

"No."

"Find out where he goes, okay?"

So Stan keeps walking with the one-legged man at his side, and pretty soon the radio cracks again, "We see where you're at, but this one-legged guy—he's still going. You have him?"

Stan says, "I have no idea where he's at."

"Well, we'd like to find him. He's wounded."

Not long after, Stan is overtaken by Kinney and the platoon officer, and they see what he's been doing with the foot, see it on the end of his bayonet.

Stan says, "I didn't do it intentionally. It was just something to do." But even as he says this, he knows it's not true; he did do this intentionally. It was something to do to keep from going crazy. The things that happen now seem to happen all at once, and the anticipation of them happening is so monumental that in the back of your mind, the fears curl and uncurl, glowing wires. Fear of explosion, fear of death by gunshot, death by bayonet, by grenade, snake bite, madness. Fear of being forgotten, by whom? By home, your sweetheart, your family. Fear of remembering, of what? Everything. The fear that you will remember everything.

They're walking and looking for the remnants of Charlie Company. About thirty of their soldiers are missing. Stan doesn't know them personally, of course, but they are part of the 1st Battalion, to which Echo Company belongs. He wants revenge. All of Recon wants revenge.

As they come into a clearing, the sun appears. Light slants down from the green canopy and joins the brown forest floor. Where the beam hits the ground, it spreads out in a pool of light, and arrayed around this pool of light are the thirty bodies of Charlie Company.

They're all in uniform, staring up at the sky. Their faces have been shot in half. Or, rather, someone has placed a rifle's muzzle and methodically pulled the trigger until half of the face of each man had turned to hamburger. The bodies have been arranged in neat rows, their hands either at their sides or folded on their chests.

Birds call in the canopy overhead; there's the sound of dripping, the *pwop-pwop* of water in the trees. He can't see the dripping, only hears it. Stan thinks of this as the jungle's voice, and it has been talking to him, saying, *You are not a man. You are an animal.*

He kneels at the bodies and looks close. He turns his head this way and that, marveling at how from one angle, the young men look fine, and then by leaning the other way, they look otherworldly, bloody, their flesh whorled in red patterns. Stan stands up and starts vomiting.

One of the guys in the company says they must've arranged the platoon after they'd been killed in the firefight and then set about ruining the faces. Stan thinks they'd been executed and then shot—the wounded and the already dying who may or may not have surrendered. He can see bullet wounds in the skulls that had not been part of the unmasking of the flesh from the faces. He starts walking around the clearing and piecing together what he thinks happened.

There are a few soldiers who had not been lined up in rows.

Stan finds one still sitting upright, his right leg bent backward, his left leg thrust forward, his rifle across his lap. He's leaning back like a man in the middle of a stretching exercise; he still has an IV bag, empty now, clutched in his hand. From the bag runs the tube, and this had been attached by needle into another soldier's arm. The medic had been trying to give his fellow soldier fluids and had been firing his M-16 at the same time. Stan can see the brass casings sprinkled around him.

Stan marvels at the ingenious nature of it, this trick of the eye that is not a trick at all, that had been created for them and that the enemy knew they would walk upon in this jungle clearing. Stan is filled first with awe at the sight, then more nausea, then rage.

They start on a steady march for the next ridgeline. As they turn a corner, Stan sees several NVA soldiers running down the trail. He fires but with no effect. Up ahead, he sees rucksacks that the fleeing soldiers have left behind. The platoon searches them for intelligence but finds nothing of value. As they are doing this, five NVA soldiers step onto the trail and fail to see Stan, Wongus, Dove, and Beke. Without a shot being fired, all five enemy soldiers are captured and turned over to the South Vietnamese, who will interrogate them.

Whether or not the five captured soldiers know anything of value, Stan knows he'll never really find out. He wonders how you can measure value in a war like this. Their orders are to kill as many enemy soldiers as they can find. Back in D.C., men like Secretary of Defense Robert McNamara have devised a strategy, and convinced President Johnson of its validity, that the North Vietnamese Army, led by the president of North Vietnam, Ho Chi Minh, can be shot and bombed into submission. On the other hand, Ho Chi Minh himself has said that for each man the Americans kill, his country will replace that man with another soldier. Stan is pretty sure there is a never-ending supply of people to shoot.

• • •

Helicopters come in, and Stan and the platoon start loading up the dead of Charlie Company. Under the soft light of the trees, they look like wax figures.

The platoon walks around the clearing, the killing zone, picking up the bodies. Someone's already laid a tall soldier on a poncho; Stan and Dwight Lane pick up one end, and Jerry Austin and Tony Beke grab the other. The body shifts and the blood that had gathered around him as he sat cooling on the poncho is coagulated—like Jello-O, Stan thinks—and slides out of the poncho through a hole and lands, *plop*, on the ground at Stan's feet. Stan sees this and starts throwing up. The men set the poncho down and they all get sick. Then they pick up the soldier again and walk him to the Huey.

His detached leg falls out of the poncho onto the ground, and Dwight Lane says, "Hey, his leg," and Stan, without thinking, says, "He ain't leaving without his leg." Then he sets his end of the poncho on the ground, walks over and picks up the leg, carries it back to the poncho, and places it on the bundle. He, Lane, Austin, and Beke keep walking and lift him up into the helicopter and are they ever glad that this is over. It's like they are sleepwalking, as they move around the clearing carrying body parts, arms and legs, putting them on ponchos in piles, and putting the piles on choppers.

Stan, Al Dove, Tim Anderson, Tom Soals, Michael Bradshaw, and Dwight Lane set up an ambush, and after an hour, out of nowhere, Stan whispers, "I have to piss."

"What do you mean, you have to piss?" asks Dove.

"Like, I have to go. Now."

Dove whispers to Stan to inch back up the hill on his belly and let 'er fly. Stan does just that lying on his left side, luxuriating in the immediate relief he feels. He crawls back down to Dove's side. Within a few seconds, Dove asks Parker if his canteen is leaking because he is getting soaked with water.

"No," says Stan. "I drank all of my canteen water earlier, and that's why I had to piss so bad."

"You mean that I am lying in your piss? I'm gonna kill you first thing in the morning!" says Dove.

Dwight Lane, listening to this whispered exchange, finds it very funny that his friends are arguing about killing each other over who peed on whom. He whispers that he understands why Dove would want to kill Stan, and then has to stifle a laugh.

Stan has his face buried in the leaves, trying to control his laughter. They have to remain silent on account of the ambush. They are very still and trying not to laugh. And Stan knows—all of them know—that there's nothing Dove can do but surrender. He must sit in the warmth of the piss until it cools around him. Stan knows that in a funny way, they're happy, giddy, even. They're among friends and they're still alive.

Stan is walking in a gray drizzle with Al Dove and Brian Riley, wrapped mummy-style in clear plastic shower curtains they've torn down from the shower stalls at the nearby schoolhouse. The curtains are their only protection from the cold rain. Their weapons poke through a part in the curtains and they make a strange sight, like translucent beasts. Stan sees a little girl standing in the middle of the road up ahead, watching the group's advance. She looks scared, filthy, and very alone. As he gets closer, he sees that she's also very young, maybe six or seven. Her hair is tangled and her face is dirty and streaked with tears. Stan takes off his shower curtain and offers it to her. She doesn't move, so he wraps it around her. But it's too long and bunches around her bare feet, so Stan takes his Ka-Bar knife and hacks away at the extra length to shorten it. She doesn't say anything. She does not ask for anything, nor does she stand back and shy away. She stands there looking at him. Mute. Impassive. Courageous. Stan feels the need to do something for her, but he simply stares at her in his confused, sleep-deprived state. He looks and looks at her. And then he has what he can only describe as an epiphany, an awakening, as if his eyes are snapping open after a long nap. He is able to see the whole lousy war through her eyes—the shooting, the killing. Images roll back and forth over her face, and he watches them pass before them—a movie of who he is, who he was, who he is becoming. An animal. A killer. A young man who is filled with hatred, as President Johnson had predicted all young men would become in the jaws of war. He has this overwhelming desire to make the girl safe.

But he doesn't know how. He wants to give her something. Clean clothes, food, a future. He has nothing to give her except his attention. Then he remembers he has a can of peaches in the canvas bag on his chest where he stores his Claymore mines. He pulls out a heavy green can of the fruit and bends down to offer it to her. The can is large in her dirty hand, which sags under its weight. "It's okay," he tells her. "Go away now," and he makes a shooing gesture with his hand. He would like someone to come and take care of her. He would like to come back to Vietnam as another kind of person and be able to offer her some peace and attention and safety. It's quiet between the two of them, punctuated by the rustle of the shower curtain wrapped around her thin shoulders. She stares at the peaches and then back at Stan, as if asking him what she should do with this. It's then he realizes he's been left behind by the rest of the patrol. He knows they are in a no-man's-land, where he could run into any number of enemy and he feels terribly exposed. Al Dove and Brian Riley, already far ahead, are calling to him, "Come on, man. We've got to go!" He finally turns from the girl, touches her gently on the head, says "Good-bye," and runs to catch up. He rounds a corner and sees the other guys up ahead. A few seconds after that, he hears gunshots behind him.

Oh my god! Not the girl. He wheels around and runs, his gear flapping around his body as his arms pump faster and faster. He turns the corner, and there she is, a tiny clump, no bigger than a pile of rags, in the street. Looking down the road, he sees four NVA soldiers fleeing among the buildings. He levels his weapon and fires at them, but he misses and curses himself. How could he miss when he'd killed so many men before? Stan runs up to the girl, looks at her, and drops to his knees, crying.

Why why why oh why. He knows why. Because he's a bad person. Because he's an American soldier. Because he's a man filled with madness. He looks down at her, still holding the peaches, her hand tightened in spasm around the can. Her fingers are incredibly slender and tiny. Why did he give her the can of peaches? He would love more than anything to reach back through time and take them back. She's dead because she accepted the American's peaches. The irony is that if he'd had no compassion for her, if he'd ignored her, she'd still be alive. He might as well have aimed his rifle at her and pulled the trigger himself. Stan looks up at the sky, shuddering, and he starts howling, a hoarse cry emptying from his stomach, more animal than human.

The rest of the guys come running back to him. And they stop when they see him. They're unsure what to do. They look at him, start circling him, as he rocks back and forth in the street and howls.

Brian Riley finally walks up and says, "Hey, man, we have to get outta here," looking around for the return of the NVA. "Let's radio this in and go." Riley then calls in the sighting of the four NVA soldiers, so that others in the battalion can be on the lookout.

Stan reaches over and picks up the little girl and cradles her. She's warm, her chest soaked with blood. He thankfully figures that she died instantly.

He walks with her in his arms across the street to an empty building. It's been bombed and reduced to rubble, but the front wall is still standing and he thinks that she'll be safe there, away from the street. Next door is an apartment building that's been bombed and is empty too. Al Dove and Riley want to leave the street, but Stan refuses. He tells them that he will not leave the girl there alone. He tells them he wants to sit across the street in the safety of another building, as a hidey-hole, and wait to see who comes passing by. Maybe the bastards who shot her, or some of their friends, or maybe her family, or someone who knows her. . . . But either way, he can't leave her like this in an empty building alongside an empty road as twilight falls now. The other guys try to convince him otherwise, but Stan won't leave. He sets up an ambush position across the road, with his M-16 trained on the building where she lies in state.

Through the long night, cold and raining, Stan thinks he hears footfalls in the dark, the steps of the approaching enemy, but nothing materializes, and as the sun rises, he gets up, feeling sore, and stretches. He has that feeling, worn-out, rinsed-out, after great strain, as if the terror of the past days had burned away his nerve endings. Across the road, he sees the rats.

They are crawling all over the girl. He can hear their scratching, and he puts it all together. *Oh god no!* he thinks. Real calm, he lifts his M-16 against his cheek, takes aim, and fires. One of the rats goes flying backward, away from the girl, and he aims again, careful to guide the round away from the girl, and fires. Another rat cartwheels from the slight frame. Stan thinks that the report of the carbine would have scattered the rats, but they are persistent in their feeding.

He starts firing more rapidly, knocking the rats down, and he keeps firing even after the last rat is dead, getting more excited now, feeling his nerve endings coming back to life, as if sprouting through his skin. He keeps pumping rounds into the dead rat bodies. He's shot them all, every one, at least several dozen, and he says over his shoulder to Riley, calm and spooky, "More ammo," and Riley, without objecting, hands him another magazine, nineteen more bullets, and Stan jams the mag up in the receiver and charges the weapon and begins firing some more. He fires several more magazines, then stops and it's quiet. Real quiet. Dove and Riley quietly tell him, "It's okay. You did good." Stan realizes he's gone berserk.

After a few moments, he gets up, walks across the road to the girl, and looks at her. He can barely stand it, looking at her, the ugly thing he's wrought by his attempt at kindness.

She is still holding the can of peaches in her tiny left hand.

Her ears and nose are gone. The rats have been feeding all night, and for a second time he has let her down. He screams.

Stan Parker's second-grade school photo, taken a year after his recovery from polio. As the son of an itinerant ironworker, Stan was used to overt displays of condescension in nearly every town his family moved to. In San Antonio, Texas, his teacher called him "gypsy-carnival trash."

The four Parker brothers in 1965: Stan, Bruce, Joe, and the eldest, Jim (Dub). Both Stan and Dub would see action in Vietnam.

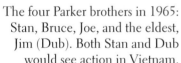

Stan at a friend's house in Gary, Indiana, in August 1966, just before leaving for Army basic training. His high school friends nicknamed him "Boots" because of the cowboy boots he usually wore. Stan believed his cowboy get-up let people know he was his own man.

A photo from the local newspaper shows Stan (third from the left) and three high school buddies— John Santos (second from the right), Tom Gervais (second from the left), and Pat Devitt (far left)— all shaking hands with a recruiter after enlistment in the Army on May 22, 1966. Stan did not discuss his decision to enlist with his parents until after the fact.

4

Stan served as part of the U.S. Army's Long-Range Reconnaissance Patrol (LRRP) in Germany after his father intervened to keep him from shipping out to Vietnam. Stan nevertheless approached his company commander every week to request a transfer.

5

6

Photo taken in early December 1967, Echo Company, 1st Battalion (Airborne), 501st Infantry Regiment, 101st Airborne Division, Fort Campbell, Kentucky, a few days prior to Vietnam deployment.

On December 14, 1967, Echo Company was transported to Cu Chi base camp, located south of the Viet Cong stronghold known as the Iron Triangle. On Christmas Day, Stan was reunited in Cu Chi with his older brother, Dub, in-country from the 101st Airborne, stationed with combat duty around the Phan Rang area of Vietnam.

7

Stan sent letters from Cu Chi to his girlfriend, Maureen, back in Indiana. "We're going to end this war," he promised in one. Later, as he saw more action, he wrote letters to her he decided not to send.

8

Stan carried Maureen's school picture (left) and that of his friend and neighbor Anna Runion (right) in the top left pocket of his jungle fatigues, right over his heart, for the duration of his tour in Vietnam. Some members of the Recon Platoon would come to believe that the pictures possessed special powers that kept them alive.

9

10

After two weeks of filling sandbags, the platoon began patrolling the area around Cu Chi, scouting for VC fighters. From left to right: Brian Lewis, Tom Soals, Lieutenant John Gay, Staff Sergeant Lindsey Kinney, Stan, and Al Dove.

11

Recon Platoon members Tim Anderson (left), Francis Wongus (center), and Tony Ramirez.

12

Specialist Dwight Lane (pictured here), Stan, and Brian Riley met each other as LRRPs in Germany and hit it off immediately. All three ended up as members of Recon Platoon in Vietnam.

13

Smoke in Cu Chi base camp following a rocket attack from the Viet Cong in December 1967. The nationwide surprise attack by the North Vietnamese on the 1968 Tet holiday was only weeks away.

14

15

Stan in Cu Chi with an M-60 machine gun, which could fire about six hundred and fifty rounds per minute with an effective range out to twelve hundred yards. "We were itching for something to happen," he wrote in a letter to his father. "Come on, do something! *Shoot at us!*"

16

On January 23, 1968, Recon Platoon and the entire 1st Battalion of the 501st Infantry loaded up on C-130s in Cu Chi and flew three hundred eighty miles to the Hue–Phu Bai area in the northernmost province in South Vietnam, following reports that the North Vietnamese Army was planning an attack over the Tet holiday.

17

Brian Riley, Stan Parker, and Bob Cromer loading up in the C-130.

The Recon Platoon on their first patrol from LZ Jane, about twenty-five miles south of the DMZ.

18

19

Al Dove from Honolulu napping with his M-60.

Charlie Pyle from Colleyville, Texas. He would be killed in action on March 22, 1968.

20

Huey helicopters darted in and out of hot landing zones, delivering soldiers and supplies and carrying out the wounded and dead. The Recon Platoon considered the Hueys that dropped them off and picked them up to be their lifelines.

21

Stan in a helicopter in February 1968 heading into combat.

22

23 24

The Recon Platoon often set up their ambushes on rickety bamboo bridges, laying down trip flares.

Stan, war-weary, with a thousand-yard stare in his eyes, April 1968. He had been in-country about five months.

25

January 1947

Texarkana, Texas

Here we are, looking into the bedroom of a house on a wooded yard in Texarkana, Texas, where a baby is sleeping fitfully in a shoe box in the opened top drawer of a dresser. Sickly, born four months premature, each day has brought a new prediction of his death for his worried parents. The baby, one month old, is named John Stanley Parker, a long, old-fashioned name he will have to grow into. It's a few weeks after the New Year, 1947. The streets are quiet and cold. On radios across town and across the country, Bing Crosby is singing "Let it snow, let it snow, let it snow." The war that consumed America for four long years is finally over.

Helen Laverne Parker, the boy's mother, age seventeen, is sitting in an adjoining room, rocking the baby's one-year-old brother, J.W., nicknamed Dub. She doesn't know how long she and her husband, John James, will stay in this rented house or even how long they will be in Texas. She had grown up on a watermelon and cotton farm in Muleshoe, Texas, about twenty miles as the buzzard flies from New Mexico. They met in February 1945 at a barn dance shortly after his return from the war. John James liked to call her his "Texas wildcat." Having survived twenty-four missions over Europe aboard a B-24 bomber, he had come home eager to put the war behind him. Three months after they met, they eloped. What Helen Laverne knows about the future, well, it's in her arms and around her: her sons' and her husband's love.

The shoe box, the makeshift crib, had been the home of a pair of John James's work boots. He's rarely home now, working in oil fields across West Texas—wildcatter jobs, mostly. He wasn't here for his son's birth. Alone and scared and in labor, Helen Laverne called a taxi to take her to the hospital and walked inside, saying, "Help me, I'm about to have a baby!"

The birth was quick and fierce. She gasped when the doctor handed her young Stanley. In hand, he seemed to weigh no more than a bird. He was wide-eyed as an owl, tiny and weak. The following day, the doctors informed Helen Laverne that he was close to death and needed a blood transfusion.

John James arrived home just in time to save his son's life. Doctors inserted an IV into his long, muscled arm and placed a tube into an incision, one of the four cut into John Stanley's pale, thin legs. The four-pound baby, buoyed by his father's blood, soon brightened, and doctors gave him a fighting chance to live. The baby would grow into a man who forever would feel his father's blood coursing in his veins, a feeling of pride he would cherish. And if we could look ahead now to the future as John Stanley Parker sleeps in a shoe box, we would find the baby, now a young man, bleeding in a ditch with a piece of jagged metal sticking out of his side, his shirt stuffed into the wound, the stock of his rifle pressed against it hard to stanch the bleeding. He's firing his weapon on full automatic, his mouth open in a roar that we can't hear but can understand: *Do not quit.* But we can't look into the future like that.

Go back to the window, to the opened dresser drawer, to the boy.

● ● ●

He outgrew the shoe box. His parents packed up and left Texas. He kept on living.

With two more babies in tow (a third son, Bruce, was born in 1950 in New Mexico, and a fourth, Joe, in 1959 in Colorado), John James and Helen Laverne migrated from oil field to oil field, now towing an enormous mobile home. It was a hardscrabble life but an increasingly secure living. There was always food on the table. When John James found skilled work as an ironworker, life in the Parker family became even more peripatetic, with John James following building projects across the country. By the time he was five, John Stanley had lived in ten cities, and as the new kid in school, he was picked on constantly.

He got his first bloody lip during a school yard fight in Trenton, New Jersey, where his father was helping build a Manhattan skyscraper. At school, John Stanley tried sticking up for Gilbert, an African American classmate, when other students picked on him because of his race. And although Stan was too little, too scrawny, to win the fight, he sensed something righteous about the battle. Gilbert was his friend—and fighting for a friend was the correct thing for a boy to do.

He got his first black eye in El Paso, Texas, in the first grade. He was a friendly and outgoing six-year-old, short for his age, with blue eyes that seemed perpetually turned up in surprise. His father was a god to him. The tall, rail-thin man could reach down and grip his skinny leg with one hand and lift him straight to the ceiling. His father called him, lovingly, "Stan," mussing his blond hair, before setting him back to the earth. His kindergarten classmates called young Stan "gypsy" and "trash." He tried ignoring those who called him names.

When he was seven, doctors delivered some bad news to his parents: he had polio. He was fitted with clanky metal braces for both legs and used crutches to shuttle himself around the dirt roads, and past the cactus, on his way to school. He was filled with energy, curiosity, intelligence, and he didn't know why his body was failing him. Seeing his leg braces, his classmates added new nicknames: "Cripple," "Clinker Bell" (because of the noise the leg braces made as he shuffled on his crutches). And worst of all, they called him "Franken-Stan."

El Paso is cattle country and cows roam the fields and roads at will. They drop their cow pies wherever they please. The abundance of this excrement became one of Stan's worst nightmares. He was regularly attacked by classmates, thrown to the ground, his face rubbed in the manure. Stan came to call these piles "Hereford pies," displaying a delicate awareness of his situation, a kind of whistling-past-the-graveyard kind of humor.

One day, he told himself that he'd had enough. He didn't know how he was going to stop his classmates from picking on him. He wondered who was watching him as he sweated and groaned as he fought his classmates. The sky? God? Someone had to be watching, he figured. *Someone.* He knew he must defend himself.

He was hopping home on his crutches one afternoon, his leg braces clinking in rhythm with his shuffling feet, when he heard his tormentors approaching, laughing, calling after him: "Hey, Franken-Stan!"

"Hiya, Clinker Bell!"

"Get him!"

Stan made a decision. He was going to run. He didn't know how, but he was going to try. He sat down in the dirt road and unbuckled his leg braces. How he hated them. They were ugly, made of scratched aluminum posts, leather, and sheepskin padding. He removed one, then the other, and tossed them aside, where they landed in a pile.

Using his crutches, he carefully pulled himself up, sure that his weak legs would snap under his weight. He stepped down, testing them. He looked over his shoulder, saw that the boys were closer than expected, and said a prayer. And then he threw the crutches away.

He wobbled at first, and then began hop-skipping forward, finally breaking into an awkward gait. At any moment, he was sure that he'd pitch onto his face and that the boys would set upon him and beat the daylights out of him. He was more scared than he'd ever been.

But his legs started moving faster—faster than he'd ever felt them move, and his short arms started pumping. Soon he could feel the dry Texas air move around, over, and past him. He dared to look down and saw tiny dust clouds rising at his feet, kicked up by his sneakers. He kept running. The would-be attackers receded. He turned and saw them pull up and watch him run away. He believed they must be amazed by his near-magical resurrection.

He ran the half mile all the way home and into the kitchen, where his mother was making pot roast, his favorite.

"Stanley," she said, taking a look at him. "What happened?"

He just stood there. "I don't know, Mother. I *ran* home."

Helen Laverne stared at him. He was her special one—the child whose existence, after his difficult early childhood, seemed just this side of magic.

"Well," she said.

And then again: "*Well.*" She smiled.

She had no explanation as to how he escaped polio's near-paralyzing grip. Neither did the doctors. But Stan explained his recovery to himself like this: he knew someone was watching as he was being picked on. He knew that anyone who might've been watching would know that he, John Stanley Parker, ought not to be beaten up anymore. He never used crutches or leg braces again.

The following year, 1953, John James found work welding on oil rigs around San Antonio, Texas, and Stan entered the second grade. His teacher was a cruel woman. As the son of an itinerant ironworker, Stan, and indeed the entire family, was used to displays of disdain by local residents they met in each town. But his teacher took the cake.

In class, she referred to Stan as "gypsy-carnival trash" and "Dumbo" because of his large ears. For no reason that he could think of, she made him stand in the classroom corner with his nose touching the wall while wearing a cone hat made of newspaper. When the hat slid down on his head, his ears stuck out even more. He tried but could not fully comprehend the depth of her cruelty or its source. It mystified him.

And then his body rebelled against him once more: he contracted rheumatic fever. Often fatal in children and damaging to heart tissue, he survived without apparent side effects after a three-month convalescence. When he returned to school, his teacher made him stand in class while she warned the other students not to get too close to him, for fear they'd catch his "cooties"—her name for rheumatic fever. On the playground, the attacks by some of his classmates became ritualistic. The older boys grabbed his shoulders and spun him around, then reached in and punched him, and when he was on the ground, they kicked dirt on him. Stan wondered who was watching him now and figured, well, nobody.

His father proved him wrong. He announced that he was going to help his son end this terror. He instructed Stan to play along with the bullies the next time they approached. One day, Stan stood at the merry-go-round and started spinning it, ostensibly happy to entertain himself. He then announced to the other boys that if they really wanted to make him sick, they should make him ride the merry-go-round and spin it as fast as they could.

One boy, one of the older ones, liked this idea and walked up for a closer look, which is when Stan shoved him forward and slammed his head into the spinning bars, knocking him unconscious. Stan was escorted to the principal's office and suspended from school for one week. It was his first lesson in the pleasure—and the cost—of seeking revenge. He was also glad to be out of his teacher's torture chamber. A few weeks later, when his father found new work in Little Rock, Arkansas, they moved away. He was free to begin again in a new city, with a new life.

Thus began a dizzying series of cross-country trips, to Minnesota, New York State, Texas. Often Stan returned from school to find the mobile home already hooked to the family's double-wheeled truck, the big engine idling. His mother had duct-taped the family's TV to the legs of the kitchen table and sealed the end of the trailer home's sewer hose, carefully securing it to the floor. She had stowed the kids' bikes in the back of the truck, among John James's welding tools. The only thing left was to lift away the trailer steps and place them in the truck.

On the road, the boys read maps and helped navigate as their father drove. John James was also eager to detour to see anything of historical or social significance. As Stan's sense of the vastness of the United States grew, so did the closeness of his family. Of the boys, Helen Laverne demanded obedience and she was vigilant about their behavior as they grew up in this fluid, ever-changing environment. Swearing was not tolerated and was answered by making Stan and his brothers wash their mouths out with soap.

No matter how much trouble he got into, though, Stan felt that his mother and father loved him unconditionally. His mother often met him and his brothers after school, no matter where they'd unhooked the trailer, with a piece of pie in one hand— and in the other, a list of household chores. In fall 1955, when Stan was almost nine, they fetched up in the pine woods and on the freshwater beaches of St. Ignace, Michigan. Stan's father had gotten a job on a project building the Mackinac Bridge, then the world's longest suspension bridge. This would be some of the happiest times of his nomadic boyhood.

The Mackinac Bridge spans the Straits of Mackinac, joining Lake Michigan and Lake Huron. Stan and his brother roamed the beaches, pretending they were at Normandy, storming German troops in World War II. At his new school, no one knew him as a kid with any problems—no crutches, no illnesses, no history of being picked on in class. He began watching after other kids less fortunate, those terrorized by others.

One day a classmate pushed a girl down in the snow. Stan helped her up and confronted the bully. Without warning, the bully socked him right in the nose. Stan woke up watching the school yard swing set come into focus. A few weeks later, when the boy pushed the girl into the snow again, Stan didn't take any chances: he walked up and hit the kid squarely in the face. That settled the issue. The girl quickly told her friends that Stan Parker was a "real Prince Charming."

The idea that such behavior could be perceived as heroic was a revelation to him. His father taught him how to stare at an opponent when facing him down, unblinking, a skill that Stan started practicing when he talked with people, even as a young boy. His father also imparted secrets about the sweet science of boxing. (They agreed not to mention these lessons to his mother.) On top of this, his father was *building* America, bit by bit. As a union ironworker, the elder Parker would climb skyscrapers in New York City, Chicago, Atlanta, Dallas. He worked on B-52 Strato-fortress hangars in Texas, Minnesota, the Dakotas, and along the East Coast. He helped build a dozen coal-fired power plants across the plains and mountain states. He built bridges in Colorado and Mississippi and across the St. Lawrence Seaway.

When Stan was eleven, the family moved to Denver, and there young Parker's life changed in a monumental way: his father told him he was no longer a boy. He told him it was time to be addressed by his real name: John Stanley Parker—Stan, for short. This felt like a matter of initiation to young Stan and thrilled him. His mother objected, but his father prevailed.

By now, he'd lived in twenty-three states and attended twenty schools. He'd been in dozens of bloody fights (and would eventually be knocked out twice on school playgrounds). He felt like a seasoned young man, capable of some self-sufficiency. He got a paper route and started delivering the *Denver Post*.

Each day on his route, a twelfth-grade student in the neighborhood would tower over him and demand a percentage of his paper route money, threatening to beat him up if he didn't comply. Stan, though only in sixth grade and almost two feet shorter than his aggressor, didn't blink. The extortionist, likely surprised by this reaction, didn't attack Stan.

When he explained the situation to his father, Stan was surprised to hear him say that this would be an excellent chance to "work on his left and right combinations." They agreed that he would fight the kid and not tell Stan's mother of the upcoming match. Stan was scared, but he was more scared of the continued harassment. His father insisted that the only way to keep the bully at bay was by confronting him.

One day after school, Stan informed the senior student that he was going to fight him. They set the date for a Friday after school.

The student looked surprised when Stan arrived in a pickup truck driven by his father, and even more so when his father got out and walked over with Stan to where he stood. His father looked at the kid and said, "This is going to be a fair fight. I'm going to make sure of that."

The senior threw the first punch, pummeling Stan, blackening both his eyes, splitting his lips, and tearing his shirt off his body. The fight was some of the longest twenty minutes of Stan's life. He figured he'd landed maybe every third punch—a losing battle.

When he arrived home, his mother took one look at his beaten face, his torn Levi's, and realized what the plan had been. Stan waited for her to get mad, but she didn't. She informed him that he was grounded from further after-school activities, and—this surprised Stan and his father—she told his father that his bowling league nights were canceled until Stan made enough money to replace the school clothes destroyed by the fight. His father started to speak, but Stan could tell that he decided better. His father looked sheepish, a rare thing.

"This fighting works for now," said his mother. "But what about when we move to the next town? Are you going to have him fight every time we move?"

In eighth grade, the Parker family moved five times, to Carlsbad, New Mexico; Queen City, Texas; Rapid City, South Dakota; back to Carlsbad; then to Grants, New Mexico, but only for the last ten days of the school year. For many other children, the peripatetic nature of this life would have doomed any sense of intellectual discipline. In the rare school conferences that his parents—most often his mother—were able to attend, teachers remarked about Stan's intelligence, noting that he was quick to read a situation, carried himself with poise, and possessed a nearly photographic memory. His IQ would later be tested as extremely high.

At school, Stan's social life was improving. He was returning to classrooms in towns where his father had worked before, and students remembered Stan from his previous fights. They left him alone.

In this migratory existence, he faced his most challenging moment in Carlsbad, New Mexico, when he got into a game of dodgeball during eighth-grade gym class.

He had managed to evade the lightning throws of an especially tall and muscular kid, who was growing frustrated with his inability to tag scrawny Stan Parker. Finally, some of the other students jumped on Stan and held him against the gym wall. The kid stepped back about twenty feet—close enough that he would be sure not to miss—and threw a blazing pitch at Stan's groin. The impact crumpled him to the varnished wood floor. He looked up, trying to squeeze the pain from his body, and saw that both the boys' and the girls' gym classes were looking on, including the teachers, who did nothing. Stan, no matter how tough he felt he had made himself, could never really grasp why the world seemed a cruel and unusual place, a place often without justice.

He stood up, feeling wobbly on his feet. His classmates watched as Stan started walking toward the boy who'd thrown the ball at him. He was walking away from Stan, waving his arms up and down, urging on his classmates for even more applause.

Stan tapped him on the shoulder. The boy turned around and Stan enjoyed the look of surprise on his face. He could tell that the kid knew what was going to happen next, and he also knew he didn't have enough time to react.

Stan threw a right fist that crashed into the boy's head. He stepped forward, grabbed the boy's T-shirt, and drove his knee up into the kid's groin. The force of Stan's blow lifted the kid several inches into the air. Stan then shoved him, and he went sprawling to the gym floor, groaning in pain. Stan looked at the boys who'd held him against the wall when their friend had thrown the ball. He held their gaze, just as his father had taught him, and told them to step up. They backed away.

Just then, something happened that would change the way Stan felt about his father and forge a lifelong bond between them.

Having watched Stan's attack on the boy, including the face punch and knee-to-the-groin, the gym teacher ran up to Stan and yelled for someone to get his "board of education." Stan had no idea what the gym teacher meant. He did sense that some type of punishment was headed his way, but he didn't imagine what it would be and was sure the boy who'd hit him with the ball would be punished too.

The teacher told him to bend over and grab his ankles. Stan did as he was told, fearful of what was going to happen next. As he bent over, he realized just what the "board of education" was. It was the teacher's paddle, actually a canoe paddle. Someone, maybe the gym teacher, had sawed off the long handle and drilled about a dozen quarter-inch holes in the long, thin blade.

The first swat lifted Stan up on his toes and rocked him forward. He couldn't believe the pain. The second blow was even swifter, sharper. He felt as if lighter fluid had been poured over his butt and set alight. The third blow made it difficult to breathe; the fifth and final blow made him feel as if he'd pass out.

He couldn't believe the teacher had hit him five times. The top of his head was on fire. He looked up and around through teary eyes at the rest of the gym class. What bothered him as much as the pain was the fact that the girls in the class were looking at him.

The pain was so intense that he'd been gripping his ankles incredibly hard, practically cutting off the blood flow to his feet. He was afraid he would fall over.

He stood up and saw the other boys and tried smiling at them, thinking that their turn with the "board of education" was coming next. He couldn't wait for the gym teacher to remove their smirks with the application of his paddle.

But Stan was shocked by what happened next. The gym teacher told the rest of the boys to go hit the shower. He turned to Stan and told him that he had better never cause any more trouble in his class; otherwise, he'd meet the "board of education" again.

Stan hobbled away, each step causing his backside to burn. He gingerly undressed and in the shower leaned against the wall. He looked over his shoulder and was frightened by what he saw. The skin on his butt was raw, and the cool water made him feel like he was burning up to an even greater degree. It took him a long time to get dressed, and then he made his way to the administration office and called his mom. He told her he'd been hurt in gym class and that he was excused to go home early. This was a lie, but the school office didn't object. He felt he was on his own.

When he got in the car, he had to slide in carefully. He decided not to tell his mother what had happened so as not to upset her. He didn't want to have to deal with what his father would say about this. His mother, he knew, sensed something was wrong. But they talked about other things, principally the stomachache that he said was bothering him.

That night at dinner, his father asked what had happened to him in gym class. He and his mother shared a look; they obviously had talked about Stan's earlier behavior. And they looked puzzled as Stan squirmed uncomfortably at the table. Finally, his father demanded to know what happened. Stan told them the whole story.

They stared at Stan in silence, looking shocked. They then asked to see the damage. He sheepishly unbuckled his pants and showed them his backside.

His mother gasped. He was bleeding through his white under-shorts.

His father sat there silently. His silence, Stan knew, was a sign of titanic things to come. He announced at the table that he would address this situation in the morning.

Early the next day, his father drove Stan to school and asked Stan to show him to the principal's office. When the principal emerged, the elder Parker demanded that he lead him to the gym. As they walked, his father explained to the principal what had happened the day before. Stan was following behind and was both dreading and looking forward to the coming confrontation. They walked into the gym, where a class was in full swing.

The students turned to look as the trio entered the gym. The gym teacher himself smiled a moment at the principal and at the man walking next to him. The smile turned to a frown when he saw Stan step from behind the two men.

His father walked up to the gym teacher and shoved him backward onto the hardwood floor. The teacher fell flat on his back and Stan's father put a boot on his chest and ground down his heel. Then he knelt down, put his knee in the middle of the gym teacher's chest, and simply stared.

Stan saw that the principal was about to say something to interrupt the proceedings, but Stan's father cut him off. He told the principal that if he had any objections, he would also find himself on the floor.

The gym had fallen silent. Stan saw that all his classmates were watching, eager to see what would happen next. Stan knew only that it would be interesting.

His father told the coach that if he ever laid another hand on his son, he would come back and beat him to a bloody pulp.

His father told the assistant PE teacher, standing nearby, to go and fetch the so-called board of education. The assistant handed it to his father. He took it and broke it over his knee and threw it in two pieces at the PE teacher, still spread out on the floor. His father then reached down and pulled the teacher to his feet and asked, "Am I making myself clear?"

The frightened man nodded. But then he couldn't help himself. He asked Stan's father if he thought he was up to fighting the entire teaching faculty the next time he walked into what he referred to as "my gym."

His father looked amused. "No," he said after a minute. "The only person I'll be after will be you." And he explained that if he did come back, it would be with thirty angry ironworkers eager to kick his ass.

"Don't think I'm kidding," said his father. He then told the teacher, "If my son ever acts out, you will leave the punishment to me. And believe me," said his father, "it won't be light." He grabbed the principal by his necktie and led him out of the gym.

Stan could tell what the principal was thinking, and so could his father, because he said, "If you're thinking of calling the cops, go right ahead." He explained that the gym teacher likely could be arrested for assaulting a minor and that he, the principal, would be arrested for being an accomplice.

He added that his son would be going home early and that his absence would be excused for the rest of the week.

When they walked out the front door, it seemed to Stan that the entire school, teachers and students, and especially the girls, had gathered to watch. Most of them seemed in awe of what Stan's father had done and the way he'd pulled the principal around by his necktie.

When they got into the car, Stan's father reached over and wordlessly touched his shoulder.

The young boy felt as if he were floating.

AARON
19 FEB 1968
101st Airborne

Dear Maureen

Well long time no hear. I know you can find a few min to stop and drop me a line. I have been in the boonies for the last 25 days now and was not able to write. But now I'm out of the boonies in a hospital over here and have some time an paper to write on. The reason I'm in the hospital is because I got wounded. I got hit in the right leg and in the right side. Anyway I'll be out of action for a while.

Them ~~___~~ (NVA) were doing us a job. Five of us got wounded and one got killed. But we got (killed) 8 the day before I got hit and five more the day I got it. I got one before his buddy got me. They really had us pined down. These NVA (North Vietnamese Army) are a lot ~~_____~~ meaner that the part time ~~____~~ (VC) down at Cu Chi.

The weather up here is real bad. Rain, Rain all the time. Gets cold as hell at night. I'm kinda glad I got wounded. Cause I not out in the rain and cold any more. It sure feels good to know I'm gonna sleep in the nice warm place again tonight. Sure will hate to go back to the boonies again when ~~____~~ when I get out of the hospital. I (and 50,9 more guys) will sure be glad when this war is over. Oh well I've only got about 297 days to go over here.

How's things in Gary? Any news ~~__~~, that

PART II

WANDERING

As we talked, I noticed a fellow mortarman sitting next to me. He held a handful of coral pebbles in his left hand. With his right hand he idly tossed them into the open skull of the Japanese machine gunner. Each time his pitch was true I heard a little splash of rainwater in the ghastly receptacle. My buddy tossed the coral chunks as casually as a boy casting pebbles into a puddle on some muddy road back home; there was nothing malicious in his action. The war had so brutalized us that it was beyond belief.

—E. B. Sledge, *With the Old Breed:*
At Peleliu and Okinawa

February 8, 1968

Hai Lang, Vietnam

Stan wakes at LZ Jane under a gray sky and in cold drizzle thinking about the girl with the peaches. She's been dead for over a day. What's painful is this: her death will last forever, and he knows he caused it. He knows there's nothing he can do to change this. After leaving her, he and the rest of the platoon returned to LZ Jane to await the next orders. The others wake now, stretch, stir in wet poncho liners, the ground around them muddy and slick, pocked with rain pools.

Al Dove unfastens the back of a Claymore mine and pinches off a thumb-sized piece of the C-4 explosive inside, just a dab, places it on a rock, lights it with his Zippo, and places his metal cup filled with coffee over the quick flame. Nothing, in fact, burns quicker or hotter than C-4. The entire white dab is consumed in about thirty seconds and the water inside Al's cup is boiling. He drinks down his coffee, watching Parker, who's quiet, withdrawn. Al's worried about Stan; they're close, and he sees more and more strain in Stan's face. Al relies on Stan for steadfastness, for his courage. Stan will not leave anyone in a fight. He will stand and slug it out until the lights dim. Al knows that; Jerry Austin knows that. They all know this about each other. They will fight to the death for each other, yet, of course, none of them wants to die.

It's strange to be living in a world now where the very reason for your existence, the protection of your buddy, is in fact predicated on your commitment to die for that person. But still, Al's worried. Stan looks exhausted, his eyes hooded by grief, by unspecified anger: anger at being in this position of fighting to live in the first place; anger at surviving, which means so much killing has been done in order to have survived thus far.

On a typical day, if you can call any of their days typical, they gulp down their coffee, slurp some beans and weenies from a cold C-rations can, repack their ammo belts with full magazines, grab more grenades from camp supply, and walk back out beyond the wire, looking for trouble. The days are a loop: patrol and carry out search-and-destroy missions, and ambush at night. The platoon's job is supposed to be the eyes and ears of the battalion, to find the enemy, to probe, size up, and report to the battalion so that the line companies—the "line doggies," the other grunt soldiers—can come in and fight.

But as February progresses, as the platoon maneuvers back and forth from LZ Jane to Hai Lang, the battlefield is around them every hour of every day. They don't sleep. They don't really eat. The filtered water they drink tastes like iodine, which tastes like blood.

Slowly, they are no longer part of this world. They start calling the world another place, as in: "Back in the world, my girl's probably, she's probably, well, who knows what she's doing." That's what they think of the war: that it's not happening in the world they know or once knew.

They don't use first names. It's Anderson. Or Bradshaw. Austin. Dove. Lane. Parker. Beke. Soals. Fowler. Pyle. Sudano.

Stan doesn't want to get too close to anyone around him. The other boys feel the same way. Somebody asks, "Who got killed?" And somebody else gives the first name—and hearing the dead guy's name makes the news more painful. They say, for instance, "Donald got it; he got killed." And it's different than if they had answered with just the last name. The first name makes it personal. It brings them closer to the person in question and if something should happen to them, it would become one more thing to forget.

Today they load into two-and-a-half-ton trucks and ride the two miles down Highway 1 into Hai Lang. They're going to scout the positions of an outnumbering force of three hundred NVA and the VC soldiers who've taken control of part of the city. This new information will be used by 1st Battalion's four rifle companies to plan an attack.

Stan and the crew bounce over the rough road, the diesel trucks spitting black smoke in their faces, making some of them light-headed—that, and the heat. Helicopters zip past, leading the way into Hai Lang and providing fire cover.

The trucks park a half mile outside Hai Lang, and the men start walking. The fighting in the village has been intense since the Tet kicked off. Other soldiers of the 101st Airborne have been here, too, fighting house to house.

Dead dogs lie alongside the road to Hai Lang. The village is in ruins, leveled by artillery fire.

They crest a hill and hear voices down in the wooded depression at its bottom. They creep forward and look down. Below them is an NVA platoon, about thirty or thirty-five soldiers kicked back alongside a river. The soldiers are eating and laughing, holding bowls of rice, chopsticks poised in midsentence as somebody tells a joke. Their khaki uniforms are dirty and blood-stained. These are not replacements to the area, Stan thinks. These guys have killed before. These are the guys who greased Charlie Company.

The platoon maneuvers into position, surrounding the NVA

soldiers, then starts firing at them from their hilltop vantage. For the first few seconds, the NVA soldiers are surprised, and then they return fire. As they do, a UH-1D Huey arrives overhead and circles the entrapped NVA, the door gunner aiming his machine gun at them. Every man is killed. In the silence after the gunfire, Stan feels an immense sense of relief for having avenged Charlie Company's slaughter. He looks at the dead men down the hill, tumbled about in awkward positions. But his relief is fleeting. He knows he will have to kill again.

Later in the day, they're walking across a rice paddy and hear, *Boom*.

They have no idea what made this sound.

It's an RPG, being fired at them by an unseen enemy soldier. The rocket *whooshes* past them. And then here comes another *whoosh*, with the explosion landing not far from where they'd just been walking in the rice paddy. They realize that somebody is zeroing in on them and start hotfooting it for the tree line. Toward safety.

Stan and Russo and the rest of them stop and look back to where they'd come from, and when they turn back to keep running, they find themselves face-to-face with an NVA soldier. He's stepped out of the trees, either to meet them or by mistake. But either way, Stan can't believe his eyes. Where'd this guy come from? Up out of the ground?

Stan's walking point, so he's the lead guy, and he knows there are others behind him. The NVA soldier is solo. Stan looks at the soldier, who's maybe seven, eight feet away. It's just crazy; he's standing there with this huge, cat-eating-the-canary grin on his face, like, "I got you," and he raises his AK and starts firing. It happens so fast that Stan doesn't even have time to lift his M-16, and the guys behind can't start firing either because Stan and Russo are in the way, or because they don't know what's going on, it's happening so fast. The NVA guy empties what seems like his entire magazine, and Stan's sure he's going to die. When the guy finishes shooting, Stan sees smoke rising from the end of the barrel. Stan's watching it, waiting for the image to fade as he waits to die. The NVA soldier is out of bullets and he's staring at his weapon, like, "What the hell?" and then at Stan, as if trying to understand why he's still standing. And now he has to reload, if he's going to shoot some more. That's when Stan lifts his M-16 and starts firing. The look on the guy's face goes from "Got you" to "Whoops." Stan kills the guy.

When the shooting stops, someone in the platoon pipes up, "Stan, you are so lucky. There's no reason for you to still be alive. You must have a guardian angel watching over you."

The next day, February 9, the weather is still gray and cold. Stan's on a three-man patrol and he smells bacon and coffee. He turns off the path and follows his nose, parting his way through the undergrowth until he emerges on a clearing where cooks from the 1st Air Cavalry Division are just putting away the makings of a hot breakfast they've served to some of their famished troopers. The food's all gone but Stan begs for something, and a sympathetic cook gives him three raw eggs. Cradling the eggs as carefully as possible, which makes it difficult to fire his rifle quickly if needed, he makes his way back to the rest of the platoon outside Hai Lang. The fighting around the village is still heavy. New airstrikes are landing close to the friendly troops, and Stan and the patrol are forced to pull back. He realizes he won't be able to cook the eggs, so he cracks them open and eats them raw. At the same time, some of the guys in the platoon get deathly ill and come down with food poisoning.

They had arrived at the 1st Cav's cooking station before Stan and got to eat some of the cooked food. Dysentery and other maladies have plagued them throughout their time in-country, so this food poisoning seems like an insult to injury. Stan's glad that he ended up eating the eggs raw. What seemed ill luck at first turns out to be good fortune. With some of the men puking and running off into the bushes with their pants around their knees, the platoon is ordered by Higher to set up a night ambush position near a railroad bridge outside Hai Lang. The severely ill hole up in a nearby French-built bunker and continue to be sick.

Dwight Lane is in the bunker and has food poisoning so badly that he's doubled over constantly in pain, and each evacuation of his bowels literally blows through the fabric of his fatigues. Meanwhile, Stan, Al, Tony Beke, and David Watts set up the ambush on the bridge spanning the Song Vinh Dinh River while the others of Recon stand guard. Al isn't sick because he didn't have any of the hot chow; his mother had sent him a care package from home, filled with Hawaiian delicacies, candy, and one of his favorites, cuttlefish, which everyone else in the platoon finds gross. It smells like what it is: salted fish.

Stan and Al can hear the groaning of the men coming from the echo chamber of the bunker and hope that by nightfall, when the NVA are expected to cross the bridge, they're able to lay quietly in their misery. Otherwise they'll be discovered before the ambush can be enacted. A large force of NVA troops—maybe as big as a battalion, numbering approximately five hundred—is expected to be on the move in the night over the bridge, trying to make their way into Hue, where U.S. Marines are fighting NVA and VC soldiers in the city.

Just before night closes in, Stan and the others organize the ambush, setting trip flares just before the bridge and then on the bridge itself.

The trip flares work pretty much like their name implies. A wire or chord is attached to the end of the flare and then tied off to a distant object. When the wire or chord is pulled, or stepped through, it ignites the flares and burns brightly on the ground, leaving almost no time for anyone trapped in the glare to evade the inevitable follow-on gunfire.

Stan sets maybe six Claymores on the bridge. The bridge isn't much to write home about. It's constructed of two I-beams, and spread between them are boards and interlocking metal planking, the same kind used to make airplane runways in the country. When they step on the metal plate, it squeaks on the I-beams, and Al's worried that the noise will give them away to any NVA soldiers lurking in the area. Stan unspools the wire leading to the Claymores, and they try to step quietly back across the bridge, which is hard in the dark. They make it all the way across and pick their way along the river back to their gun positions and wait.

They're maybe fifty yards from the bridge. Al positions the M-60 machine gun with a clear line of sight; others in the platoon take up their places where they can have the most effective killing radius. Now they sit and wait. At about eight o'clock in the evening, some of them hear the first creak on the bridge, then silence, then another creak—another step—and the first trip flare goes off.

The bright light in the otherwise deep darkness is blinding. What's revealed is a tableau of khaki-clad men frozen in confusion on the narrow bridge. Then they start to move, turning this way and that. Al watches as maybe two dozen men make a decision to proceed all the way across the bridge. The men in his position open up with the small arms fire, which creates even greater confusion among the NVA soldiers. Other trip flares go off as even more of their compatriots come in from behind them, and now the bridge is haloed in a globe of hissing light. The NVA stumble around, disoriented, trying to figure out which way to go. The scene is so sudden and dramatic that all Al Dove can do for about ten seconds is stare and take it in. He can't bring himself to shoot because it seems too easy. He sits there and does nothing. Parker's yelling at him while he's emptying magazine after magazine into the disorganized NVA.

"Al," he yells, "fire them up!"

Yet Al is quiet. This pause lasts for maybe only ten more seconds, but in the firefight, it seems an eternity. So often he's pulled the trigger on the machine gun and killed lots of men, elevating the barrel to lob the shots and kill them that way. This time, Al is waiting for the NVA soldiers to dive to safety off the bridge. He's waiting to find a way where he doesn't have to kill them. When he comes to, he starts yelling at Parker to stop firing his M-16 and set off the Claymores.

But Stan can't find the clacker handles that operate the Claymore mines. He's pawing at the ground along the riverbank, looking for them.

The NVA soldiers turn around on the bridge, and start running back the way they've come. Al swears to himself, feeling even worse, because now the enemy is getting away from him, and the question he has to answer is whether he will shoot them in the back.

He can't. He didn't come to Vietnam to shoot anyone in the back; he just can't. He's under some belief that honor is at stake here—his own and even the honor of his enemy. But what is he supposed to do? He can't let them get away—or can he? Yes, he can—he could if he wanted to—but there is the pull of the duty of the entire Recon troop to kill as many of the other guys so they can't be killed by them. So to stop their stampede off the bridge, he starts firing ahead of the soldiers, ricocheting rounds off the concrete wall that faces the end of the bridge, and then he starts shooting at the bridge itself, hoping to turn them around. This way they'll run back toward him, face-first, and in this way he can shoot them in the chest or the face instead of the back. Al can see his rounds spark on the bridge and on the concrete wall, and he waits for the NVA soldiers to start jumping into the river instead of running ahead, straight into his bullets. But they don't. Not one jumps in the water, and he doesn't know why. Instead they run straight into his fire. They run into it, and they tumble off the bridge with a splash illuminated in the faintest brush of light. Al is swearing even louder, asking himself why they are running into his fire, and he will live with this white light of the trip flares burning on the bridge for his whole life. He keeps shooting. They keep running into the fire and falling. He can't imagine how many men he's killed, but he guesses it's a lot. Two dozen? He can't wait for the morning to count the dead bodies and to give the number up to Higher; he looks forward to this with a sad mixture of pride and regret.

The next morning, some of the other guys want to dive for the dead and ask him to stay on the bank to provide cover in case the NVA stages a counterattack. Al is disappointed. A part of him wants to go down to the river and find the bodies himself. He's killed them; it should be his job to do the cleanup.

In his place, Dennis Tinkle, Tim Anderson, and Sergeant Kinney go diving. And it's a shocker to them all when they find just one body. After all the shooting and anguish, all the worry that he was killing them in cold blood by shooting them in the back, and now to find evidence of just one kill. It's beyond disappointing and even insulting—that so much existential inner debate should result in no evidence that the killing ever occurred. Al and the rest figure that the dead hit the rain-flooded river and floated downstream and were gone. Dennis Tinkle surfaces with the one body, holding it by the ankle, with the boot still attached to the foot, and he's able to lift the body, or at least most of the leg, out of the water. They carry the guy up the bank and lean him against a tree and tie him up there. They call in to Higher and report that their body count has elicited exactly one confirmed NVA dead and he's tied to a tree. You can't miss him.

On about February 14, the heavy fighting around and near Hai Lang is nearly over. So many are dead now, Americans and South Vietnamese civilians, NVA and VC. Who knows who did what? A slaughter, everything is dead: body parts here, body parts there, trouble in the mind. After a while, it starts to pile up, add up, accrue. Stan is running out of room on that shelf in his brain where he puts all the sadness.

The men are haunted by *things* that will become ghosts but are not ghosts yet. They are images, moods, gestures that are moving from the physical world to the museum of memory. For Al Dove, the *thing* that will become a ghost is the sight of a man running away from him, as if the man is already knowingly running toward ghosthood, toward the future a few moments later in which he will cease to exist and become part of a past that almost no one will remember.

One of those people who will remember is Al Dove, who will commit this last moment of the man's life to his museum of memory. The man's shiny black shirt flapping, his black pants flapping.

The man who is about to become a ghost comes out of a hooch from which Recon had received sniper fire and starts walking away from Al, Stan, and Jerry. He may not even have seen the three paratroopers; he's out for a walk, it looks like. Stan and Jerry see the man as someone who's carrying a weapon; Al doesn't see this weapon, he sees the man as unarmed but he suspects he's an enemy fighter. Either way, as is the case with these memories in this museum, each man will remember in his own way, and differently. The man is striding along, like nobody's business, on this wide thoroughfare shaded by trees. It's pleasant outside, a nice day. But because Al's all pumped up, and generally pissed because he's seen so much dying, he yells at the carefree man to stop. Al feels that the man's nonchalant nature is an affront while he, Al Dove, is forced to march and walk through this death day after day. Al yells again for the man to stop and when he doesn't, Al fires a few rounds ahead of the guy, maybe by eight feet, and they kick up the dirt of the road. And the guy doesn't turn around or look around. No; he starts running, and then he picks up speed. Al is now yelling, "Stop! Stop! Stop! *Goddamnit, stop!*" Al raises his rifle and fires a quick three rounds. The first two miss. Al, Jerry, and Stan are now pretty sure he's VC: he's male, he's wearing local clothing, and he's running. In the time it takes for the round to leave the barrel and travel the six hundred feet to the man, zeroing in on his back, getting closer, and, *impact*, entering the right shoulder and exiting out through the man's heart, blowing pieces of his heart out his shirt front—in the time it takes for this to happen—Al knows that what he's done is wrong. But there's no calling the bullet back.

Come back, bullet. Come back.

Hell no. I can't come.

After shooting the guy and wishing he hadn't, Al runs up and turns him over, or what's left of him. What astounds Al is the way the third round, the only one that hit the guy, has nearly torn him in half. His top half is lying facedown; his bottom half, his hips, are facing upward. As he studies the man, he sees that he's young, in his twenties, near his age. He's standing there and an old woman comes charging out of a nearby hooch and she's screaming. The old woman's saying something to Al, and Al says, "Van, what's she saying?"

Van, the interpreter, translates: "She's saying that he's a mute. A deaf-mute. He can't hear."

Al about collapses on the ground, all kinds of thoughts running through his head: "I came here to protect children and people, not to kill them." He wonders how he can repay the man's family for his mistake and knows just as quickly that no repayment is possible. He already feels that he'll barely be able to live with himself. This moment perhaps answers all kinds of questions for Al about how he will live the rest of his life. He will grow into old age as a genuinely sensitive man and accept Jesus as a savior. He will believe in UFOs and end times/Armageddon, and spend quiet, air-conditioned hours in his California home Googling the existence of either. As a loving father, he will spend time with his son playing video games, namely aerial combat, and he will marry a loving woman whose health will require his constant attention as her in-home caretaker.

And then there is something else that happens to Al, if he had any doubts about the meaning of his presence in Hai Lang. One night out on ambush, Al spots a dog in a graveyard walking around looking lost, and the guys in the platoon start to shoot at the dog, trying to hit it. They don't want to kill it; they want to hit it just to see if they can. They don't realize that hitting the dog will likely kill it. Their sense of cause and effect is warped. Al loves animals, especially dogs, and he's seething that any of them are shooting to begin with. To put an end to this, he raises his M-60 and fires off a round to scare the dog away. But at the last moment, the dog changes direction and walks right into the bullet and drops dead. Al wants to scream. But he swallows his scream, which travels somewhere deep inside him, just as Stan's own image of his dead mother has gone up into the moist attic of his head, jostling around up there under his heavy steel hel-met—Mom, up there, and Al's scream about the dog up there too, baking under their helmets.

After shooting the dog, Al doesn't understand his place in the world. When he pulls a trigger, he sometimes worries that something else will go wrong. Growing up in Honolulu, his friends had been Japanese, Chinese, and Filipino; he feels sim-patico with Vietnamese people by extension of these friend-ships, and an important part of him feels that he's in Vietnam to save the Vietnamese people from . . . communism? Well, yes, but more immediately from danger itself: gunfire, bomb-ings, from whomever might want to do the Vietnamese people harm. Al knows he will keep killing as long as he's in Viet-nam, and he'll kill to keep his buddies alive. When he's tired, they carry his ammunition belts for him; when they're fight-ing, he covers them with the heavy fire he lays down with the machine gun. The men call him "Dova"—Doe-Vuh—as in, "Dova, how's your ammo?" They don't ever want him to run out. He can shoot from his hip and lob rounds into groupings of enemy soldiers.

At times, thinking of his father—an Irishman who'd drifted from the mainland United States to Honolulu and married his mother, a Hawaiian—fills him with anger. At age nineteen, he's over six feet tall, pure muscle, dark hair, dark brooding eyes, long arms—a street fighter. With each firefight, he's scared, but he's afraid to admit this to the platoon. He thinks that if the other guys only knew how much time he spends being scared, they'd think less of him. At the same time, he thinks he got exactly what he wanted when he joined the Army. He got adventure. He's grown up feeling ashamed of his father for failing to see combat in World War II. His dad was a baker in the Navy and never saw a day of death. Al lied to his boyhood friends, saying, "Hell, my dad flew fighter planes against the Japanese," in order to keep up with their stories about their dads.

Later, after leaving the war, hoping for some reconciliatory moment with his father, Al will take a pistol off a dead NVA soldier he'd just killed. He will clean it and carefully store it among his things, waiting for the day when he can return home, thinking that he will present it to his father and they will talk. Or at least, they won't fight and punch each other. When that day came, he did give his father the pistol. And one day his father will take this same pistol, walk around to the back of the house, and blow his brains out with it.

Paul Sudano, a medic, is walking when he sees an arm in the shape of an L lying on the ground, sticking out of a hole. It's just the arm, disembodied but connected to a body because . . . it moves. The hand opens and grabs a rifle that's lying nearby, the fingers flex open and close around the wood stock, and the hand slowly pulls the rifle into the hole. Sudano and radioman Tom Soals walk up to the hole and yell, "Okay, come on out!" And they're wondering, of course, if the soldier's going to shoot, spraying them at knee level with gunfire.

But no.

Silence.

"We said come on out!"

They're speaking through their South Vietnamese translator.

They're tired, but mostly they're losing their minds. They are so tired that they can't even remember sleep.

One of their platoon-mates walks up and throws a grenade

in the hole. It explodes and the hole collapses. Sudano thinks, *That's the end of that guy, right?*

He gets ready to leave; no need to investigate further. "What a mess in there, right?" And then they hear some voices coming from the collapsed hole, and they start digging and digging. They find an arm, a hand, and a bloody braid of long gray hair. They start pulling the body parts free from the tight grip of the hole and uncover two old women, horribly damaged. Their brains are falling out of their heads. And they find the soldier too, who'd been hiding in the hole and precipitated the grenading.

He's fine, of course, and isn't that the sonofabitch of it all: for the soldier to be fine? Sudano knows this is a fight between him and the soldier and that these women have nothing to do with it. The women are in bad shape; they're convulsing and won't make it. A soldier walks up and says to Sudano, "Anything you can do for them, doc?"

"No, not really," he says. "I haven't been resupplied. I don't have enough as it is."

He does the math: if he spends field supplies on these wounded Vietnamese civilians, he may not have enough supplies to treat wounded Recon members. He makes a decision: he can't treat the women. They may die, but he doesn't know what else to do.

They call a medevac and it lands and takes them away and god knows if they'll make it. As he's standing by the LZ as the chopper lifts, Sudano is already haunted by this moment, as if it's lived inside him for years.

Back at LZ Jane some nights, they sing. They look up at the dusk sky, light a cigarette, somebody bitches about his girlfriend, the letter she wrote, the one that says "I'm leaving you for William," and forever after, a name like William or Daniel, a name that just seems so much fancier than any of the names they have, names like the Rock or Kickass or Short-Timer, those fancy names of guys who are laying their girlfriends back in the States, making them moan, nobody says those names. It's terrible to wait for sleep and think of their girls getting laid by other men. And there they are, stuck, frozen, in a place where every day seems the same, and where each hour might be their last.

They change the words to the songs they sing.

They change "Kansas City" as sung by Little Richard to:

> Going to Vietnam, Vietnam here I come.
> They've got some crazy little people here.
> And I'm going to kill me some.

Amid the steady rain, the trees seethe with leeches. Stan wakes one morning with one stuck to his eyelid. It has grown enormous, thick as a hammer handle.

At first he thinks he's gone blind. He reaches up and touches it and says, "I can't see!"

That's when the firefight erupts. First the mortars, then the small arms. They are under attack. The platoon begins returning fire. Stan is pulling hard on the leech, stretching his eyelid far out from his eyeball, screaming that he must get it off so he can see. At the same time, with his left hand, he's firing his M-16 into a tree line.

Finally, the leech breaks free and disgorges its night's meal. Stan's buddies look over and think he's been shot in the face—he is covered in blood. He tries wiping it away, but there is so much of it. All the while, though, he is still firing his rifle. And then, as quick as the battle started, it ends. Nobody has been hit.

On February 18, in the morning, Jerry Austin gets another kill. He is walking along the dirt road toward the village of Trung Hoa and up ahead spots a VC soldier walking toward him. Reports are that a large number of enemy soldiers have amassed near the village.

Jerry can see that the guy has a 1918 Browning automatic rifle (BAR) over his shoulder, and Jerry guesses he's VC because he's not dressed in NVA khaki. The man sees Jerry watching him and hightails up the road to a small hooch. He goes around it and slips down into a hole in the ground next to it. Jerry doesn't see any of this happen, of course; by the time he runs up to the hooch and dips around the back, the man's in the hole. A sergeant comes up behind Austin, and they're standing there, thinking, *What next?* The sergeant decides, "Okay, so throw a grenade in there," and that's when a grenade comes pitching up out of the hole, aimed at both of them. The bastard's trying to hit them! Austin can't believe what happens next: the stupid grenade hits the sloped dirt apron around the hole, lands there, and then begins to roll back into the hole. It drops in like a long putt on a golf course and explodes. Luckily for the guy in the hole, he'd thrown a concussion grenade meant to stun instead of shred and kill.

"Go get him," says the sergeant, and Austin walks over there and stands quiet and listens, tilting his head the way you would over the blowhole of a whale. He can smell the earth scorched by the explosion and hears the faintest groaning from inside the hole, an "oh, oh, oh." Jerry reluctantly reaches down and is surprised to find the guy's feet; he somehow turned around after throwing the grenade, probably to get his head away from the blast. Jerry pulls on the boot and the guy emerges, as if being born backward. He's all blown up: his ears are bleeding, his eyes are bleeding, he's covered in dust, and he's barely conscious. He's dying quickly. The sergeant looks him over and looks for anything that might be of souvenir value. He sees the belt. "Get me that belt," he says.

"I was thinking I'd like the belt," Jerry says.

"I outrank you, I get the belt."

Austin reaches and unfastens the buckle. He pulls the leather through the loops, and the man's hips lift at the last pull and fall back. The belt dangles free, long as a snake, and Austin hands it to the sergeant. "Thank you," he says. "Now kill him."

Austin looks at him. He's never killed anybody up close before, and the sergeant says again, "Now kill him," and Austin lifts his rifle and shoots him in the chest and he's dead. He reaches down and grabs the soldier's BAR, an American rifle prized for its reliability and ease of use. Jerry thinks it sure is nice to have this new rifle. He thinks it sure is weird to kill a guy like that, so up-close and personal.

About twenty minutes later, Stan and Wongus are walking a trail at the edge of Trung Hoa. They've been on ambush a few nights in a row, and it feels kind of good to be doing this, walking along, when somebody starts shooting at them. The bullets snap by, sounding like the crack of a leather belt near your ear, just like *that*. That's the sound of the projectile breaking the sound barrier. Two Viet Cong soldiers jump up from the weeds by the side of the trail and start running away. Stan and Wongus shoot at both of them. One dies quickly, falling dead in midstride; the other keeps running, maybe a dozen steps, before he drops and hits the ground. He turns and starts returning fire. Stan and Wongus drop to the ground beside the first dead guy, and crawl behind him for cover as they start shooting back. The VC fighter's bullets start hitting the dead guy, *whap whap*, and his body jumps at each impact.

Wongus says, "What do you think we ought to do, Parker?"

Stan says to keep shooting. And then pretty soon another six or seven VC soldiers start shooting at them. Stan kills one of them. Then one by one, the VC soldiers break contact and disappear back into some trees. That's the most frustrating thing of all: these bastards never stay and fight. The shooting stops and Stan looks up the trail, about fifty feet, and to the left.

"Holy mackerel, Wongus," he says, "look at that."

The enemy soldiers were in such a hurry to get away that they had forgotten their rucksacks. Stan counts seven of them, lined in a row. He says to Wongus, "Get on the radio and tell 'em we found these," thinking that maybe this is a valuable intel cache that somebody should know about. A message comes back on the radio to wait for reinforcements to arrive in case this is a ploy to draw Stan and Wongus into the open for an ambush.

There's nothing to do but wait. And waiting in the forest can be both nerve-racking and boring. Stan can't stand it. He says to Wongus, "You know what? I'm going to run out here and grab a couple of those rucksacks."

Wongus is incredulous, "You're going to do what?"

Stan says, "Cover me. I'm going out there."

"Parker, are you crazy?"

"There could be all kinds of souvenirs in those things," Stan says.

"Souvenirs? Man, leave it."

But before Wongus can finish, Stan is up and stepping onto the trail. The funny thing is that his feet won't move. It feels like they have been nailed, or glued, to the earth. He tries to take a step forward and trips and stumbles. He regains his balance and tells Wongus once again, "Cover me," but again he pitches forward, off-balance.

Stan tries a third time to walk, saying yet again, "Cover me."

By this time, Wongus is practically rolling his eyes at Parker.

"What're you gonna do," he asks, "trip again?"

At the same time, Wongus doesn't know why Stan can't walk.

Stan is equally confounded. He's sitting looking at the booty rucksacks, thinking, *Don't this beat hell?*, when, just then, the rucks start exploding, one by one, all seven of them, and debris starts flying everywhere, mostly paper, and roots and rocks, as each rucksack explodes.

Stan and Wongus duck down, and when they lift their heads, they quietly watch the smoke drift away. After a moment, Wongus says, "I'm sure glad you didn't drag one of those damn things back here."

And then something catches their attention. An NVA soldier jumps up from the brush about a hundred feet away, along the side of the trail, and he's holding the detonators in his hand, with the wires leading to the small craters where the rucksacks used to be. He starts to run away down the trail but gets tangled up in the wires. He falls and then gets up. Stan and Wongus shoot him in the back, and the guy falls dead.

Wongus turns to Stan and says, "Your guardian angel, Parker. He was with you today. He nailed your feet to the trail."

And Stan starts to believe him. Well, he already believes in the love of Jesus Christ, but he doesn't think of himself as a proselytizer. After this episode, some of the other guys will start staying close to Stan. They will walk right behind him, wanting to be in his safe zone, his angel-heavy zone.

At night, before he sleeps, he'll pray:

"Lord, I'm so tired, you've got to let me sleep."

And: "If I go to sleep, I know we're going to die."

About thirty minutes after Stan and Wongus narrowly escape the exploding rucksacks, the platoon comes under sudden fire in the village. Stan figures they are facing several hundred NVA and VC soldiers. The platoon is stopped among some hooches, with several rice paddies at their back. The enemy fire is coming from their front, and it occurs to Jerry Austin and others that the NVA and VC are trying to surround them. Austin rushes across a road to stop the flanking maneuver but finds himself outnumbered by dozens of fighters closing on him. Any minute he expects to be shot.

From his position across the road, Stan hears a call for help and recognizes the voice. It's Austin yelling that his weapon has jammed.

Stan and Angel Rivera have been shooting at a group of NVA swarming on their left but quickly shift their fire. Stan springs to his feet and Rivera follows. Stan hollers at Rivera to get down and cover him. Stan runs several hundred feet into the grass and is suddenly standing next to Jerry. Jerry looks over at him, surprised. He had been sure he was about to be killed. The look that passes between them is electric; both men feel it. They are convinced that *right now* they are about to live or die together. They have never been so close to anyone in their lives. Jerry turns away from the fight and works to get his rifle operating again.

Stan shoots the approaching NVA, one soldier after another, rounds cracking past his own and Jerry's face as Jerry struggles with his M-16. At last, he gets it working, and he and Stan shoot as more soldiers charge them in what appears to be a suicidal charge. The enemy force finally breaks off, and Stan helps Jerry gather his gear and they move back to Rivera. Not long after, Dennis Tinkle and Terry Hinote get hit. Hinote drops, a wound to the shoulder. Tinkle gets it worse: the gunfire rakes him, sweeping him off his feet, where he drops in a courtyard in front of a thatched house. He lays screaming and writhing in his own blood, which is pooling around him. Recon calls for a medevac but the request is refused—the gunfire is too heavy.

The morning is worsening by the minute. When the platoon captures a wounded NVA soldier, he tells them their objective is to overrun and kill all Americans. A little after one p.m., Alpha Company arrives by chopper to reinforce the outnumbered platoon.

Heavy machine-gun, RPG, and small-arms fire rattles across the several hundred yards of ground separating the NVA and VC from Recon and Alpha Company. As far as Stan can tell, one of the guns is about fifty yards away across a rice paddy, across a narrow dirt road, next to a hooch. Now that he's got his bearings, Stan can see the bunker where the attack is coming from. It's constructed of stacked logs and sandbags. There's a machine gun firing out of a hole in the wall; there's another gun beside the bunker; and three or four NVA soldiers shooting AK-47s, as well as a couple of RPG gunners.

Stan says to Russo, "We've got to do something."

He thinks for a minute. "I'm going to destroy that bunker." Stan holds up a LAW (light antitank weapon). It weighs about six pounds and fires a rocket meant to destroy tanks.

"You're too far away," Russo is saying.

"I'm going to charge it."

"Parker, I'm telling you, you are a dead man if you do."

Stan likes Russo. He has this energetic way of talking. Russo, all business, says to Stan, "They're going to cut you down, man."

Stan says, "I don't give a crap," and he means it. "Let them kill me, you know? I'm tired of it. I'm tired of this. I'd be better off dead anyway." And Stan sits back. There, he's said it, though he never meant to.

He adds, "We'd all be better off dead. This life is terrible. We're already dead. We just don't know it yet."

Russo says nothing. Stan hopes Russo will speak up. That he'll point out that wishing to be dead, to get killed out there in the fields of fire, is not a natural thing to say, that it's bad for your health. That it's a sign of a crazy man. But Russo is quiet.

Stan gets up and turns and over his shoulder says to Russo, "Give me cover fire, and holler back to the rest of them guys— cover me!"

So Russo hollers back, "Hey, listen up! Parker is going to assault the bunker. Give him cover fire!"

Stan strips off his ruck, grabs up the LAW, his M-16, and when he stands up, all hell breaks loose. The air is filled with bullets. At the other end of the rice paddy, the leaves and bushes and trees are jumping as the fire coming through them shreds the foliage. Then the leaves get blown away and there's nothing for the bullets to hit. It's a clear, drilling path from them to him.

He's zigzagging, running this way, that way, and the bullets are whipping past him, just nicking past him. The paddy water is flying up at his feet, and there are RPGs swimming low over the ground, dropping lower and lower and plowing into the water and exploding. With some of the explosions, Stan does a somersault as if to get over the sound of the explosion itself, like a circus performer, and he rolls out of this and extends back up onto his feet and keeps running. It's the damndest thing you ever saw, Parker sprinting atop the narrow dike along the paddy with water on either side. And Wongus there, saying something like, *He's got that angel with him today*. Stan's running and huffing and puffing with the LAW clenched in his left hand, firing his M-16 with his right hand, when suddenly he feels the LAW lurch ahead of him. It's been shot out of his hands. He stoops down as he approaches and scoops it up and keeps running. The fire increases. He falls on his butt and gets up and reloads. A bullet enters his head. But it's not his head, it's his helmet; it enters on the right side and zings right around the helmet on the inside the way you would run your finger along the inside of a bowl to lick the frosting clean. And then the bullet exits, spinning Stan in a circle. He falls face-first into the muddy rice paddy. He sits up. His hairline stings. He'll look at that later. Oh, hell, he can't help it; he takes off his helmet and looks at the hole going in and the hole going out and he can't believe his noggin's intact. He runs a finger along his scalp where it hurts and traces a line right around his head. He puts his helmet back on and sits there. He doesn't think he can run much farther. He's pressed his luck too much already, and he says, *Lord, you've got to help me out. Come on, I'm almost there*, and he leaps a few more steps forward and lands behind a dike. He's in about six inches of cold water but he's safe behind the berm. The NVA are pouring fire into the dirt, and he thinks, *I am in a fix now*. He thinks to himself that he'd better kill these bastards now or for sure they are going to kill him.

He's about sixty feet from the bunker where the machine-gun and small arms fire is coming from. Sixty feet. That isn't so far; in fact, he's too close. He rises up to shoot, and immediately the NVA gunners open on him. He raises just the M-16 over the berm and dumps more rounds in the direction of the bunker. *Bwipp bwipp bwipp*. That was useless. He can't take the bunker with small arms fire; he needs to fire the LAW. He's got one round in the weapon. That's it. One and done. He realizes he's stuck. Every time he falls back to avoid the next fusillade, he can hear the guys behind him yell, "Are you hit?" He spots a cooking pot, picks it up, holds out his M-16, and places the pot on the barrel, the plan coming into focus now. He extends his arm and raises the barrel, and the pot begins to dance on the end of the barrel as the gunfire swarms it. He drops it back down, not wanting to get his M-16 shot up. But he realizes he has a second, maybe two, when the NVA are going to be shooting at the pot and during that time he might pop up and fire the LAW. He raises the pot another time and it's attacked. *Whang whang whang.* Drops it. Raises it again. Drops it. Now he immediately sits up, sights down the barrel of the LAW, pushes the plunger, and watches the twenty-inch rocket sail like a line drive, headed for the narrow aperture in the NVA bunker through which they've been shooting. The rocket enters the hole and disappears.

The bunker blows up. The sky is filled with yellow smoke, burning pieces of thatch. Stan figures everyone inside and near it has to be dead. He looks up at the sky, squinting. "God that's beautiful," all that fire, all that destruction, all that will no longer be shooting at me, and in the silence—for his ears are blown out by the gunfire—comes a crackling noise like the sound of leaves burning, of autumn nights at home. Pieces of the bunker and parts of dead enemy start falling back to earth, smacking the ground and the muddy rice paddy water around him. He looks over the berm and no bullets meet him. It's quiet except for the nice crackling noise.

And then the ammo that didn't blow up in the bunker starts to cook off in the fire—RPG rounds, mortars. The random firing is the loudest yet, and Stan, dazed, no doubt in shock, puts a fresh magazine in his M-16 and grabs two other mags, gets up, and starts shuffling toward the bunker. There's debris flying out of it now, whirring and whizzing—jagged bats leaving a burning house. He sees something moving ahead, limbs moving through the burning debris, and he can't believe that any of the NVA are alive. He walks up and dumps a magazine into them, killing them. They are dead, and he keeps walking. He's walking to where the crackling is coming from, and it's a large hooch, twenty by twenty feet, and it's been the VC command headquarters. There's more movement, this time out of the corner of his eye, and it's Russo running to congratulate him on assaulting the bunker. Stan turns to greet his friend just as the other human being reaches out too, as if to embrace him. The two men look at each other and realize they have never met, that they are total strangers, and that, in fact, they are bound by the rule to kill each other—a rule they did not write but now inhabits every fiber of their being by virtue of finding themselves in this rice paddy.

Stan reaches out for the man's arm, and the man reaches for Stan. They recoil, as if in horror. Stan looks at the face, the eyes, the khaki uniform, and the crisp red star on the soldier's helmet. Both are startled and turn and run away and then they both turn back and face each other at nearly the same time. They stand and stare, confused. *Sonofabitch, is that an* NVA *soldier?* Stan has run back to where he'd dropped some ammo. He bends to pick it up and fixes to draw down on the NVA soldier when he sees the guy throw something at him.

It comes sailing toward him, a high arc, nice lift. And Stan's pretty sure the guy has played some Little League baseball, like him too, the way he's delivered the throw from the outfield. But the ball is actually a grenade and comes to stop in the dirt at his feet. Stan can hear the fuse inside fizzing like two bees trapped in a jar, getting louder. He looks up and he can see the NVA soldier looking at him. Stan is actually down on one knee with his right hand out, his left glove hand ready to scoop up the baseball, and instead he thinks, *I better stand up and shoot this guy.*

He's about four feet from the grenade.

It explodes.

At the last available moment Stan turns to his left. His right side—his shoulder, ribs, and hip—is shredded with shrapnel. His whole right side starts to burn. His eyeballs are filled with orange light. A flash. And sailing backward, he sees blue (from the sky), green (from the trees), and white (from the smoke filling the air) before he hits the ground. He's never been in so much pain. In fact, he doesn't even really hear the explosion until after it's over, until after he lands on his back, looking at the blue, the green, the white, and he's intensely aware of himself— where he ends and where the rest of the earth begins—because everywhere there's pain. He looks at the green and thinks that the green is not pain. The blue above him is not pain. He blinks and finds it amazing that even his eyelashes hurt at their very roots, right around the pale rim of skin surrounding each lash. He can't believe he's alive.

With the grenade's explosion, he falls back with such force and makes such a splash that the cold water in this bit of rice paddy splashes up and over the smooth mud sides of the paddy's dike, the way the water can overrun the top of a tub and slop across the floor—except now the water comes back. It comes rolling back into the pool that he's fallen into, and since he's lying on his back and looking at the sky and since his mouth is open, still in a silent scream, the water runs into his mouth. It tastes like worms and dirt and metal. He starts coughing. But he realizes that maybe he should be quiet and not make so much noise because he doesn't know who's still in the area. He can't hear Russo or the rest of the platoon, some of whom are engaged in another firefight, during which Rivera, Dove, Russo, Ron Kleckler, and Lindsey Kinney will be wounded. And because he can't hear anything, Stan thinks that he's died and that his life is draining slowly, perhaps into the pool of water; he's still able to be aware of things, but he's growing less and less aware. The truth is, he can't hear anything because he's lying in six inches of water and his ears have filled with it, so that everything has that faraway, tinny sound of a boat motor on a summer lake somewhere, of gunfire and grenade and a LAW rocket ringing in his ears as if the water that had entered his ears had trapped the sound inside his head. Then the sound starts rushing out, and he is sure that this is another sign that he is dying. In fact, what it means is that his eardrums are burst. His head is ringing and aching.

He realizes, *I can't be dead, because dead men can't hear anything*, and he is hearing something—something approaching him, and he lies back in the water. The water gets in his eyes, and he wipes them with his hand. When he moves his hand away, he sees, silhouetted against the sky, a tall, thin NVA soldier looking down at him, studying. Stan freezes.

It's the same guy who threw the grenade.

He slowly lifts his rifle at Stan.

Stan is looking up, straight up, into the small metal hole in the end of the rifle. It's about six feet away, a perfect black hole, and he's staring wide-eyed, trying not to blink. The guy's khaki uniform, the leather boots, his hank of hair hanging out from under his helmet. Stan's trying with all his might not to blink as he looks right into the barrel, his whole life shrunk and focused right to this point, about a quarter-inch in diameter, so close. All the fighting and traveling and the snowy mornings walking to school and getting beat up in the school yard in New Mexico and his mother lashing the bikes to the truck and trailer, their home, as their father drives away to a new ironworking job and a new patch of dirt to park the trailer while he works and eventually they move on again. Stan moves on through time and space, even when he was a little boy, moving, always in two places, where he's just been and where he's headed to. He was even born in two places at once, on the Texas/Arkansas border in that place called Texarkana, with the state line itself painted as a white stripe up the middle of the courthouse steps. Now he lies in the water staring right at the guy and the guy is staring at him, and Stan knows he's trying to figure out if he's alive. Stan's thinking, *He's fixing to shoot me. I'm a dead man again.*

The NVA soldier points the AK close to Stan's cheek like he's going to fire. Then he drops it away from his face and looks, really looks, at Stan. Then he places the rifle back, moves the pad of his finger over the trigger, begins to press, when a sound, or something—movement?—distracts him and he turns his head. Then he looks at Stan, drops the rifle to his side, and turns on a trot and disappears from Stan's view. It's been like lying in a grave and looking up at a rectangle of sky. Stan feels himself breathe for the first time in several minutes.

He doesn't dare move for twenty, thirty seconds. He doesn't want to move at all. He doesn't feel like he can move; he hurts everywhere.

He sits up now to take in the damage and looks at the holes in his green commando sweater, and it's been shot up, though there's no blood where the holes are. His web gear, the chest-mounted pouch he was wearing when he took off running to assault the machine gun, is gone. He doesn't know where he lost it. And he looks around for the trains, he can hear them. Now there are at least four of them, one coming from each direction of the compass, north, south, east, and west, and it seems they will intersect in his head, the roaring sound is so loud. But then other sounds become apparent—sounds of shooting, men shouting, the sounds filling the void where he's been living for the last five minutes.

He cranes around and looks back in the direction he'd run from and sees someone waving at him "Get down!" Small arms fire erupts from the place that Stan had assaulted because the NVA have come to reinforce their destroyed position. The shooting's coming from about fifty feet away from Stan, across the dirt road that runs through the village. He can't see it because he can't lift his head to look. It grows in intensity, and he stays ducked down.

I can't stay here, he thinks, and he starts to elbow-crawl up out of the water, pulling himself up to the drier edge of the dike so that just his legs are in the water. He's managed to end up at the spot where he last had his M-16 and reaches up slowly to pull it down from the dike just as more bullets strike around him. He crawls right up against the dike for protection, trying to think of a next move.

The thing is, he can't believe how transitory the pain is. First it's there one minute, and then gone. And then back like a plate of hot steel laid on his bare skin—his leg mostly. His leg's burning up. He thinks it's broken. He thinks his ribs are broken. He reaches down with his hand and rubs his leg, and it comes back to him covered in blood. He thinks, *My, look at that*, and feels around, like a man frisking himself, up at the top of the leg and down as far as he can reach, which isn't far, to check that everything is there. And that's when his hand brushes past something, something sharp and jagged, and he stops: *Whoa, what's this?* His fingers stop on the hard shape, and he looks down and discerns that it's a piece of metal, shrapnel. He pinches it between his thumb and forefinger and thinks, *Now or never*, and pulls. It slides out of his leg meat and emerges as a piece of knife-shaped steel, about as long his forefinger. He lifts it and looks at it and decides that it belongs in his shirt pocket as a souvenir, so he reaches inside his shot-up commando sweater and drops it in there and pats it and thinks, *There, that's done.* When he moves his hand, it bumps into something else; something is sticking out of his ribs on his right side. It's a bigger thing, sharper. He pulls that out, but this time, the effect is different: the hole where the steel had been suddenly fills with blood, oozes, and starts dumping blood down his side. He thinks he should put the metal back into the hole and almost tries to, then shakes his head, trying to clear his thoughts, and realizes he's going to bleed to death or at least pass out. He jams his left forefinger into the hole on his right side so he can leave his right hand free, his trigger hand, and he figures out a way to bandage himself. He's got his left arm across his stomach with his finger jammed up between his ribs, and with his right hand, he bunches his shirt into a kind of plug shape about the size of the hole, removes his finger, and stuffs the shirt into the bloody hole. *Oh man does that hurt, but it hurts so good, in a funny kind of way.* He reaches into a pocket and unrolls a cloth bandage that he wraps around his rib cage, around and around a few times, tighter and tighter, cinching himself up, battening the shirt around the hole, and, brother, does it continue to hurt. But the bleeding slows. That's good. He picks up his weapon and places the stock of the weapon against the wound and scooches up against the side of the dike, leaning into it. The weapon's stock presses into the wound, applying steady pressure, which he's pretty sure is going a long way to stopping the bleeding altogether. He sits there leaning into the dike with the shooting going on overhead and doesn't know what's going to happen next. Somebody's going to have to come and get him. He can't elbow-crawl backward from his position. After about ten minutes, Troy Fulton inches up to him; he's made it all the way from the houses where the gun battle started, up to Stan. Stan hadn't even seen him coming. He's so glad to see Troy again. His voice is calm. He looks at the bandage job Stan did on himself and says, "Parker, that's real good handiwork." And then he says, "I can't do anything more for you," and he explains they just have to wait for the medevac and that the ground fire is too heavy right now.

"Can you give me a shot or something?" Stan practically begs him. The pain's getting worse.

"No, I can't, because you need all your faculties here. If I give you a shot, you're liable to pass out on me."

Oh, sweet Lord, I ain't going to pass out, thinks Stan.

"You just sit tight. We'll get somebody to you in a little bit."

A little bit? This surprises Stan. "You're not going to leave me, are you?"

"No," Fulton says, and then he starts crawling backward, over the ground from whence he came.

Stan is looking at him, saying, "I thought you said you weren't going to leave me."

"Well," says Fulton, trying to explain to the increasingly agitated Stan, "I'm going to be back for you. I'm not going to leave you here."

"But right now, you're leaving me here, right?"

"Well, yeah," Fulton says, as if to say, *When you put it like that*—

"How long?" says Stan. "How long before somebody's back?"

"I don't know, thirty minutes, an hour. We'll be back."

"Don't forget about me being here!" cries Stan. "Don't go off and leave me." What's really bothering Stan is the prospect of being left behind, of not being carried onto the chopper, of not being airlifted from this terrible place.

"We won't leave you," says Fulton. "I guarantee you."

"Okay," Stan says finally. He's shivering. He drifts off and wakes when somebody shakes him. It's Dwight Lane and Brian Riley come to get him back to the rear, to a safe place behind the screen of trees along another rice paddy, where the helicopters are going to land. Stan is incredulous. He's coming out of the initial haze of the pain and remembers that Lane and Riley are two of the shorter guys in the platoon. How are they going to carry him?

"What happened to those six-foot guys we've got?" Stan asks.

"They said we'd do a better job of dragging you," says Riley.

"Dragging me? You mean, you're going to drag me back there? I thought you were going to carry me."

"There's too much shooting going on," says Lane. "We got to stay low. We're the shortest, and we won't get shot at as much."

"Hang on," says Riley, and each of them grabs one of Stan's shoulders and starts dragging, half-crouched, half-crawling at times, with Stan bumping along over the rough edge of the paddy along the tree line. Stan can feel every heartbeat in his chest. He's throbbing with pain. Lane and Riley drag him for a while, and then they stop and turn and shoot at the place they've come from. They drag Stan another fifteen feet and stop to shoot. They do this several times, and finally Stan yells out, "How about I do the shooting and you guys keep dragging?" All the starting and stopping is killing him. The pain makes him feel like he'll pass out.

With Stan firing and the men dragging, they finally reach the trees. Troy Fulton rushes to Stan and asks, "How are you feeling?" and Stan says, "I'm hurting all over. Can you give me something?" That's when Stan looks over to his left and right and sees the other wounded laid out, Tinkle and Hinote. Tinkle got it the worst: he got the machine-gun fire across his legs, right below the knees. It didn't take his legs off, but it sure messed them up.

He's screaming at the top of his lungs. Stan realizes he's been listening to Dennis Tinkle scream like this the whole time he was lying against the dike, after assaulting the position. Poor Dennis. Stan feels sorry for him. He'd gotten so used to his screaming that he wasn't even hearing it anymore.

The chopper lands. Stan thinks it's beautiful the way the blast pushes down yellow grass in a perfect disc shape. He thinks he will live if he can get on the helicopter and be medevaced to the hospital at Quang Tri City, about thirteen miles away.

The helicopters are taking ground fire. Stan is aware that it's dangerous but not aware that he's in danger. He's in shock. Somebody lifts him to the door and he sees there are other men inside, maybe worse off than him, and he says, "You don't have to take me now. I can wait." He's not bleeding so much. He's in pain, but he knows he's not dying. He remains behind the dike with the helicopters taking off and landing and finally one lands for him, and he's put on and he thinks, *Freedom. I'm out of here.*

He's about three hundred feet in the air when stuff starts popping up through the deck of the chopper and exiting up through the overhead, and it's pretty clear that this is gunfire from the ground. And he's thinking, *This is not my day. They're definitely trying to kill me today. I'm not going to live to see the end of this one."*

The chopper starts spinning.

The chopper pilot turns and looks at Stan and says, "Hang on, we're going down."

When he wakes up, he doesn't remember the crash. He only knows he's on the ground. Men are running around him. Soldiers in khaki, NVA soldiers. How did he get on the ground, and why is the helicopter about fifty feet away from him? How did he get so far away?

Everything's silent.

For the second time in several hours, he can't hear anything.

The helicopter is lying on its side, crumpled up. He still hasn't pieced together that this is the helicopter he has just been in. The rotor blades are broken off. There's gunfire, and Stan sees that soldiers—NVA—are running by him, shooting at the helicopter. They're running past him like he's dead, or insignificant, of no threat. He looks up, and here come two Huey "Hogs," gunships bristling with high-speed mini-guns and rocket pods. They're firing at the NVA soldiers around the crash site. Stan worries he's going to be shot. One of the Hogs circles and a guy in the door leans out and waves at Stan to stay down.

The Hogs are doing figure eights in the air, and everything starts exploding around Stan. He's waving at the guys in the choppers to say, "Remember, I'm here! See me, see me!" The Hogs peel off, revealing, in the middle of the sky between them, a Huey medevac. For a moment Stan thinks it's going to shoot him. But the chopper wheels around and is facing him broadside and a soldier sitting in the side door says, "Come on, man. Hurry up!" and Stan realizes, *Oh. I gotta get out of here. I gotta walk, but I don't think I can walk.* The guy in the door keeps waving, and then all of a sudden he grabs his chest and falls over, out of the open door and hits the ground. He's been shot. Stan can only think, *Why didn't they land closer?* And the chopper's door gunner on the machine gun swings around and starts firing right past Stan at an oncoming enemy he can't see but can imagine running toward him. He needs to hightail it out of here. But he starts yelling that he can't walk. He feels *someone* pick him up from behind and start carrying him, pushing him, toward the helicopter, whose rotors are still turning, the turbine still whining above the grinding of the gunfire. Who the hell is pushing him from behind? He feels a presence but doesn't

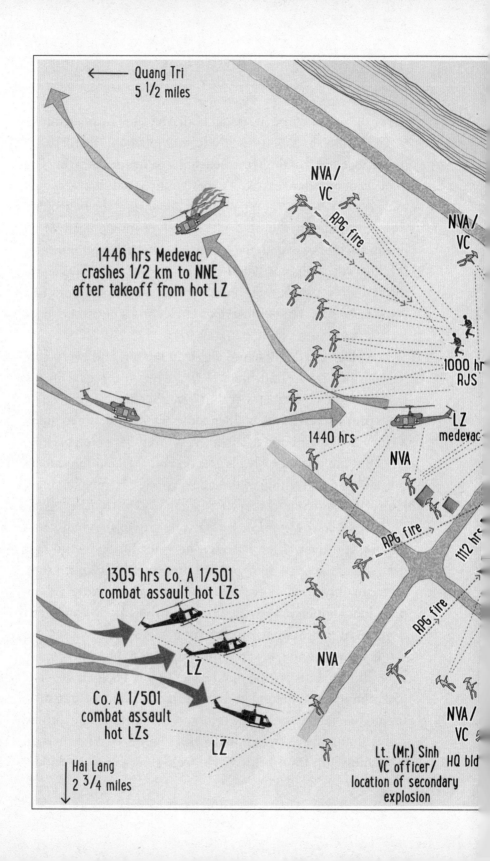

← Quang Tri
5 1/2 miles

NVA /
VC

NVA /
VC

RPG fire

1446 hrs Medevac
crashes 1/2 km to NNE
after takeoff from hot LZ

1000 hr
RJS

1440 hrs

LZ
medevac

NVA

RPG fire

1112 hrs

1305 hrs Co. A 1/501
combat assault hot LZs

RPG fire

LZ

NVA

Co. A 1/501
combat assault
hot LZs

LZ

NVA /
VC

Hai Lang
2 3/4 miles

Lt. (Mr.) Sinh
VC officer/
location of secondary
explosion

HQ bld

ASSAULT OF RECON PLATOON, 1/501, TRUNG HOA
FEBRUARY 18, 1968

Buildings
Roads
Path or dike
Rice paddies
Combat assault
Medevac
U.S. soldier
NVA or VC soldier

Song Vinh Dinh River

Recon
0938 hrs RP
0910 hrs R2
R1
0845 hrs R1

Recon
1045 hrs R WIA 2
1210 hrs NVA POW
1335 hrs R WIA 6
Recon
R2
NVA/VC

Hwy 602
1 1/8 mile →

1340 hrs Stan Parker assaults heavy machine-gun bunker with M72 LAW rocket: 1345 hrs WIA

R WIA 2

RPG fire

Machine-gun bunker
RPG fire

Approx 1/4 mile

Map based on sketch by Stan Parker

ASSAULT OF RECON PLATOON, 1/501, TRUNG HOA
FEBRUARY 18, 1968

Abbreviation Key

R1 = Recon 1st Squad

R2 = Recon 2nd Squad

RP = Recon Platoon

RJS = Recon, Jerry and Stan

R WIA 2 (T&H) = Recon WIA, Tinkle and Hinote

R WIA 6 (P, D, R, K, KL, R) = Recon WIA, Parker, Dove, Russo, Kinney, Kleckler, and Rivera

LZ = Helicopter landing zone

NVA/VC = North Vietnamese Army/Viet Cong locations, machine-gun, small-arms, and RPG fire

TIMELINE

All hours shown in military time ·

Order of movement of Recon 1/501, to the NNE on dirt road: North side of road beside water canal, 3rd Squad SP/4 Jerry Austin point man, SP/4 Bob Cromer slack, then rest of squad, followed on north side of road by Recon HQ section; south side of road, 2nd Squad, SP/4 Stan Parker point man, SP/4 Guido Russo slack, then rest of squad, followed along south side of road by 1st Squad, SGT Tony Beke point man, SP/4 Charlie Pyle slack.

0845 hrs: (R1) Recon 1st Squad, point man SP/4 Jerry Austin takes fire from VC scout at edge of village armed with 1918 BAR; Austin engages VC scout, kills 1 VC.

0900 hrs: (R2) Recon 2nd Squad takes lead position with continued movement NNE along south side of road beside rice paddy.

0910 hrs: (R2) 2nd Squad point man SP/4 Stan Parker makes contact with enemy force of unknown size; 2 NVA killed.

0928 hrs: (R2) 2nd Squad point man SP/4 Stan Parker kills a third NVA soldier.

0930 hrs: Recon Platoon breaks contact, pulls back for head count of members, and establishes better position of engagement.

0938 hrs: (RP) Recon reengaged in heavy fighting at same location.

0940 hrs: Recon calls in arty on NVA location.

1000 hrs: (RJS) SP/4 Jerry Austin becomes separated from main Recon force, weapon malfunctions while he is charged by 25 to 35 NVA, and he yells for help. SP/4 Stan Parker hears his call for assistance from about 75 yards away and leaves his position and assaults through a barrage of enemy fire to get to Austin's location.

1045 hrs: (R WIA 2, T, H) Recon 2 U.S. WIA: SP/4 Dennis Tinkle (3rd Squad) and Terry Hinote (2nd Squad) both with multiple gunshot wounds (MGSW). Recon requested medevac, but medevac request denied because of heavy enemy fire in the area.

1100 hrs: (RP) Recon receiving small-arms, machine-gun, and multiple RPG fire.

1105 hrs: Recon encircled by large NVA/VC force with fierce close-quarter fighting.

1112 hrs: (R1) Recon silences sniper but still engaged in small-arms fire and heavy enemy force.

1125 hrs: Company A 1/501 notified for combat assault to reinforce Recon 1/501.

1210 hrs: Recon captures 1 NVA WIA; POW states their objective was to overrun and kill all Americans.

1230 hrs: Air support requested by 2nd Brigade HQ, 101st Airborne, and denied. Recon in contact at "extreme danger close" quarters with attacking NVA/VC force.

1305 hrs: Company A 1/501 conducts helicopter combat assault into hot LZs and reports 3 WIA.

1315 hrs: Recon engaged overwhelming NVA force at 50 meters or less to immediate front and sides with massive amount of small-arms, heavy machine-gun, and RPG fire.

1325 hrs: Company A, 100 meters from Recon right flank; both Company A and Recon engaged large NVA force located between them.

1335 hrs: Recon pinned down by NVA automatic weapons fire.

1338 hrs: Recon receiving heavy machine-gun, small-arms, and RPG fire from heavily fortified bunker to immediate front. Also small-arms fire from left and right flanks and rear.

1340 hrs: Recon uses machine-gun and small-arms fire to repulse enemy attack.

1345 hrs: SP/4 Stan Parker assaults through machine-gun, small-arms, and RPG fire to within 20 meters of fortified bunker and fires M72 light antitank weapon into forti-

fied NVA machine-gun bunker. Reinforced bunker explodes with secondary explosion resulting in 8 NVA KIA. Secondary explosion destroys building to right of bunker. After the explosion, Parker assaults bunker with automatic weapons fire to fully cease enemy fire. While assaulting, Parker WIA with multiple shrapnel wounds (SW) to right leg, rib cage, chest, arm, and face. Firefight engagement subsides but intensifies again with small-arms and rocket fire from left and right flanks. Five additional Recon members WIA: SP/4 Albert Dove with SW to head and face; SP/4 Guido Russo with SW to leg and buttocks area; SP/4 Angel Rivera with SW to right leg and foot; SGT Ronald Kleckler with GSW/SW to shoulder; and SSG Lindsey Kinney with SW to shoulder and arm.

1350 hrs: Company B 1/501 notified for combat assault to reinforce Companies A, C, and D and Recon 1/501.

1403 hrs approx.: First medevac lands, extracts two Recon WIA, Tinkle and Hinote.

1410 hrs approx.: Second medevac lands, extracts Recon and Company A WIA.

1440 hrs: Third medevac is called in, picks up additional wounded and Recon WIA, SP/4 Stan Parker.

1446 hrs: Medevac chopper receives heavy machine-gun fire in tail and engine and crashes after flying approximately ½ km to NE.

identify a person. He can feel the warmth of the other person's body, the person who does not say anything to him. *I don't know who you are, and I don't know where you came from, but I'm sure glad you're here.* They're getting close to the chopper. Stan can see the look on the gunner's face; he's looking past him, at something that is approaching from behind. Two NVA soldiers quickly come running past Stan and take aim through the open door up at the pilot in the left seat. The gunner in the door can't swing his machine gun around because the angle is too severe and he can't shoot the two enemies who've approached. If he does, he'll shoot Stan and his friend. Stan still has his M-16 and he lifts it and fires, killing the soldiers. The copilot is yelling, "Come on, come on!" He's on the left side of the chopper, closest to Stan, and he's got his .45 pistol out and shooting people as soon as they run up. He's shooting through the windscreen, which shatters. Stan falls onto the deck of the chopper and is pulled up into the cabin as it lifts immediately from the grass and wheels up and away. More rounds are coming up from the ground and piercing the deck. The chopper begins rocking back and forth, violently swinging side to side, as the pilot jams the stick and takes evasive action in the midst of so much ground fire. "Hang on, man!" he yells, and Stan is pretty sure he's going to be shot down a second time. He blacks out. When he wakes up, the pilot announces they're landing. Stan can feel heavy rain on his face coming through the door onto the deck where he lies. The chopper's on the ground. People are running out to it with a stretcher, and they slide Stan onto it. As they take him away, he asks, "Where's the dude who helped me get on the chopper?"

The door gunner looks at him. "What?"

"The guy that helped me to the chopper, where's he at?"

"What are you talking about?"

"You know, when I got up and I was coming to the chopper and I'm getting on . . . "

"Yeah?"

"And then I shot the two guys."

"Yeah, that was so cool. You saved our day. I didn't think you could do it. You wasted them both right there, man."

"Yeah, but the guy that was with me, helping me. Where's he at?"

"You were all by yourself, man."

Yet there is no trace or sign of the person anywhere. As he's pulled from the chopper, he looks back and sees it's empty.

He's wheeled into the military hospital in Quang Tri wearing the commando sweater he'd been shot in. He'd bought the sweater at a PX back in Fort Campbell, Kentucky, a few days before deploying. That seems a long time ago, though it's been only nine weeks.

The sweater's filthy and full of holes. The nurse takes medical-looking scissors and starts cutting the sweater off him. "Hey, not that," he protests. "Not my favorite sweater."

The doc, walking in, says, "You won't be needing this sweater."

"I will be wanting that sweater," Stan insists. "Please don't cut it off."

The nurse stops cutting with the scissors, and Stan realizes in his haze that he's falling in love with her. No other way to explain it. She's so pretty. She's so clean. He can smell her hair even from several feet away.

"You really want to keep this sweater?" she asks him, this time looking serious. "This is going to hurt."

"That's okay," he says. He just wants to sit and look at her.

She'll have to remove the sweater inch by inch away from the wounds across his body, the heavy strippling done by the shrapnel. His back, if she could see it right off the bat, would look like a duck or grouse when you've shot it up close and the pellets have driven the feathers into the flesh. She starts pulling the sweater away from the wound in his right rib where the grenade fragment went in an inch or so and where the blood has dried. You would think the movement of the fabric away from the flesh would make a sound, but it silently peels way. The entire right side of his body is lined with small, bleeding holes.

He looks at her and says, "When I get better, I'm coming back to see you."

"Okay," she says, patting his hand. "Sure you will."

Stan lies back on the bed, exhausted. The nurse walks away with the sweater.

A couple of days later, he's in bed and when she walks in, he can smell her hair again. She says, "I've got something for you," and he says, "What?,'" and she holds out the sweater.

It's been sewn up and cleaned and made whole.

Stan feels like crying. He can't believe she has done this for him.

But she's done it. She's his perfect angel. She starts asking "Where are you from?" and "Where do you hurt?" and she says, "You're going to be okay, don't worry." Stan can't keep still; her presence stirs something in him. And it's not just between his legs; she has made him feel *alive*. He's wiggling on the bed, and she reaches down to his right wrist to take his pulse, to the vein there jumping under the skin, and she says, "What are you doing?" And "Will you be still?" and she stops and announces, "I've got you figured out." She throws his arm aside and says, "You just want me to hold you, don't you?" And he says, "Well, is there anything wrong with that?"

She looks at him a moment and says, "Oh," and reaches down

and grabs his arm with her hands and squeezes and says, "Does that feel better?"

Stan can't respond; he's speechless. "Just don't let go," he says. "Just don't let go." Her touch. Stan is lying in bed, against a white sheet, which smells like bleach, and feeling the young woman's touch on his arm.

He already knows he will have no way of describing this to the guys back in the field.

1962–66

Minot, North Dakota, to Gary, Indiana

How long has he been gone from Indiana? What day of the week was it when he boarded the bus in Gary for Fort Leonard Wood? The past is receding. It was a warm Thursday in August 1966, yes. He can count the days that've passed too: 559 of them, but these seem hardly able to contain what he has seen, heard, tasted, and done. His childhood now belongs to another man entirely, yet each step he takes in combat feels to him an affirmation of his father's and mother's instructions about how to live bravely. He feels he's been brave; he hopes he's been honorable.

In Minot, North Dakota, when his family moved there during his freshman high school year, Stan mustered enough courage at the homecoming to dance with girls he felt (and he was ashamed of this) were better than him. Nonetheless, he'd asked them, and they seemed to enjoy themselves. His father was building nuclear missile silos, and townspeople typically, and derisively, called a boy like Stan Parker a "missile kid." Stan had no inkling of the transgression he'd committed by asking the girls to dance.

    At a subsequent football practice, the coach said he had a special kind of training for Stan. He told him to warm up by taking a lap around the football field. As he ran, he saw the entire football team lined up on the sideline, about fifty players in all. The coach waved Stan over.

The coach pointed at the players. He said that it should be no problem at all for Stan to run the entire length of the field while keeping hold of the football as the team rushed at him. If he dropped the football, he would have to start over again.

The coach added, "This shouldn't be a problem, Parker, if you just show us some of the fancy footwork that you had at the school dance."

A light went on inside Stan's brain. He was being set up by the coach, an adult, whom he had assumed would have his interests at heart. The coach gave him a pat on the helmet. "Get going," he said.

Stan started running, focused solely on the end zone. As he got to about the twenty-yard line, he saw the players peeling off from the side. They launched themselves at him, aiming for the football, trying to dislodge it so he'd have to start all over again.

He gripped tight and kept churning. He wasn't big, and he wasn't an experienced ballplayer. In fact, he'd been put in only a handful of times by the coach at the tight-end position. One by one, the players crashed into him.

The body strikes by the bigger players knocked his breath away. Some of the hits flattened him to the ground, and he struggled getting back up. The big linebackers reached down and pulled him to his feet, and then they shoved him toward the next oncoming player, ready to knock him down. At the end of the field, he couldn't see the end zone itself but another kind of place. A *place he had to reach.*

He would not stop.

He was hit by a player he didn't see coming. The impact made him black out a moment. He opened his eyes and saw the players circled around him and looking down. He struggled back to his feet. And started running again.

He ran a few more yards and was knocked down again. This time he woke up under the goalpost. And then he saw he'd made it. He hadn't dropped the ball. The players gathered around again, this time grumbling. A hand extended itself through the blurry cloud of faces, and Stan saw that this was the coach and that he was smiling. Maybe he had proven something after all, Stan thought. He grabbed the hand, and the coach pulled him up. He ached, but he hadn't stopped running.

In 1964, when Stan was a junior in high school, his parents worried that he and his brothers, approaching adulthood, needed a place they could call home for longer than several months at a stretch. When John James found work building the Bethlehem Steel Works in Gary, Indiana, they towed a new mobile home to a large lot in a new trailer development called Black Oaks, several miles from the Gary lakeshore, and set up housekeeping. The Parker family would spend the next two years at Black Oak, a community filled with union-organized steel and construction workers. By now, at age sixteen, Stan had attended twenty-three schools and lived in forty-three states.

That winter of 1965, he saw his first AR-15, a semiautomatic rifle, in a gun store. The AR-15 was cousin to the government-issue M-16, which, he'd heard on the news, soldiers were carrying in a place called Vietnam. Stan hadn't heard much about the place. He did like the looks of the AR-15, though. Snow was falling outside the gun store window as he stood and stared at the gun. The attraction to the shape of the rifle was nearly physical. And then when the store clerk handed him the weapon, there was something incredibly exciting in holding it. The gun seemed capable of transporting him to a new life. But when he handed the gun back to the clerk, he returned to what interested him most for the coming senior year: meeting girls. Witty and charming, he nonetheless hadn't had much luck with them at Calumet High.

The summer between his junior and senior year he toyed with the idea of dating three girls at once. Anna Runion was a neighbor in the Black Oaks trailer development and two years younger than him. Her father was a union pipefitter, and she too had seen the world from the rear window of the family's work truck. When Stan found out that Anna already had a boyfriend, this doubled his resolve to win her heart. At the same time, he started doting on another classmate, Carol Hamilton, a friend from art class. If things with Anna didn't work out, he figured he'd date Carol. Beyond that, and not ready to limit his affections, he started flirting with a sophomore, Maureen Bell, who attended Lew Wallace, a rival high school. Stan called her Mo.

Years later, all Mo could remember about meeting Stan Parker was that he'd appeared at her side as she was shopping with her girlfriend at a local clothing store and that he wouldn't stop talking—about everything. It seemed he'd been everywhere in the United States. Throughout Stan's senior year, he and Mo went to movies and afterward drank Cokes and malts at the Blue Top Drive-In. All the while, Stan was considering his life after graduation. What was he going to do? Work like his father as an ironworker at Bethlehem Steel? Join the military?

His older brother, Dub, had just graduated from high school and was at Fort Bragg in North Carolina with the U.S. Army's 82nd Airborne. *Shouldn't I join too?* wondered Stan. He felt he had a duty to join, and, increasingly, it seemed that his country, and the Vietnamese people, would need guys like him. At school during lunch, he couldn't believe it when he heard some of the guys talking about getting married just to get out of going to Vietnam. By the end of his senior year, he had decided to join up.

He didn't want to be drafted and get an assignment he didn't like. "If I'm going to join the Army," he told his mother, "I'm going to do one thing: *fight*."

When he told his mother about his plan, she objected mightily, as did Maureen. His mother made him promise that he would not, under any circumstance, join the U.S. Army, and Stan promised that he would honor her wish. Reluctantly. Stan felt that this didn't leave many options for him. Gary was an increasingly dangerous city in a year that was turning more violent. Some of his classmates would be killed—drug deals, muggings, murders—before they could graduate. Steel bars lined the windows of some of the homes and businesses along the main street. You didn't linger at stoplights. The country was coming apart at the same time some of its people were coming together. Martin Luther King Jr. was saying his thing, and the Black Panthers were holding up weapons at rallies. The country was simmering.

The news that night, that month, that year, was not good, but the color images were perfect. You could see someone get shot, as if it were happening in your living room, as you looked up from your TV dinner. For the first time in history, America was watching a war as it was fought, in near real time.

Dub wrote to Stan from Fort Bragg and told him he was trying to get orders to deploy to Vietnam. Every month the 82nd Airborne Division was sending paratroopers as replacements to the 1st Brigade, 101st Airborne Division, or to the 173rd Airborne Brigade. Dub said he hoped to leave soon. The two brothers agreed to keep this news from their dad and their mom. Dub told Stan that their mom would go nuts if he joined the Army too.

• • •

When he thought about joining the Army against his mother's wishes, he decided he'd rather ask her forgiveness than approach her again for her approval. He didn't mention his decision to his father; he didn't want to place him in the middle. At the same time, he felt that secretly his father approved of what he was doing.

Back at home, after signing up at the Army recruiter's office, Stan couldn't wait to tell Dub about what he'd done. Dub was home on leave, thinking every day about the fact that soon he'd probably be fighting in Vietnam. Stan admired how simultaneously calm and ready for adventure his brother always seemed. Dub was sitting on the couch, watching TV, when Stan walked into the living room and said, "So, guess what I did today."

Dub, looking up from the TV, said he just had no idea.

"How about, 'I joined the Army!'"

Dub sat up. "You're kidding me, right?"

"I'm going to be a paratrooper—*and* I'm going to Vietnam."

Dub thought for moment, the news sinking in. "Wow," he said. And then, "Congratulations." Stan could tell his older brother was proud of him. But Stan suddenly saw a worried look on his face. "Have you told Mom?" his brother asked.

"No, but I'm going to. At dinner."

"She's going to be mad."

"Now don't you tell her—let me do that."

Dub didn't say anything.

That night at the dinner table, as their mother and father were passing around the food, Dub blurted, "Hey, does anybody know what Stan did today?"

His mother paused, a hot dish of food stopped in midair.

"No. What?" she asked.

His dad said, "What'd you do today, Stanley?"

Both Parker parents were used to their second eldest son getting into mischief. But Stan knew they wouldn't be prepared for the news he had for them.

"Ah, well," Stan began, "me and Gervais and a few others, we were just messing around today—"

Dub interrupted. "He went and joined the Army!"

Stan couldn't tell if his brother was angry at him for joining or just giving him a hard time. Maybe he was being driven by a fear that he'd be hurt in Vietnam. Stan told himself again that nothing bad would happen to him in the war.

Stan waited for his mother's reaction. She was looking at him, hard. She seemed about to cry, which pained him.

His dad nodded at him. "Congratulations," he said. "You remembered what I said about draft dodgers?"

"Yes, sir, I did."

His mother said, "I don't want to talk about this."

And then she said, "I can't believe you did this without talking with me!"

"I did talk with you," said Stan, "and you said I couldn't join."

"I told you not to join. And you shouldn't have!"

"Well, I did," Stan shot back.

She looked over the table and gave his father a stare, a look that said, Stan could see: *This is all your fault. You and your teaching him to fight at such a young age.*

Stan crossed his arms and sat at the table, waiting for whatever happened next. His mother was mad. He knew that. Perhaps madder than he'd ever seen her.

She got up and took the dishes to the sink and began washing. She didn't speak to him for a week. It was going to be a long summer, waiting for basic training to begin.

After enlisting that spring in 1966, Stan and Gervais drove around Gary, feeling different about themselves, older. They pulled up to Mac and Ed's, a burger joint where Stan had worked his junior year, hoping that someone might ask what they were up to so they could say they'd just joined the Army. They tried to imagine what kind of new life they would have. Overhead, the drive-in's speakers played a discordant mix these days: Frank Sinatra's "Strangers in the Night," the Stones' "Paint It Black," Percy Sledge's "When a Man Loves a Woman," and Barry Sadler's "Ballad of the Green Berets." The music drifted down from the eaves on Stan and Gervais and the boys, and they peeled out of the lot, singing.

February 26, 1968

Hai Lang, Vietnam

After seven days, on February 26, Stan is released back into the field. Or, rather, he lies about the pain he's in and talks the nurse into releasing him early from the hospital. She doesn't want to, telling him his ribs and leg haven't healed. "I *have* to get back to the guys," he says. "I just have to."

She relents. "You take care of yourself. I don't want to see you back here again," and he says, "You won't, I promise." A few hours later, he lands in a rice paddy and hops off the Huey, feeling sore but elated to be back. It's as if the charging of the bunker never happened; well, it happened, but it's in the past and he's sure it's no prediction of what the future will bring.

He heads out on another mission, this time with Delta Company, and the news is the LZ's going to be hot—they'll be shot at as they land.

They're flying, and it's fun to dip and glide over the trees, feeling the cooler wind coming though the cabin door as the blue sky slips by in panels.

Russo's standing on the skid of the Huey, facing backward, talking with Stan, who is standing inside the chopper and facing forward. They start taking fire from the tree line, and Stan can see the pilot's getting ready to land, so he tells Russo to turn around. Russo keeps standing there, both feet on the narrow skid, one in front of the other, like a man walking on a beam. The chopper drops to a near hover, still moving forward, over a rice paddy, heading for a dry patch at the edge of the paddy to land. Then the pilot yanks the stick and the chopper jerks, and Russo gets a look on his face, like, *Oh, no.* His feet go out from under him, and he drops suddenly on the skids, right on his gonads. He hangs there, sits a moment, and then slowly tips over like a top-heavy toy and plummets straight down, headfirst, into the rice paddy, twenty feet below. Much of him disappears except for his legs. He's stuck headfirst in the mud.

Now the shooting from the tree line grows fiercer. Stan looks down, thinking, *Oh my god, Russo,* and all he sees are Russo's legs kicking back and forth like a cartoon, the rest of his body swallowed by the paddy. He figures Russo's got thirty seconds, a minute, before he drowns. The pilot lands and Stan and the rest jump off and start wading into the paddy to rescue Russo. The gunfire is increasing by the minute, and Stan finds it amazing that no one's been hit. He looks up and sees a second chopper coming in. He hadn't seen it before; it'd been trailing them. The pilot, Stan realizes, has to be one vigilant individual. He wheels around and starts steaming for Russo, who is still stuck in the mud, his legs still kicking, though not as fast. The pilot drops the nose of the chopper and the craft is tipped to such a severe degree that its rotors are digging into the paddy ahead as it rushes forward, throwing up a tremendous fan of water, which begins to glisten like a rainbow.

Stan looks up and sees that the chopper's blades are headed right toward them and he thinks the rainbow fan is the most beautiful thing he's ever seen. He says, "Hey, fellas, check this out. You want to see this before we get killed." He thinks the blades are going to slice them up like bologna. It's the most impressive, glorious sight he's ever seen. Just before the chopper gets to them, the pilot pulls up over Russo, and a long nylon strap is dropped out of the cabin door. They lasso Russo's ankles and cinch it tight and do that thing with their hands, "All clear," and step back. The chopper's engine begins to whine and the strap tightens around Russo's ankles. Stan can look up and see the chopper rising and Russo's legs seem to stretch and, finally, Russo pops free.

He comes flying up out of the mud, straight up, headed right for the bottom of the helicopter, and he nearly hits it, all of that pent-up tension on the strap being released as the chopper itself suddenly rises with Russo dangling at the end of the strap, spitting mud, swinging back and forth.

He's waving his arms, sputtering things Stan and the others can't understand. The chopper drops down so that Russo's hanging about eight feet above the water and an arm comes out of the cabin with a knife and cuts the nylon strap. Russo is set free, and he flops outward in a spread-eagle position, faceup. He's staring at the belly of the helicopter and falling away from it, when he lands on his back in the paddy, *whack*, and sinks from view. Stan and the crew run over and lift him up and start dragging him from the water as the bullets whiz past. Stan thinks it's still amazing that no one's been hit. They get to a safe place and slap Russo on the back. Soon he's coughed up all of the mud and water, and they start laughing. It is sure good to see him, and then they're returning fire, fighting again.

One day in Recon Platoon, a member of the platoon shoots himself in the foot with his M-16 to get out of the war. Puts the muzzle against his boot and pulls the trigger. The bullet enters, and when it comes out the other side, it takes the soldier with him, clean out of Vietnam and back home to Kansas. Good-bye, friend.

That's one way to get out of this mess.

The other way is to fight, live, and get home.

Two days after Stan returns to the platoon, they fight their way into a village and start to burn down a thatched hooch.

It's raining like hell; it'll be hard to burn anything. But nonetheless somebody says something like, "Burn it all down." But they can't get any of the hooches lit. The thatch is wet and doesn't ignite. Stan's thinking he's not comfortable with this anyway, so he and some of the crew are relieved. Then one of the men finds a stack of wide, deep baskets, and somebody lights these on fire, and then more baskets are discovered. A lot of them turn out to be stored with rice. In all, they guess they'd discovered about fifteen hundred pounds of food, enough, they believe, to feed a group of guerrilla fighters. Pretty soon somebody says, "Let's burn the rice too," and they start lighting the baskets and the rice and then throwing handfuls of rice in the growing fire. Stan protests, along with some other guys, saying, "This is somebody's food," and someone else says, "It's probably VC or NVA food," and Stan reasons, "Well, we don't know that; we can't know that." The platoon has been turning discovered food and supplies into headquarters, radioing whenever they find something. Stan had no idea what anyone did with the rice after that. But this burning just seems wrong. It seems random, like they're playing God. He's pondering this when the rice starts popping in the fire.

Pop! Pop!

At first, a few of the guys jump, thinking this is gunfire, and then they start hollering and dancing around the fire. While this is going on, an old man comes out of the smoldering hooch and looks at all of them, trembling.

Stan can see that the old man is terrified they're going to shoot him. After all, they're burning his rice. And he starts pointing at the ground and Stan realizes he's pointing at the rice. The old man lowers himself to his hands and knees and starts picking up grains of rice and putting them into a pouch he's made of his shirt by pulling it out from his body and holding it open. He goes from rice grain to rice grain, one at a time, tweezering the individual grains between his blunt thumb and finger and wiping them against his shirt front, holding them up and looking at them, and dropping them into his makeshift pouch. He's talking to himself and crying.

All Stan can think of is his mother, and how, if she saw him, John Stanley Parker, right now, she'd probably tan his hide, give him a whipping, and he'd be glad for it. He thinks back to his own family, back to the day of his grandfather during the Civil War, how Sherman came through and killed his family's sheep and burned the land, and Stan wonders, *Who am I? Am I like that? No, I am not like that.*

He gets down on his hands and knees and starts crawling alongside the old man and he starts picking up grains of rice too.

Somebody says, "What are you doing, man, come on!" and they throw more rice on the fire, and Stan yells, "Knock it off!" and a few of the guys say, "Why are you helping the gooks?" All Stan can say is, "You know what . . . ? You know what . . . ?" He's at a loss. And finally he says, "Enough is enough." He can't take the killing anymore. But he'll keep killing, if needed; he knows that. He thinks how bored he's grown amid so much adrenaline, so bored that a few days earlier he watched a few of the other guys throwing a knife at a dead guy they found on a trail. Stan told them to stop throwing the knife. They grunt and complain and kick over the rest of the rice baskets and walk away. The old man is so grateful to him that he calls out his entire family, who materialize from the woods, and Stan shakes their hands one by one. He can tell they're so happy that he didn't kill the old man, and he can tell that the old man is so happy too. He reaches up and gives Stan a big hug. Stan has tears in his eyes when he turns and walks away. These are *people*, he thinks.

This is one of the worst things you can do, he thinks, burning an old man's food.

On March 2, the platoon relocates southeast some twenty miles from LZ Jane to a larger base at LZ Sally, about eight miles northwest of Hue. Days earlier, U.S. Marines had recaptured Hue from NVA and Viet Cong soldiers. From LZ Sally, the platoon will shuttle by chopper across wider swaths of territory, engaging enemy fighters in the area. The platoon will perform at least fourteen combat assaults, their sense of time and place bending even more, the hours broken into abrupt departures, violent arrivals, ambushes during which your heart beats so fast it seems the enemy might sense its rhythm on the night air.

On March 9, Stan, Wongus, Kinney, Dove, and Kleckler set up an ambush on an itty-bitty rise overlooking a trail, back in the trees, hidden in the green shade of the falling daylight. They arrange trip flares and Claymores while Al Dove sets up the M-60 on the rise. They settle back and wait for the kill.

"You know what?" says Stan to Wongus.

"No, what?"

"I'm dog-ass tired. Let's convince these ARVN rangers to watch guard duty all night," meaning soldiers from the Army of the Republic of Vietnam.

The rangers are solid soldiers, but Stan and Wongus aren't

going to completely trust their lives to them. Yet they have to sleep. They are so worn out they can't stay awake.

Wongus is not sure. He says, "If you think you can pull it off," meaning if he thinks he can get them to agree.

"Well, let me try."

Stan walks up to the two ARVNs, looks at his watch, points, and says, "You guard now to 3:00 a.m."

And right away the ARVN soldier says, "Oh, not me," which Stan ignores, and says to the other one, "And you take the guard duty from 3:00 a.m. to 6:00 a.m."

"No can do," says the soldier. "No can do."

"Yeah, yeah," says Stan. "We're going to rest. We're tired. You know, this is your country. You got to take some of the—"

"Oh, no no!" the soldiers protest. They stop talking. They hear a sound on the trail.

Movement.

"Son of a bitch," Stan says. He knows they won't be sleeping now. They won't be living and breathing maybe in five more minutes. Hard to tell.

And then he has second thoughts, wishful thinking brought on by the fact that more than anything else on earth, he needs sleep. So he wonders if the sound is made by a water buffalo, the poor beast being forced to trundle down this dark midnight trail by the NVA, to clear it of the trip flares he and the others just placed there.

"Here comes the buffalo," Stan says. "Get ready"—and to himself, thinking, *Don't worry; it's just buffalo. There ain't no firefight here.*

The ARVN are really protesting. They seem to know something Stan doesn't, which is what a buffalo sounds like coming down a trail, as opposed to what a human sounds like.

"VC!" they're saying.

"VC, come on, really?"

185

Stan starts to reason that there's no way that a VC soldier, or soldiers, would be making this much noise, *crunch, shuffle, crunk, snap,* coming through the vegetation. Stan thinks it's just the ARVN soldiers' way of getting out of guard duty by implying that there's something really dangerous happening right now.

One of the trip flares pops.

It's not but fifteen feet away, and standing in the glare is an NVA soldier caught looking suddenly up and to the right, directly at Stan and the group. He's got his AK strapped over his shoulder, not at the ready at all.

In the light, Stan and Al and Wongus, and the rest, including the ARVNs, squint and make out another soldier, standing behind this first one, and then another one standing behind him. Another beyond that. Stan thinks, *Holy cow, there must be fifty of these guys.* He realizes they're outnumbered, and that's something you don't want to be in an ambush. If you can't have surprise when you're outnumbered, you don't want to pull the trigger; let 'em pass. Fight another day.

Stan and the rest are lit up too by the trip flare, an illuminated target, and the shooting starts from behind him. It's the two ARVN soldiers, they're the first to react; they apparently do care that this is their country. They drop the solo NVA soldier where he stands, and he falls away, out of the light of the flare.

In the excitement, somebody yells, "The Claymores, blow the Claymores," but Stan's about a hundred feet from the Claymore clacker handles. Wongus yells, "Dammit, Parker. Get the Claymores," and Stan says, "Wongus, you know where they're at too!"

"Yeah, but you set them out!"

Wongus and Stan see tracers streaking in from their rear, passing through the large group of NVA soldiers in front of them. It's Dove, dear Dove, shooting his M-60 machine gun. Stan thinks it's now or never. He dives into brush alongside the trail and starts crawling. He crawls to the place where he thinks he left the clacker handles. He jumps up, and standing on the trail are two more NVA soldiers, and they too look at him surprised. In war, why is the look just before death one of surprise when it should be expected? Stan raises and fires. He shoots them dead.

Stan ducks back into the brush, thinking, *I guess I got out a little early*. He moves up the trail and jumps out again, this time surprising two more NVA soldiers. He shoots and kills these guys. He can hear movement and NVA voices in every direction. He's scared. He walks into an NVA soldier, and before the guy shoots, Stan stabs him in the chest with his bayonet. Another dozen soldiers appear and Stan shoots four or five of them. The rest are startled and Stan keeps shooting. The remaining few scatter into the darkness.

As he keeps moving toward the clacker handles, more NVA swarm in. He fires his M-16 and keeps moving. After ten to fifteen seconds, he crawls up to the clacker handles, grabs them, and jumps into a hole to get out of the way of the coming blast. He squeezes the handles and the mines go off, sending ball bearings everywhere. Two men jump into the hole with him.

Stan can't really make out who these people are. "Who are you?" he asks, squinting, realizing they're two NVA soldiers. They must've jumped into the hole to avoid the blast. There's a parachute flare dropping down in the sky over them, illuminating their faces. Stan shoots one of them, and the other scrambles up over the lip of the trench, rolls out, and runs away in a crouch. Stan bears down with his M-16, trying to get a bead, and he's about to fire when he senses that the shape has reversed direction and is headed back toward him. What now?

He's ready to shoot when a body, the object that had seemed to reverse direction, flies into the hole.

It's Wongus. Stan breathes a sigh of relief. He'd almost shot

Wongus, but he doesn't tell him this. *Oh my god*, he thinks, *I was this close.* Wongus says, "Who the hell just ran by me?"

Stan puts it together and tells him "That was an NVA soldier."

"What's he doing over here?"

Stan nods at the dead soldier slumped in the hole and says, "That's his buddy."

And that's when Russo crawls up to the hole and slips in. Stan says, "Jesus, Russo, don't scare us like that!" Russo's got the radio on his back. The radio's heavy, about the size of a small aquarium, and called a Prick 25 radio, nicknamed for its real name, which is PRC-25. Russo holds up the handset and starts talking into it, real quiet, "Battalion, come in."

He's talking quietly because he and Stan and Wongus realize that it's gotten very quiet on the trail. Not a sound is coming from the dark around them, except for the moaning of the dying who've been shot in this ambush over the past few minutes. It's a terrible sound.

Stan thinks something's going to go down; he just doesn't know what yet. Russo's on the radio with Sergeant Kinney, who's a hundred feet up the trail, and Russo hands Stan the radio and says, "For you."

Kinney says, "Parker, battalion wants to know who you ambushed. They want some evidence. Who are they?"

And Stan says, "NVA. Who do you think it is?"

"Do you know who they are?"

Stan can't believe that Kinney's asking him such a dumb question. He must be getting pressure by Higher to get intel on enemy troop movement.

"Oh, hang on," he tells Kinney. "I'm going to ask them." He says very quietly to the dark, "Hey, who are you guys?"

Back into the radio, he says, "Come on, man."

"They want to see if you got anything," meaning Higher wants to know if there's any intel on these dead soldiers.

He adds, "Go out and look at a couple of them."

Wongus and Stan worry, of course, that some of these guys might still be alive. They won't know until they're out there, when it's too late.

Off in the distance, maybe a quarter mile away, Stan can hear gunfire every once in a while—the fighting's still going on some-where close—but around him, all the NVA are dead. He con-vinces himself of this.

More parachute flares go off overhead, drifting to earth, swing-ing their weird silver light over everything. Kinney says, "And we got some incoming too," meaning incoming artillery, or, in the vernacular, "arty."

Stan tells Russo to holler out if he gets word on the radio that arty's coming in. "We don't want to get out there and get hit."

He and Wongus set out crawling through the bush. Wongus has his .45 out, leading it ahead of them as they crawl. They're both nervous. It's dark ahead on the path, especially this close to the ground.

He stops. "Parker, what weapon you got?"

"I got my M-16."

"That's too big. It'll make too much noise."

"How's this?" Stan pulls out his Ka-Bar knife, and Wongus nods. He sets the M-16 aside and keeps the knife at the ready in his hand. They start crawling again.

They haven't gone far when they come to the first pile of shapes on the ground. And in a blast of sudden light—para-chute flares again, burning above them and dropping—every-thing around them is revealed. It's like somebody has suddenly turned on a light in a room filled with dead people. Wongus freezes. They're surrounded by bodies. Wongus sees that he's nearly crawled onto a dead guy, his face just inches away from the dead man's.

Wongus whispers, looking around, "So how do we know these guys are really dead?"

"We don't," says Stan, ignoring Wongus's fear. It seems to Stan that every one of these soldiers around them is dead.

They stand up a bit but keep stooped in a crouch.

"Here," Stan says, "grab this fella's ankle."

And he and Wongus grab a soldier by the ankles and pull, and he's so light they nearly fall over. They regain their balance and start pulling in tandem, walking backward as they do. Russo, fifty feet behind them, starts hollering that the artillery is on its way.

The shells drop close, not real close, but enough to make the ground rumble around them. He and Wongus start running to get out of the open.

They run so fast that they run right past Russo and keep going up the trail. They're disoriented. They stop and Wongus looks around, and says, "Russo, where are you?"

"Hey, you guys, I'm back here!"

Stan and Wongus walk back down the trail, dragging the dead soldier by the ankle. When they show up, Russo says, "You guys ran right past me." The soldier is small, and Stan and Wongus are standing there still holding him by the legs. Stan feels stupid. What are they supposed to do with the guy? He's wearing a small leather case on a strap over his shoulder, and they open it; there's nothing inside. None of the intelligence that Kinney earlier told them that command wanted.

What they've got here is a dead guy they don't know and will never know; he's nothing to them now. Minutes ago, he meant everything.

At daybreak, though, the numbers are staggering. They've killed forty-eight enemy soldiers. That's a lot. The dead are lying in piles where they were standing when the trip flares went off and exposed their presence and the machine-gun fire poured on top of them.

As they collect the corpses into one place and count them, they start arranging them in various poses, carrying and dragging the bodies around the clearing, propping them up under the trees with cigarettes in their mouths, some with their legs crossed and looking off in the distance. Others look like they've fallen asleep on the leafy ground. Some of the soldiers don't even look dead except for a few small bloody holes, which Stan has to look for. The platoon has spent so much time and energy and pure focus trying to kill the enemy, and now it seems important to reanimate them, bring them back to life. They are experiencing a collective breakdown, an inside-out-turning of their world.

In an hour, as they leave this place of carnage, Stan—all of them—will look back over their shoulders as they step among the blood and bone and realize how strange, how *otherworldly* their actions have been. They've snapped.

News of this large ambush is all over the radio net; it's being viewed as quite a show. A chopper lands in the clearing, and aboard is a major who's come for a look-see at the body count before the colonel tours this battlefield.

The major rolls out of the Huey in his clean uniform and strides across the makeshift LZ. The men, filthy, sweating, look up from their handiwork of arranging the dead. The major whips around the clearing, seeing the dead enemy soldiers propped up in the grass, against the trees, out in the open, many of them with their rifles, their AKs, pointing off in random directions. But some of them are pointing at the major. And some of them look *alive.* He thinks he's just walked into an ambush, that Stan and the guys have been used as bait. He turns to head back to the chopper.

"They're dead," someone calls after him.

"Dead?"

"Yes, sir."

"What are they doing"—he points around the clearing—"like *that*?"

He's truly confused. And it dawns on him. "You can't do that!"

"Why?"

"That's, that's—what do they call it? Defamation of . . . no . . ."

"Desecration of a corpse," somebody pipes up.

"That's right, desecration."

Desecration? thinks Stan.

"You guys could be in trouble over this."

"No one ever told us this," says Stan. He hadn't thought of this action as being anything but . . . something to do. These guys were dead, weren't they? What are the rules when the rule is to kill every man you see who is trying to kill you?

"You've got to fix these guys," the major says.

"What do you mean, 'Fix them'?"

"There's going to be some other guys coming here, and if they see this?"

So Wongus, Stan, and others start running around the clearing trying to make all of the corpses look dead again. It's not as easy as it might seem. They grab this one soldier, and he's tightened up in rigor mortis, hardened into a sitting position with his AK-47 gripped in his hands. Stan tries to pry the rifle away, but he won't be quit of it. Then he lays him on his back and tries to push him straight down to the ground, to, in essence, flatten him out, and that won't work either. He stays on his back, frozen in a horizontal C shape.

"You know what?" Stan announces. "This ain't going to work. We got to get rid of these guys."

So they start dragging them off the trail, hiding them in bushes. The dead stare intently at plants and weeds just inches from their faces; some still don't look dead at all but appear to be asleep. And that's when the colonel's helicopter lands. They're only about half done with the job of hiding the dead.

Stan's ashamed. He now feels that what they've done is not right, but he's taken part in it, and there you have it. The colonel walks up to him, and Stan has a boot touching the chest of one of the dead men to hold him flat as the colonel talks.

The colonel tells him what a fine job they've done, killing so many of these bastards so thoroughly, and every time Stan lifts his boot, the dead guy starts to sit up, and Stan has to step back down and apply pressure as the colonel rattles on. The colonel doesn't notice. After about fifteen minutes of chitchat, the colonel reboards the chopper and lifts off. The clearing falls quiet, and the men gather their things and start walking, just to get the hell out of there. Stan vows never to do anything like that to the dead again.

They move on. It's a Thursday, March 14, and Stan and Al Dove are lying on the sunny banks of the Song Bo River, their pale feet trailing in the soft current flowing beneath them. Stan spies something across the river and sits up.

"Dove," he whispers.

"What?"

"I said, *quiet*. Look. Over there."

He nods his head upriver, trying to indicate with the degree of his head's tilt how far upstream Al should be looking.

Al sits up slow and sees it too.

NVA soldiers are sitting on the riverbank opposite them, upstream by about fifty yards. Not too far. Strange that they haven't spotted the Americans, but you never know in these things. It may be that the NVA don't expect to see any Americans sunning themselves along this riverbank, just as Stan and Al didn't expect to see them upstream either.

Stan and Al are looking at two NVA soldiers, whose weapons are on their laps and are also dangling their feet in the water.

Stan says, "Okay, now, Al, on three, I'm going to take the guy on the right, farthest upstream."

"I got the one on the left."

"Okay, let's go."

And Stan starts counting slowly and quietly, and on three, he and Al open fire. They shoot in two small bursts, and Stan watches one of the guys in his group fall over, the one he was shooting at, but the other one is unscathed, not shot at all, and Stan has a hard time believing that Al Dove has made such a bad shot.

At the same time, Al's complaining, "What happened, Parker! I thought you were going to shoot!"

"I did shoot."

"But what happened?"

"I don't know. What happened to you?" Stan's watching the one dead guy he shot lie there in the sun. A moment ago he was alive, of course, now he's very, very quiet.

"Parker, I got only one of the guys."

"Me, too."

And Al points at the guy he shot, closer to them, along another part of the bank, and both Al and Stan realize that they'd been shooting at different groups of NVA soldiers, and each one of them had killed just one of them. All of the still-living soldiers start to run away; they go up and over the bank and disappear. Stan and Al realize that they're probably in trouble because where there are two NVA groups, there is probably another larger group. The two of them think about what to do next.

The rest of the Recon Platoon is spread out about a quarter mile away. They are waiting for nightfall and the setup of another ambush. They've got about an hour left before it gets dark. They'll eat in the light of the day, and then in the cover of darkness, they'll move down the trail, or up the trail, and set up an ambush. But those guys are of no help now; they're too far away to assist Al and Stan. They are on their own.

Upstream, nearly a hundred and twenty-five yards away, hangs a cable bridge, close to seventy-five feet in length. It's made of two strands of cable strung across the river, each strand at waist height, and from it hang more wires and an uneven deck of crude wood planking; some of the boards are not even nailed down. Stan sees that about twenty armed NVA soldiers are running toward the bridge, headed at Al and Stan to attack them.

Stan gets up and starts running.

"What are you doing!" Al yells after him.

"We've got to stop these guys," says Stan. He's running and firing across the river at the NVA soldiers who are keeping pace with him. Stan's trying to get to the bridgehead before they do because it will form a natural choke point and he can stand there and lay down suppressive fire and prevent them from crossing over and killing them both. Just as he reaches the end of the bridge on his side of the river, he looks down and sees a hole up ahead.

It's only about two feet deep, and if you knew it was there, you could easily avoid it. Stan sees the hole has sharp spikes sticking straight up. Punji sticks, about eight of them standing up in the air, the bamboo wood dried and hard and hacked to a very sharp point by machetes back in some village sympathetic to or run by the Viet Cong.

At the last minute, just before Stan realizes he's going to step into the punji pit and impale one of his feet right through the heavy sole of his combat boot, he dives forward and lays himself out in an effort to halt. He's got both hands gripped on his M-16 before him like a stick, one hand on the barrel and one hand on the stock, and he drops it down over the punji hole so that the length of the rifle will stop his descent.

It only half works.

His right hand stays up with his weapon out of the hole, but his left hand keeps going down. His wrist first rests atop a bamboo point for the briefest of moments — which not even the quickest camera could catch — then the wrist keeps going. Stan keeps falling, following his left hand down into the two-foot-deep hole, and the bamboo spear enters his wrist and travels through skin and muscle tissue and tendon. The point reaches the other side of Stan's wrist and presses against his skin, from the inside, and then pokes through and appears, covered in the thinnest veil of blood.

Stan stops.

Sucks in a breath.

He's lying with his head in the hole, smelling the damp dirt, and behind him, across the river, he can hear the NVA soldiers headed his way. He's trapped, pinned. Speared. Literally pinned to the bottom of the hole like an insect.

He looks at his wrist. The spike is attached to the ground at the bottom of the hole; it's probably buried three or four feet deep to make it especially secure. Stan studies the spikes around the one that's going through his wrist and sees they are smeared with excrement, likely human; a homemade bioweapon. Stan's got about twenty seconds before the NVA soldiers head his way. With him stuck in the hole, they'll shoot him dead for sure. He thinks that Al Dove will try to save him, and poor Al, outnumbered, will get killed too.

With his right hand, Stan maneuvers the M-16 around in the hole. It's hard because he's gripping the barrel with his right hand and he's afraid that if he lets go, he'll come tumbling down even farther onto more sharp spikes. His left hand is useless. He scooches his right hand back along the barrel until it's on the receiver and then on the trigger guard, and he inserts his finger onto the trigger. Pressing forward and readjusting his body, he carefully places the muzzle against the base of the sharp spike that's sticking through his left wrist and presses on the trigger. The weapon fires and shoots the sharp spike in half. He's suddenly free and deafened by the blast of the weapon. He pops up wild-eyed, the piece of spike still in his wrist, and looks around.

He scans the bridge and sees the NVA soldiers running across it. He's still got the M-16 in his right hand and starts to fire. He's got his left hand held out from his body with the six-inch length of stick poking through the wrist; it's awkward and hurts, and he's surprised it isn't bleeding more.

The NVA soldiers start returning fire. He kills three of them and they fall onto the bridge. One tumbles off the few feet into the swift river. And then Al Dove arrives and starts shooting too. Trapped at the bridge entrance, the NVA soldiers retreat. Al and Stan slump down against a tree, breathing heavily, sweating, amazed they've gotten out of this jam. The afternoon is quiet, the river peaceful. They watch it slide past as a familiar soft whir rises downstream and a helicopter comes into view to pick them up.

The next day, March 15, Stan is back in the same hospital he entered earlier when he'd been blown up by the grenade. The nurse he'd fallen in love with at the time walks into his room, where he's hooked up to IV lines feeding him antibiotics and fluids, and when she recognizes him, she does a double take and, Stan thinks, she's about to walk back out of the room. He's glad she gathers herself and tells him, gently, "I told you to take care of yourself." She means it. His injury seems to upset her, though he imagines she doesn't remember his name, except by looking at his medical chart. When she leaves after checking his bandage, the examining doctor tells Stan he's impressed he had the presence of mind to shoot his way free. The six-inch-long stick, where it enters and exits his wrist, bears a collar of blood around the wood itself, but beyond this, the wound does not communicate the violent moment that created it. Surprisingly, Stan can still wiggle his fingers. The pain, though, is unrelenting.

On one end of the stick, where he'd placed the barrel of the M-16 and fired, the wood is frazzled, cracked. The doctor tells him he will have to pull the stick backward, with the point end leaving his body last. He injects Stan's wrist with painkiller, and Stan watches as the doc grips the stick between thumb and forefinger and begins to pull, with the same speed and attention you lift a garden stake from firm ground. It slides out silently. Stan spends two weeks in the hospital pumped with antibiotics, flexing his hand, as the dime-sized hole heals, dimming later in life to a scar he'll carry hidden under his watch's wristband. In heavy rain or when summer turns to autumn, the wrist will ache and he will think again of the nurse, the punji stick, the girl who died because he gave her peaches.

When he's able to write, he sits in the hospital bed and composes a letter.

"Dear Mo," he begins, and he tries describing what he's seen, but the more he writes, the more he's certain he can never send this to Mo. He writes,

I am torn between letting you know what it is really like over here, and not saying anything at all.

I have been thinking more and more about you a lot here lately, even to the point of thinking about you when I should have my mind fixed on searching for the enemy.

I have desired to write to you this letter but realize at the same time that you are too beautiful, soft and too delicate to be tarnished with my fearful stories.

But I feel that if I do not inform you or someone of the misery around me, dealing with death on a daily and nightly basis, I may not live long enough to get the chance to write to you again to express just what it is like over here. . . .

I have been WIA twice already and Recon is suffering tremendous casualties and so the way things are going over here, with the constant endless fighting, I have more days of expecting to be killed than living to see another day.

I really want to live and get out of this awful dreadful place alive and in one piece and go home. . . . But one minute I hate this place, but the next minute I like it here. . . .

I know that Vietnam has changed me and I am not the same guy you knew before, but I know that down deep underneath all this ugliness, I believe that I am still normal and a good kind person at heart. And to help me keep my sanity, I need to write and say something.

He's certain he can't send her this letter. He starts over:

My Dearest Mo, You ask me in one of your letters what it was like over here. I mentioned a few things in one letter past but was reluctant to write and be too graphic and possibly upset you and have you stop writing me. I have a confession for you. I have not been completely truthful with you in prior letters with the total numbers of enemy (NVA/VC) being killed on behalf of myself and my buddies in Recon.

I purposely keep the numbers low because I figured that if I told you the truth in the numbers of enemy dead, you might think less of me for being somewhat proud of our job of killing bad guys. I want you to be proud of me and not ashamed or frightened of me. That is what we are called upon to do over here and I hope that you have not thought the less of me for doing so.

He continues:

Our living conditions are the worst I have ever experienced, seen, or heard of. They are absolutely primitive, archaic, deplorable, and totally unbelievable. I hope that you can comprehend what I am writing and really appreciate what I and the others here are being subjected to as we are exposed to such unimaginable conditions. We are living and acting like animals and each day life gets worse.

The insanity of this place is easy to absorb. The inhuman, dreadfully appalling misery here makes insane behavior seem sane and feel normal. As a paratrooper, I, as well as those around me, are trained to kill and have adapted to that characteristic habit very demonstratively. I hope that I get out of here alive and when I get back home that I will be able to conduct myself in a sensible, rational, respectable manner and act normal again especially if I am able to see you again. And be accepted as the person I was a lifetime ago when I left home, and not the person I have become in order to survive here. . . .

Because I and the others have attained the quick subliminal reaction to kill so easily, no doubt, a civilized person back home would view our reaction as a neurotic, habitual, irrational, illogical psychological disorder. . . .

But ironically, for some unexplainable reason, as bad as I hate it here, at the same time I like it here and I and some of us are talking about extending our combat tour or volunteering to come back once we get home. We feel like this is where we belong, even though we hate it here. . . .

I just want to get out of here alive and see you, if that is possible. And that when I finally get home, I can be accepted as a normal young man who consequently was required to grow from the adolescent boy I was when I got here, almost overnight, into the hard core young man of resolute convictions I had to become.

Just like the law of the Old West, there are only two types of people here in the Nam, "the quick and the dead."

In the end, he decides he can't send this letter to Mo either. He scribbles out her name and writes across the top, "Dear Brothers . . ." and gets to the meat of his feelings:

It's hard to find a beginning for this story in the fact that I can remember it in every detail at any given moment. We are lucky to live from one day to the next.

He writes in detail about the dead girl with the peaches, the rats, his screaming. He sends the letter to his younger brother Bruce, back in Gary, Indiana, who's enjoying his junior year of high school.

On the day that Bruce comes home and opens the letter, he reads it and is filled with fear. That night, and for nights thereafter, he has trouble sleeping. He starts worrying about his two brothers fighting in a war he doesn't know much about but which he sees nightly on the news. Whenever a news report comes on about the combat, Stan's father stops wherever he is in the house, cocking his head to listen for one word, any word, about Stan and Dub. Thankfully, so far, that word has not come.

Bruce is confused by how Stan has closed his letter.

"Hug a girl for me," Stan instructs Bruce, and he tells him to, of course, ask the girl's permission, and to remember every sensation of this hug, and to write it all down and send a description of these sensations in a letter back to him.

He wants it all. "The smell of her hair," he explains to Bruce. "Her softness. Even the color of her clothes."

Stan is so far gone from the world back home he can no longer remember it. After two weeks, he's shipped from the hospital back to the field. He can't wait to be among the platoon again.

Specialist Charlie Pyle, from Colleyville, Texas, is killed on March 22 while Stan is in the hospital. He's blond, handsome, and beloved by his platoon. His death, like the wounding of John Payne, who in January was accidentally shot by one of his own platoon-mates, is a blow to them all. Ever after, in the platoon, they will mark time by saying things like, "This happened after Charlie Pyle was killed."

On the day that Pyle dies, the platoon gets a call from Higher that a blocking force is needed to protect Charlie and Delta Companies, which are slugging it out with a large NVA force. It's midday; they'll be exposed on open ground as they advance toward Charlie and Delta. Al Dove doesn't like the situation at all. It feels to all of them that they're about to walk into an ambush.

They're accompanied by what are called PFs, or Popular Forces—militia-type Vietnam soldiers. Nearly every village they pass through, the PFs emerge with more stuff—booty, pots and pans and chickens, items they've lifted from the villagers as they make their way.

In order to move quickly, Al and the platoon are forced at times to walk along the dikes that line the rice paddies they pass, but that lifts their silhouettes above the horizon and makes them easy targets. When this seems too dangerous, as it does almost immediately, they wade directly through the paddy, in places sinking deep in muck. Progress is slow.

"What's up there in the tree line?" someone in the platoon asks. "Did anyone just see something?"

Charlie Pyle, walking on point, has gotten ahead of the main force of the platoon, with Tim Anderson struggling to keep up. Behind Anderson, Michael Bradshaw is also slogging ahead, feeling increasingly that they should've chosen a route that would've taken them closer along a nearby tree line. He and Charlie are close friends; they met eighteen months earlier in jump training. He wants to keep up with Charlie in case any shooting starts so they can defend each other. Tim Anderson doesn't like the terrain either, and he wishes that Pyle would stay close in formation. But that's Pyle, he thinks. Always gung-ho.

The heavy rice plants are nearly waist high and whisper as the men pass through them. Bradshaw looks up from his position and sees two NVA soldiers jump up and run along the tree line. They're running, he guesses, to get in position to fire off a better shot as the squad walks ahead. One of the Recon guys gets spooked and starts shooting ahead of the rest of the platoon as it moves forward, and he hits two of his own platoon-mates in the back; they have to be medevaced out. Their advance into the hamlet is turning into a problem pretty quickly, and the shooter is sent to the rear of the line.

The main part of the platoon has just about entered a hamlet when the firing starts. The NVA open up, and Charlie Pyle goes down. He disappears in the rice. In the chaotic firefight, ten other members of the platoon are wounded: Marvin Acker, Ronald Bard, Tony Beke, Warren Jewell, Dennis Kilbury, Richard Lapa, Brian Lewis, Guido Russo, Francis Wongus, and Luis Zendejas.

Dwight Lane, Mike Bradshaw, and Tim Anderson conclude at the same time that Charlie's been hit. The experience is so personal that both Dwight Lane and Tim Anderson will wonder, years later, if they weren't alone, all by themselves, when they found Pyle. Bradshaw is crushed when he sees Charlie fall. He starts crawling through the rice, looking for his friend.

Dwight Lane is about twenty feet away when Charlie drops, and he crawls up first, just in time to watch him die. Charlie's blue eyes are still open. Dwight can't stand this and he reaches over and tries closing them with his fingertips. He can't make them close. He thinks of all the movies he saw as a kid, when the gunfighter reached over and did this for his newly dead buddy. Dwight thinks, *This don't work like it does in the movies*. He won't remember later how long he sat there with Charlie, hours or minutes. Time had stopped. When he removes his hand and looks at Charlie's face again, he begins to cry, and in doing so, he dooms himself to a life of remembering. He hears somebody yelling—it's Warren Jewell, and he's yelling that he's hit and needs help. Dwight starts crawling on his belly toward his screaming friend.

After he leaves, Tim Anderson crawls up and finds Charlie alone, and he figures that he's the first to discover him. Tim had been sitting with Tom Soals and Sergeant Westerman, in the rear, about 150 yards away, when he heard the shooting and realized that Charlie, walking point, might be under fire. He told Sergeant Westerman that he was going to see what had happened. Tom Soals, Westerman's radio operator, said he wanted to leave too. Westerman ordered them both to stay put, but Tim took off in a fast crouch.

When Tim finds Charlie, he sees that he's dead and that his eyes are spookily open, and he decides he'd better close them, but they won't stay shut. To prevent Charlie from being hit by more enemy fire, he decides to drag him over the two-foot-high dike that separates them. He radios Westerman for help, but Westerman says that he and Soals are pinned down by fire. Every few minutes, Soals holds his radio in front of him as protection from the bullets, knowing, at the same time, that it's futile.

Anderson reaches over the dike and grabs Charlie's arms and pulls them out straight and eases the tall, thin body over the dike and it slumps back to the ground, next to him. He drags Charlie another thirty or forty feet to a place where he hopes the enemy won't see him if they come looking.

After he leaves, Dwight Lane returns, having bandaged up Jewell. He's confused why Charlie is gone, but he doesn't have much time to consider this. They're taking heavy fire from the tree line. He picks up Charlie's radio and calls Tom Soals to call in an artillery strike. Soals relays this to Westerman. Dwight can see a cement building nestled in some trees and he guesses that's where the enemy is sitting.

Westerman comes back on the radio. "That's awfully close to you, isn't it?"

"Yes, but that's where they're at."

Westerman tells him to duck.

The artillery strike arrives like a thunderclap. The ground explodes about fifty yards ahead of Dwight, and shrapnel buzzes past his head. Something slams his helmet. The impact knocks him over and he lays on the ground, blinking, collecting himself. He sits up and finds a four-inch-long, one-inch-wide piece of smoking metal—shrapnel. He figures that if it had hit his helmet point-end, he'd be dead. As it is, he feels like he's been bludgeoned with a rock. He picks up Charlie's grenade launcher and sets the butt-end on the ground and starts dumping one grenade after another at the tree line. He thinks, *I'm not gonna make it through this night, but I'm gonna try.* When it's dark, he will crawl ahead and find Tim Anderson and Michael Bradshaw sitting with Charlie's body. They will drag him a bit farther into the shadows, out of possible enemy fire, and then in the stillness of the night, creep back to Westerman's position.

Like Anderson, Bradshaw, and Lane, Al Dove starts looking for Charlie as soon as he realizes he's been shot. As he crawls ahead, though, Al hears someone else calling out in the tall rice plants that he's fallen in, and he decides to detour to see if he can offer help. Al can't see him and doesn't know who he is, but he follows the sound of his voice, saying "Keep on talking!" in an effort to keep the man engaged and alert. He's got his .45 pistol out and ten grenades in a pouch at the ready.

"Where are you at?" he yells.

"I'm over here, over here!"

And finally Al finds the man lying in a bloody, smooshed-down place in the rice plants. It's a guy named Lapa whom Al knows, but not well.

He is hurt bad in the leg. In fact, Al can see Lapa's femur shining through the hole in his thigh—gunshot, through and through. Lapa's not bleeding a lot, but he can't walk and Al's got to move him. Somebody, positioned not far away, is throwing grenades, and they're exploding close by. Al can't figure out if it's friendly fire or not—maybe the rice plants are crawling with other soldiers, enemy and friendly.

Al takes off his long web belt, wraps it around Lapa's chest, and then fastens the belt in a makeshift harness, which he places around his neck. With the belt straining against his windpipe, he starts crawling and dragging Lapa behind him. He's more tired than he's ever remembered being in his life, but this has been his perpetual state for weeks. He's pretty sure he can't keep crawling, but he does.

An explosion goes off very close, and Al feels something

burning the back of his neck. He can hear a sizzle sound. At first he thinks one of his own grenades has gone off, but no; he'd be mangled and dead if that had happened. He panics and says to Lapa, "I can't take you. I got to get ahead and see what's up there." He feels they're vulnerable stuck together like this, literally belted together. He takes the belt from around his neck, moves up through the rice paddy, and pulls out one of his grenades, and his neck starts burning again. He reaches back and pulls out a piece of shrapnel and pitches it aside, and sits and waits, but there's no enemy out there waiting to kill them. He makes his way back to Lapa, rehitches himself, and continues dragging him. Lapa cries out in pain but is mostly silent, and Al tries to maneuver in such a way that he's not dragging Lapa's left leg through the dirt, where the gaping hole is in his thigh, until they reach the safety of the tree line.

The next morning, Jerry Austin and Tom Soals move forward and find Charlie and prepare him to be taken out by chopper. Jerry bends down and hoists Charlie across his shoulders and they move quickly back through the rice plants. Jerry lays him carefully on the ground and Soals moves the body onto a poncho and checks for wounds. Tom can't see any blood on his uniform. He feels along Charlie's shoulders and ribs and spies a small hole under his right arm. Tom guesses that the bullet had entered there and continued through Pyle's heart, which must've stopped instantly, and which would explain the lack of bleeding. Pyle, they surmise, had likely died instantly.

In the hours since his death, rigor mortis has set in and Tom tries to position his body so it will fit on the poncho. Tom has to bend the stiff arms back over Charlie's head and place them at his sides. He finishes with the second arm and steps back and looks at Charlie, thinking, *He's a thing now, he's not a person. He's not Charlie Pyle anymore, but I will never forget him.*

The platoon gathers around and they load Charlie onto a chopper. The chopper lifts away and he is gone. His departure happens so quickly that no one really has time to think that they are really saying good-bye. They stand looking at the place in the sky where Charlie and the helicopter used to be. They never see him again.

Now, at the end of March, so much of the world seems so far away that to remember it is to perform an act of conjuring, a trick of the mind. "How can they send us here without telling us what it would be like?" Stan wonders. "We have become animals, living in the dirt."

If Stan sees that a platoon member does not have any mail, he, or any of the others, will leaf through their own, and suddenly, as if surprised, say, "Jeez, here you go, Beke. Looks like this one's for you." And Beke will reach up for the envelope and take it and read the address and then say, "No, there's some mistake there; it's not for me," and Stan might say, "No, I think *that* one's got your name on it." This is part of the ritual, the offering and the refusal. And the boy, Al Dove or Tom Soals or Tim Anderson or Dwight Lane or Jerry Austin or Tony Beke will begin reading the letter, taking in the other man's news as if it's his own. He can sit back afterward, tapping the envelope against his knee and looking off at the green hills, nodding, as if everything he's read really had happened to him, that in some wonderful way he really did have a sister who'd just gotten into Middlebury, that his father had been promoted, that his girlfriend will love him forever.

Not all the news is good, though. Stan gets a letter from his beloved Mo—she's now a senior at Lew Wallace High School—and she writes that she's dating another boy. This spirals Stan into a funk, and the platoon has to intervene and remind him to get his mind back into the war or he's going to get himself killed. But when he tells the platoon that he's so distraught that he's going to rip up Mo's junior and senior pictures, the other guys swiftly veto this action. They tell him they want to be able to look at her photograph, and just because she's not Stan's girlfriend any longer, she's still a young woman, a person with sweet eyes, a nice smile. Her photo possesses totemic value, endowed with rich powers. The other guys tell Stan that he can't destroy Maureen's pictures because this might endanger them all. Her photographs, they tell him, as well as the ones he's carrying of Anna and Carol, are the reasons they've been spared. There's a feeling among some of them that to go into the next firefight without them in Stan's shirt pocket might get them killed. He doesn't destroy the pictures.

One day Stan is walking down the trail on the way to an ambush and says, "Riley, do you realize right now there are women walking down a street in America who are going about their business and they don't know we're here?"

"I know it."

And then he asks the question that is always on their minds: "Do you even remember what a woman looks like?" Some of the guys keep their girlfriend's perfumed letters in the plastic bags that their radio batteries are shipped in. They take them out at night and pass them around. Somebody will say, "Gimme a hit of that," and the guy will stick his nose in and breathe deep. It seems impossible to them that there is something so sweet left in the world.

● ● ●

Rain falls all day and all night as they walk. Nothing is ever dry, and nothing ever changes, and yet nothing ever is the same.

Stan and Riley sit down to rest. It's then that they realize the rain has stopped falling after days of steady downpour.

"Riley, you hear that?"

"Yeah, what?"

"It's stopped."

"God, you're right."

"Oh, god, Riley, it feels so good."

Finally, Riley says, "Do you still have those pictures in your pocket?"

Stan carries five: two Mo had given him; two from Anna, on whom he's long had a crush; and one from his art class buddy, Carol. Anna had written to him once: "Do you sleep in a barracks building over there?" There is so much he wants to tell her now to set her straight. These pictures remind Stan that there is another world to which he might return, if he can survive. When he looks at them, he thinks, *This is what home looks like. Home.* He is certain they are a link to sanity.

"I still got those pictures," he tells Riley, "right next to my heart." He taps his shirt pocket.

"You mind if I look at them again?"

"No, I don't mind."

"And you won't mind if I say whatever I want to?"

"I won't."

Stan pulls out the dog-eared pictures, and Riley holds them up against the blue sky and looks at them. And then he begins talking to them, saying things like, "You are so pretty," and so on. He says to Stan, "You know what's the first thing I'd do?"

"What's that?"

"I'd drop my rucksack."

"Hell, that'd be the second thing I'd do," Stan says with a laugh. "I wouldn't even bother with that."

"You're right about that," says Riley, handing the photos back. "You won't ever tell 'em if you see 'em, right?"

"I won't tell them, Riley. I promise."

On March 31, five days after Stan returns to the platoon from the hospital, President Lyndon Johnson sits down before the American public on national TV and reports on the apparent success of U.S. forces repelling North Vietnam's surprise Tet attack.

The attack, he says, "did not collapse the elected government of South Vietnam or shatter its army."

"It did not produce," he says, "a 'general uprising' among the people of the cities as they had predicted."

"The Communists," he explains, "were unable to maintain control of any of the more than thirty cities that they attacked. And they took very heavy casualties."

And then, at end of his speech, the president delivers a shocking announcement: "I shall not seek and I will not accept the nomination of my party for another term as your president."

When the platoon hears this news over Armed Services radio, they think Johnson's throwing in the towel, that he's giving up on *them*. The boys feel they're *winning*.

They feel they have the enemy *on the run*. They feel they're killing so many enemy soldiers that surely Uncle Ho in Hanoi is about to give up—but not them. Dammit—*why give up?*

News reports in general have been getting depressing too.* Saying that Tet has changed Americans' perception about the

---

* Reports of the March 16, 1968, massacre of some five hundred civilians at My Lai by the 23rd Infantry Division soldiers wouldn't come to light until November 1969, with the publication of news reporter Seymour Hersh's stories.

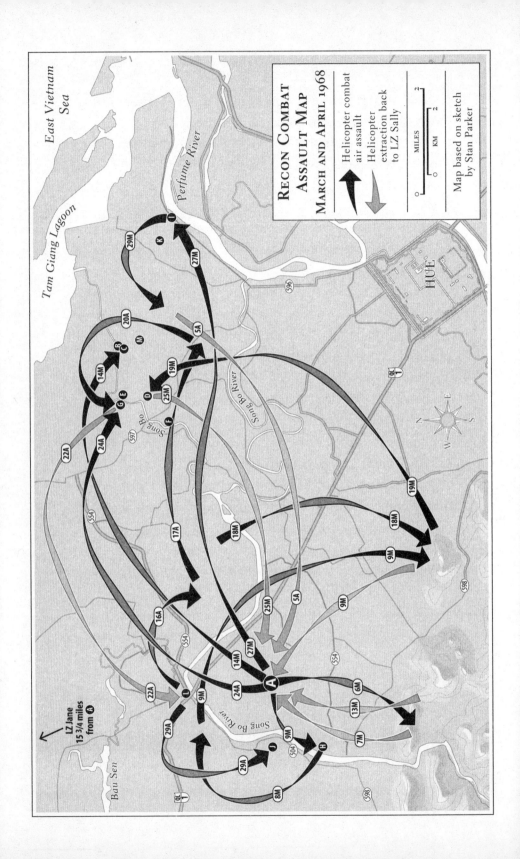

RECON COMBAT
ASSAULT MAP
MARCH AND APRIL 1968

Helicopter combat
air assault

Helicopter
extraction back
to LZ Sally

MILES

KM

Map based on sketch
by Stan Parker

East Vietnam
Sea

Tam Giang Lagoon

Perfume River

HUE

Song Bo River

Song Bo River

Bau Sen

LZ Jane
15 3/4 miles
from Ⓐ

war. Saying we can't be winning if these little bastards can do this: attack an entire country in just one night!

When he learns that Americans back home believe they are losing the war, Michael Bradshaw, like others in the platoon, is incredulous. They're decimating the VC and NVA. Before the offensive, the VC had often vanished after short, intense fire-fights. Now they've been taking a stand to slug it out, and conse-quently are suffering large casualties.

Some forty thousand NVA and VC—compared to some four thousand U.S. forces—are now dead. That's a lot of dead Com-munists.

Yet old Johnson himself is on TV, looking as if he's wound tighter than a two-dollar watch, and acting as grim as a high school biology student during rat dissection week—there he is staring into the camera, giving up, quitting, kaput. He no longer wants to be president.

When the boys hear this, the news is hard to digest. Have they been winning? they wonder. Have they?

The president seems to be saying that no matter how many boys he pours into this war, the boys won't win.

Is this true?

The president seems to be saying that the killing will continue and continue.

During the coming weeks, the platoon will wonder if he's right.

On April 20, the platoon is along the Song Bo River, about four and a half miles northeast of LZ Sally, keeping to the left flank of Charlie Company as they, with Bravo Company, sweep through a close-by hamlet. It's a pincer maneuver converging on the vil-lage, ostensibly trapping enemy fighters inside.

Jerry Austin is walking point, quietly, heel-toe, heel-toe, alongside Paul Sudano. Darryl Lintner's right behind them. Lintner has just joined the platoon, one of the replacements for the wounded and the dead. He's new; he's a cherry. A firefight virgin. The enemy fires from some trees, and Darryl Lintner drops immediately.

Austin runs for a little mound, not enough to conceal him, but he dives for it anyway, and Michael Bradshaw and John Arnold come running and dive behind the too-small mound and hunker closer to the ground. Austin hears Lintner yelling, "Medic!" a cry in the noon sun, and then it's quiet and then again: "Medic! Medic! Medic!" And Austin and a few of the others try to get up to run to Darryl, and that sweet kid yells, "Get down, get down!" as more fire comes from the tree line. And then Darryl is quiet and they hear no more from him because he's dead.

When the firing stops, Austin and Arnold creep out and drag Lintner back and he's white as a bleach bottle. His skin has already turned that plastic color, his face shiny and smooth and very white.

Dammit, that's the hell of it all, they all agree, he was such a super guy, the kind you'd want your sister to marry. His wife sent him sweet-smelling letters with money inside—money!— and Paul Sudano kidded him, "Lintner, where *are* you gonna spend all that money way out here?" and they'd stare out at the sun's silver glare on the trees—hot, silent emptiness—and Darryl blushed. Darryl, such a sweet kid! The hell of it is, Darryl is killed before he's been in-country long enough to be an old warrior, to make this business of killing a way of life. Hyperalertness hadn't set in; he was still Darryl Lintner from Perryville, Missouri. What killed him was that he hadn't done enough killing first, to know enough how to stay alive.

When Stan hears about Darryl's death, he goes nuts. He loses his mind. His reaction is way out of proportion to the degree to which he knows Lintner. He feels that he and Darryl might have gotten to know each other had they met back in the world. He'd said to Lintner shortly after his arrival, "Stick with me, kid," even though they were the same age. "I'll take care of you." Kind of nonchalant. Yet he'd meant it. That's about it, though: "Stick with me, kid. I'll take care of you." Sounding like an old man. When he first met Lintner, he did one thing that he didn't usually do: he learned Lintner's first name, and he called him by that. He wishes now he'd never learned his first name. Darryl.

He's about a quarter mile away in the same firefight when he hears the gunfire. When he makes his way over to the position where Lintner has been killed and Tom Soals tells him what's happened, Stan wants to walk into the village and kill every living being who has a weapon in his hand.

He starts running toward the village where the shooting has been coming from, ready to fight. Friendly and enemy fire fills the air. Someone tackles him and says, "Stan, no, there's arty coming in; it's about to get bombed." But Stan doesn't care. He gets up and starts running toward the village just as the first rockets land and blow up the village, and Stan cartwheels hard onto the ground. In the pause, he steels himself and starts running again, and he is knocked down when the next salvo lands. He gets up again and keeps trying to reach the village. He wants to run in there so badly and kill the village itself, but each time he's thrown back by the artillery barrage. He never makes it to the village, and finally someone tackles him again and says, "Stan, you can't." He thinks, *The hell I can't; they killed him*, and thinks, *I'm ready to die*. But his punishment is to keep living. He tries to forget Darryl's name. He tries to unlearn it. He can't, of course. He promises himself he will never learn another person's first name in the platoon.

There's a bad firefight on the morning of April 29, the gunfire cracking the hot dawn. Stan is walking down the trail in a sleepless trance, ahead of Francis Wongus.

Wongus yells to Stan to slow down. "Get back here! Hurry up!" Wongus wants them to walk together for security.

In a hurry, Stan rounds a corner and, just twenty feet away, sees an NVA soldier standing there, staring up at the sky, and he's whistling a song, which sounds like all songs even though technically it's Vietnamese whistling. When he turns at Stan's approach, Stan lifts the M-16 and fires the soldier up, *BRRRPPP*, and drops him. Stan jams in a fresh mag and moves forward in a crouch. But when he gets to where the soldier was, he can't find him. He's gone.

Where'd he go?

Stan sees the AK at his feet; there's blood on it, and there's the guy's rucksack. Wongus walks up and looks around and says that he's going back up the trail to tell Higher that they've engaged an enemy and are going after him. He tells Stan to stay right there and don't go looking for this guy alone.

"Okay, okay, okay," Stan answers, but ignores his warning. He wants to get even for Lintner, Kass, Pyle, and all the others.

He walks into the bushes with his M-16 aimed ahead, his bayonet leading the way.

Stan follows the blood spatter into the thicket, tracking the guy. He can make out a path in the leaves where it seems the man dragged himself forward, looking for a place to hide.

The undergrowth is so thick Stan has to get down on his hands and knees and crawl along the guy's blood trail. There are so many branches grabbing at him, and the passage is so narrow that he lays his rucksack and M-16 aside, removes the bayonet from the rifle and keeps moving, parting the vegetation with the bayonet's sharp tip. He crawls into a clearing in the jungle no bigger than a big living room rug, only this space is filled with bloody leaves. Stan's thinking, *If I were this guy, this is where I'd be hiding.* He looks around the clearing but can't see him. He's just about ready to stand up when he does one last scan and stops. He sees a set of eyes, just eyes, glaring at him, and he freezes. He immediately realizes the soldier's body is covered with leaves—he's pulled the leaves up over himself; if he had covered his eyes, Stan never would have spotted him. As it is, there are eyes peering through the loose scrim of leaves, unblinking, and aimed right at Stan, about six feet away. He springs out of the brush wall like a tiger and in midair reaches out with both hands and grabs Stan. He realizes the NVA soldier must not be that badly wounded, given his strength as he tightens his hands around Stan's neck. Stan doesn't even have time to raise his bayonet and stab him. They hit the ground and roll.

Stan keeps reaching up and stabbing but hits nothing but air. Then the NVA soldier has a knife out, and he's trying to stab Stan. This doesn't look good. Stan notices he doesn't have his bayonet anymore. Where'd that go? He reaches for the guy's hand, trying to wrestle the blade away, and as he does this, Stan remembers a move from his high school wrestling matches. He gets on top of the NVA and they roll again. Now the NVA soldier is sitting atop Stan and starts whacking at him with the blade as Stan rolls his head back and forth, trying to get out of the way. He's getting cut on the arms and the chin, and then Stan does another reversal and ends up sitting atop the guy again. The guy reaches up with just one hand and clasps Stan's throat and starts squeezing. With the other hand, he's batting away Stan's stabs with the bayonet. The guy's really squeezing, and Stan's vision starts to narrow; he's getting tunnel vision from the lack of oxygen. He's being choked to death. Stan sees small stars circling the rims of his eyes. He has to change the game quickly and decisively. Stan reaches up with his left hand and slowly pushes the guy's free hand out of the way, and when there's an opening, he stabs at the man's neck. He thrusts three times and on maybe the second thrust, warm blood spurts up on Stan, all over his face and chest. He can taste it, and in his oxygen-deprived state, he's not quite sure what's going on. He keeps stabbing.

Finally he sees the world coming back, the aperture opening up, his peripheral vision returns, and even though the guy is dead, or certainly dying, his death grip hasn't loosened. Stan has to reach up and pry the man's fingers from around his neck. He throws the hand aside, the arm flops away, and Stan rolls off and lies on the ground gasping. He still feels close to passing out as Wongus crawls up. Stan tries talking, but he doesn't have any voice; it's been squeezed out of him. He's covered in blood. Coming into the clearing with Wongus is Brian Riley. They look at Stan and are pretty sure that he's been badly wounded. But because there's so much blood, they can't see any wounds. Wongus and Riley grab Stan by the feet and drag him backward and then help him up. They retrace his steps by following the blood trail and find Stan's M-16 and his ruck, and they each take an arm and shuffle back to the trail. Only ten minutes have passed since Stan shot the NVA soldier and stabbed him in the jungle. If other NVA have been nearby, surely they'll be coming close to check out the source of the firing.

The three men rejoin a group from the platoon. When they wipe some of the blood away, they discover that Stan hasn't been stabbed deeply but he's been cut up pretty bad and needs treatment and stitches to prevent infection. A Huey is called in and Stan is loaded aboard. As they take off, he looks down and sees the green ground passing beneath him and the guys looking up at him, and they are gone. That's the last he will see of many of them. That's the last day he will serve as a member of Echo Company, Recon Platoon.

In the aftermath of the Tet Offensive, the Viet Cong fighters, the poor farmers, the teachers by day who pick up a gun at night to fight as guerrillas, the indigenous people who have never wanted anything in their country except independence from the Chinese, the French, the Japanese, and now the Americans—these people have suffered enormous losses. The Tet has made them fight in the open alongside regular NVA forces, in cities and villages and in fighting that resembles set-piece battles. Accustomed to fighting and fading away to the jungles to live and fight again, they have died in huge numbers. Vietnam will never recover from these losses, and for the remainder of the war, the next seven years, the government of North Vietnam, aided by organized cadres of thousands of women, will send troops down into the South, along the Ho Chi Minh Trail, to supplant the lost VC fighters.

After getting out of the hospital on May 20, 1968, after his third wounding, Stan faces the prospect of leaving Vietnam. When you get wounded three times, this means you have three Purple Hearts. And when you have three Purple Hearts, you're through. You've done your time for Uncle Sam in Vietnam.

To avoid a mandatory exit of Vietnam, Stan refuses to accept his third Purple Heart. This has the effect, from an administrative perspective, of making it appear as if the third wounding has never happened. He'll be able to serve the remaining seven months of a twelve-month combat tour in the 101st Airborne Division. But in another part of the division.

A day after leaving the hospital, May 21, still limping and in pain with healing stab wounds across his back and arms, he's reassigned to the 1/327th, 1st Brigade, at Camp Gia Lee, several miles from the 101st Airborne's large headquarters at Camp Eagle. He'll serve as a photographer in the Army's Press Information Office—a desk job, essentially, but he'll take it. Four months earlier, he'd passed through Camp Eagle when he was new to the country and when Eagle had been called LZ El Paso. He's returning to the beginning of his journey, bearing this time the haunted look of the war-weary, "the thousand-yard stare."

Two months spent sitting at a desk takes its toll. Stan realizes he hasn't been shot at in six weeks and he's stir-crazy. He asks to join a line unit as a combat photographer and reunites with Dwight Lane and David Watts in their platoon, part of 1st Battalion, 327th Airborne Infantry. He relishes this reunion with his buddies but realizes his attraction to combat and its adrenaline infusions is an addiction. He increasingly fears being asked to leave the war. On December 17, Stan's twelve-month tour of duty in Vietnam ends and he has to return to the States. He'll serve the remaining seven and a half months of his three-year enlistment assigned to the 82nd Airborne at Fort Bragg, North Carolina—predictable garrison life, filled with administrative tasks. He dreads the prospect of boredom.

In the meantime, he's returning to Gary, Indiana, for Christmas on a thirty-day leave and reuniting with his father and two younger brothers, George and Bruce, along with his older brother, Dub, also home from Vietnam.

Stan fears his homecoming. The truth is, he can barely remember what it feels like to live indoors or eat warm food.

He's worried if he'll adjust to civilian life. As he boards the military transport in Bien Hoa, he's scared. Fourteen hours later, he lands at Travis Air Force Base; transfers by bus to the Army air terminal in Oakland, California, forty-seven miles to the southwest; and boards still another bus to cross the bridge over San

Francisco Bay to the city itself, home to war protests that had been a counter-soundtrack to the gunfire and screams that had filled every corner of his year in Vietnam.

Each transfer and bus ride is another wicket, another cycling back into civilian life, the days behind him slamming shut. By the time he enters the bright, fluorescent concourse of the San Francisco airport, he's on edge, walking as alertly as if he's moving down a wooded trail. It's only 9:00 a.m., but it feels like midnight in his head. He feels as if he's been awake for years.

Other soldiers back in Vietnam had warned him about San Francisco—about how, when you land there, you had to remove your uniform to avoid being hassled. But Stan stays in his Class A dress uniform. He orders a Coke at a restaurant counter, thinking, *What have I been through?*

He catches sight of a television in an airport lounge and is reminded of how little he knows about what's gone on in America in his absence. Robert F. Kennedy has been killed; there have been riots in Chicago outside a hotel at the Democratic National Convention. There's been a protest march with several hundred thousand people at the Pentagon. Stan feels a million miles away from these events, which is strange, he reflects, because he—or his experience—is at the center of the national debate. *Should we be in Vietnam, and what are we doing there?* "Doing there?" What does that question even mean? We're trying to stay alive, that's for sure; that's one thing we're doing there. He can tell everybody a bit about that. Should we be there? He doesn't know the answer. But here's the thing: he *wanted* to be there. He wants to be there right now.

Some kids his age dressed in jeans walk by; one of the guys is wearing a bandanna and says to Stan as he passes, "Hey, man."

"Hey, pardner." Stan's hoping they keep walking. He doesn't want any conversation about Vietnam.

The kid looks at Stan. After a moment, he says, "Hey, did you kill anybody over there?"

Stan just kind of winces. He doesn't know what to say. He wonders, *How does he know? Do I look like a killer?*

"Hey, I'm talking to you. Did you kill any children?"

He's just numb and doesn't quite get why this guy is on his case.

"If any of your buddies died, I hope it was painful," the kid says.

That's too much. Stan can't take it any longer. "You say one more thing, I'm going to come out of this chair for you."

"Yeah?"

"Right here, right now. I know a hundred ways to kill you. Pick one."

He'll later consider how immediate his response is, as if he's been suddenly engaged in a firefight.

A businessman sitting at the next table interrupts.

"Knock it off," he tells the kid.

"Am I talking to you?"

"You're not, but leave him alone."

The kid and his friends reluctantly walk away.

"Thank you," says Stan, thinking he's found an ally.

"You know, I don't support you or the war either," says the businessman, "but what they were doing—it wasn't right."

He returns to his newspaper, leaving Stan sitting there, alone with his thoughts, which are grim. He senses his homecoming will be anything but heartwarming.

When he boards the commercial plane in San Francisco, he marvels at how nice it is to sit on soft cloth seats and look out a plane window at something other than a battlefield. He can faintly see his reflection in the glass. Does he look like a Vietnam veteran—a killer? He still has the squared-away haircut, the hard tan, but is this the look of a killer? He knows he'll stand out in a crowd of civilians.

As he did two years earlier when he boarded the bus back in Gary and contemplated this question, he still believes he's someone who serves, who loves. Yet he's killed so many. It's hard to square this circle.

Stan has discovered there are three people you fight for: your buddy, yourself, and your family. You fight to stay alive so you can see your family again. He sits on the plane missing the camaraderie he'd felt among his platoon. It's an ache. It is love. He would like to bolt from his seat. He would like to get up and walk back into the war.

The nice woman sitting in the seat next to him does something surprising. She calls for a flight attendant.

"Excuse me," she says, "I'd like to find another seat."

Stan is unsure at first that this nice person is talking about him.

"I know," says the attendant. "We tried to find a seat for him where no one else had to be next to him."

"Excuse me," says Stan. "I'm sitting right here. I can hear what you're saying."

The nice lady gets up and follows the attendant. Stan sits there, dumbfounded. He looks at himself in the reflection of the window: Do I look crazy? Do I smell? Why does this person hate me?

Vietnam, he thinks. *Vietnam. This nice lady doesn't want to know who I am.*

He returns home on December 20, 1968, determined to spend his thirty-day leave happily and eagerly reacquainting himself with his former life. He's thrilled to see his brothers and his father, who appears to have aged considerably in the two years since his mother's death.

His mother's absence is a palpable presence. He misses her terribly. Except for his family, he feels out of touch with almost everyone around him. He wants to avoid situations where he might have to talk about what he did in Vietnam. At the same time, he *does* want to talk about it. Only Dub understands what he's experienced in combat.

He's bothered by the fact that he doesn't have an idea what he's going to do for a living when he gets out of the Army. His father says he can get a job working in Gary, at Bethlehem Steel as an iron-worker apprentice. They're hiring, and the pay's good, so why not? Maybe it's not a bad idea to stick around home and settle down.

What he thinks most about is the fact that he's still alive. He real-izes his job in Vietnam had been to stay alive and that the platoon accomplished this job by killing. Upon reflection, he understands that it's not the killing he did that bothers him; it's the dying. By this, he means he's troubled by the deaths he's witnessed, seeing so many eyes close for good.

He misses the fighting. In his heart there's a hole that he can't fill.

He tries to fill the hole by going to bars and fighting. Other nights, tired of this, he poses as a college student. He'll tell the girl at the bar, when she asks what he does, that he goes to college. For so many, this would seem an innocuous statement. But for Stan, at this time in the American epoch, it's like migrating to a new country. It feels to him that he's telling a huge lie, which he is, of course, but attached to the lie is immense embarrassment. It's also nerve-racking to pretend to be someone he's not. This rubs against the grain of who he is, beginning in his childhood when his father made him stand up for himself and fight for his right to be himself, even pitting him against the high school kid who'd extorted him on his paper route when he was in sixth grade and the kid was a senior in high school. That was what his dad taught him: fight for yourself. And so that's why pretending to be a college student is so hard, aside from the fact that he doesn't know anything about what it's like to be in college.

He feels like a dumb kid from Gary, Indiana, who went overseas like a sucker and killed and bled and now he's home and pretending to be a college student because he feels shunned for serving in Vietnam. Yet at the same time, it's been the most important thing he's ever experienced. And to boot, the young women he meets have this sixth sense that picks up right away that he's been over in the Nam. One of them asks him what his GPA is in college, which seems an odd question, and he eventually realizes he's being asked because the girl doesn't believe that he's a student. He chooses a GPA of 3.5, something respectable but not off the charts; there's a part of him that is a very honest liar. Or the girls ask what college he attends, and he might say Arizona because of his dark tan. If by chance the girls knows the place, well, that's horrible and he's sunk. But still, even the pain of this is better than identifying himself as a Vietnam vet. In short, the homecoming experience feels like death or a series of deaths: he died many times in Vietnam, or at least parts of him died there, and now he must die again each time he sees the look in the girls' eyes when he tells them he's been in Vietnam. It's a look of contempt and fear and curiosity.

One day he's walking to the mailbox outside his house and meets a neighbor, a World War II veteran, grabbing the mail too, and the old codger says, "Hey, there, Stan Parker, haven't seen you in a while," and Stan thinks, *That's funny, because I haven't been home in quite awhile.* He begins to explain that he's been in Vietnam and lets on that it wasn't so easy over there. The fighting was less front line to front line and, well, the body count was really important. As Stan is going on about the intricacies and the weave of this war, such as only one veteran can explain to another in a brotherly shorthand, the old guy cuts him off and says, "That's all right, son, we don't need to talk about any of that. I spent four years fighting in Europe. Your combat in Vietnam lasted twelve months." And the old codger, the World War II veteran, turns and walks back to his house. That's pretty much a showstopper, and Stan never again speaks about Vietnam with this neighbor, nor, for that matter, with any other veterans at a VFW or American Legion Hall. He doesn't feel welcome in these places, and over time he'll discover that other Vietnam veterans feel the same way about these World War II–era fraternities.

On Christmas Eve, he goes out late and gets into a helluva fight, a fight to end all fights, and the fighting feels good.

It's been a long night when he walks into the diner near dawn for some breakfast. Sitting in the restaurant is a guy named Carl Calhoun, whom Stan has known since early high school. They've never gotten along. And in that way by which high school differences can grow into unspoken adult grievances, Calhoun has this grudge against Stan Parker. Maybe he doesn't like the way he walks, all that swagger, or the way he combs his hair, but when Stan walks into the diner, he finds his youngest brother, Bruce, sitting in a booth and Bruce tells him that Carl Calhoun is gunning for him. "I'm around," says Stan. "I'm not hard to find." He doesn't give this much thought. Carl will fight him or not fight him. It's like Stan is not really in this world. He's walking through it, but the things he walks past don't really touch him.

As Stan passes through the restaurant, he catches sight of Carl, who glares at him. Stan takes a seat in a booth with a couple of his friends and watches as Carl gets up and leaves. *Fine,* Stan thinks. *If you don't want to be in here with me, that's fine.* He starts talking with his buddies.

About that time, one of them says "What the hell!" and Stan looks up to see his brother Bruce standing face-to-face with Carl Calhoun. Calhoun reaches out and punches Bruce in the face. Bruce drops to the floor, and Calhoun walks out of the restaurant.

Stan's reaction is instantaneous. He's up and crossing the room and bursts into the street. Snow is banked along the sidewalks. Stan walks up to Calhoun, who starts to say something like, "I'm going to give you a chance to leave or I'll punch you too," when Stan hits him hard. Carl doesn't finish the sentence. He goes down on the sidewalk. Stan picks him up and slams him against the rims of his own car. Calhoun tries to get up and into his car, and when he opens the door, Stan says, "Oh, you want in this car?" And he starts slamming the door on Carl's head. He falls unconscious.

One of Carl's friends walks up and says to Stan, "You think you're pretty bad, beating up a guy you've already kicked the shit out of? Why don't you try me?" And before this guy can say anything, Stan hits him too. He jumps on him and hits him again as he lies on the sidewalk. Another of the Calhoun crowd steps forward to challenge Stan: "So you think you can kick my ass?"

"Come over here, and I'll show you."

The guy walks up. Stan really doesn't know what the guy's thinking. He gets to Stan and just stands there. Stan waits for him to take a swing, but he doesn't. Maybe he's losing his nerve, Stan can't tell. He drops him with one punch.

This last guy's girlfriend is standing next to him when this happens, and she starts screaming. She walks up to Stan and punches him in the face so hard he literally sees stars. He didn't know women could hit so hard. His knees buckle, but then he regains his balance.

A crowd has gathered on the street and somebody grabs Stan

from behind and says, "That's enough." He can hear sirens. Somebody says "Cops!" and whoever is holding Stan lets him go. Stan runs back inside the restaurant and finds Bruce, who's still groggy, and then he runs back outside and gets in his car, his GTX, and waits for Bruce to come out so they can get away.

Bruce comes out of the diner, looking around; he can't find the car.

"Bruce," Stan yells. "Over here!"

The sirens are getting closer. Bruce gets in. Stan throws the car into reverse and is about to speed away when a cop car pulls in behind him and then another blocks his way out front. The cops jump out with guns drawn and yell, "Out of the car, now!" Right behind them is an ambulance, lights flashing.

Stan gets out of the car.

"Who did this?" the cops shout. There are three bodies on the pavement, bloodied and not moving. The crowd yells back "He did!" and the people point at Stan. The cops are taken aback. One guy did so much damage? One guy? One of the cops tells Stan, "You're under arrest," and gets out the handcuffs. Stan doesn't resist. The fighting happened so fast, Stan barely remembers the punching. He had just reacted.

"What about my car?" he asks as the cop puts on the cuffs.

"What do you mean, your car?"

"It's brand new," says Stan. "Everything I own is in that car. I'm not going to jail without it."

"How do you propose we get it to jail?"

Stan says, "Let me drive it."

"You think we're stupid?"

"I don't think you're stupid. Just follow me."

Another cop chimes in, "I got an idea. Pull your boots off."

"It's wintertime," says Stan.

"If you want to drive, pull your boots off."

Stan takes off his cowboy boots.

The cop says, "Get in."

Stan gets in the GTX. The cop reaches in with handcuffs and locks Stan to the T-shaped Hurst shift sticking up through the car floor. He cuffs the left hand to the steering wheel. And then they cuff Stan's left foot to the clutch. The cop stands back and says, "Now try to get away."

Stan's thinking, *You idiots; all I got to do is drive away.*

But that's not what he's going to do. He has no intention of running. He follows the cop car to the station. The cops go into the station, and some other cops unfamiliar with the situation come out and tell Stan to get out of the car.

"I can't get out of the car."

"Get out of the car."

"I tell you, I can't get out of this car."

"Why not?"

"I'm handcuffed in here."

"Really? Where are the arresting officers?"

The original cops walk out of the station, ready to unlock him, but none of them can remember who has the correct key. It takes several minutes to get everything sorted out and to free Stan and his brother.

"We're in trouble now," says Bruce. "You're going to jail."

"I ain't going to jail," Stan told him. "That other guy started the fight."

His brother doesn't have to tell him he'd beaten up Carl Calhoun pretty bad. Stan knows it. He and his brother march into the police station, empty their pockets, and spend the night in jail.

In the morning, they call their dad.

"Where are you at?" asks their father, worried.

"I'm in jail," said Stan.

"What are you doing in jail?"

"I got in a fight."

"Didn't I tell you not to get your brother in trouble? Is he with you?"

"Yeah, Dad, he's right here in jail with me."

"Okay, all right. I'll be over there in a little bit."

Stan doesn't know if his father will be upset. When he shows up, he asks, "Did the other guy punch your brother?" Stan says that he did punch Bruce.

"You did the right thing. We'll tell the judge that."

His father posts bail and calls an attorney, who asks him the judge's name. His father tells him and the attorney says he won't take the case. "I don't want any part of this. Let your public defender take care of it."

As far as Stan and his father figure out, the judge who will hear the case does not like Vietnam veterans. He is apparently famous for being hard on veterans returning from Vietnam who disturb the peace. On top of this, he doesn't like people who drink alcohol. In short, Stan is about to go before a judge who has a rep for hating vets. True or not, that's the rumor, and he and his father don't know how to meet this challenge. The attorney tells them both that Stan is looking at going away for maybe three years on felony charges of assault and battery based on the severity of the attack. Carl Calhoun has had to be put in a body cast and hospitalized; his recovery is expected to take months. The others were all taken to the local hospital with major trauma. Stan and his father are unsure of what to do.

Shortly after, a man starts calling Stan's house and leaving messages to call him back. Stan ignores the calls. He's still going out at night to drink on the town. He knows his court date is nearing, and while it seems he'll be heading to jail, he isn't quite sure what to do about this except to do nothing. His father says the man wants to talk with Stan about his "predicament."

Stan finally calls him back. "What's this about?" he asks.

"You got in a fight about a week ago?"

"Uh-huh. That's right."

"I happened to watch that fight, I was impressed. I ain't never seen anybody knock out three people so fast."

"Uh-huh."

"You're good."

"You want to hire me as a fighter or something?"

"No. But I looked into your case. You've got a felony against you. You're going to jail."

Stan waits, doesn't say anything. He feels he's moving into uncharted water.

"You need to see me," says the guy. "I can help you."

Stan agrees to meet the mystery caller. A few days later, he's parking outside an abandoned-looking warehouse on the outskirts of Chicago. He walks inside and finds himself in a waiting room. Soft light filters through high windows. A couple of beefy fellows in suits lounge around, reading magazines.

"Can I help you?" one of them asks.

"My name is Stan Parker."

They press a button on an intercom. "Hey, boss, Mr. Parker's here." They send Stan right in.

Stan looks around the paneled office. From the anteroom, the place had looked like a dump, but this office is really something. Nice paneling. A leather couch. The mystery man turns to look at Stan.

"Have a seat. Can I get you anything?"

"I'm fine. You wanted to see me about this fight I'm in?"

"Let me tell you what's going on. Your name is John Stanley Parker. You've just come back from Vietnam. You're highly decorated. You got in a fight the other night. I watched it. You punched the lights out on those guys. I ain't never seen a good fight like that. But you got arrested, and I watched the entire thing. You're going to jail."

Stan takes this in. "Well, that's what my attorney says."

"You're going to jail. But I can help you."

Stan's confused. "Have you got another attorney for me?"

This seems to amuse the man. "If it comes to that. But I have another angle—let me try it first." He holds up an envelope. "It's this right here."

Stan sees the thin envelope is sealed. "What's inside?"

"None of your business what's in there."

"Well, what am I going to do with this?"

"When you see the judge . . ." He pauses. "Now, listen to me. It's very important that you follow instructions. I know you can do it, because the Army's full of instructions."

Stan nods.

"When you're sitting in court, you don't tell your attorney about this. You don't tell anybody about it, or word can get to the judge before you hand this to him. You can tell family members, but nobody else."

"Okay."

"Now the judge is going to ask, 'Does anybody have anything to say before these hearings take place?' And you're going to say, 'Your Honor, may I approach the bench?'"

"Okay."

"Go ahead, let's try it. I'm the judge. Let's practice."

He turns to one of his men and tells him, "You're the attorney."

Stan steps forward to the guy playing the judge and says the words and pretends to hand the guy an envelope.

"Do it again," says the guy.

Stan does this several more times. "All right. You got it," says the guy. "Now I'm going to have a couple of my men in the courtroom just to make sure things go right."

Stan drives home, dying to open the envelope. His father at home asks him, "What'd he say?"

"He said, 'Give this to the judge.'" Stan holds up the envelope.

"You're kidding me. What's inside? No, don't open it. Do you think there's money in there?"

"There could be money. I don't have any idea what's in there."

"We won't open it," says his father. And with that, his father sticks the envelope in the kitchen freezer behind some peas.

A week or so later, Stan is in the courtroom, dressed in his Army uniform. His father is there, his brothers Bruce and Dub, and a few high school buddies. Carl Calhoun is brought in in a wheelchair, bandaged from head to toe. All Stan can see are his eyes glaring at him through the bandages. Stan glares back. He looks around and sees two of the guys from the warehouse office in the back of the courtroom. They're watching him. Stan sits down, nervous.

The judge looks down from the bench and says, "Does anybody have anything to say before these proceedings take place?" Stan clears his throat and stands up. "Your Honor? Permission to approach the bench?"

Stan's lawyer is surprised and pulls him down by the arm. "What are you doing?" he asks.

The judge waves the attorney away. "Mr. Parker, let me tell you something. You might be in your uniform here today, and you might be a decorated Vietnam veteran, and you might say you've done a lot in defense of your country, but let me tell you, that doesn't work in my courtroom. Do you understand? Now approach the bench."

Stan walks up. "Your Honor, I've been instructed to give you this." He hands over the envelope.

"By whom?"

"A gentleman told me to give this to you, and you're to read this before we start these proceedings."

The judge opens the envelope. Stan sees that it doesn't contain money, which he's glad of. The envelope contains just three pages of typewritten script. He watches as the judge rifles through the pages.

He looks up at Stan. "Did you read this?"

"No, sir, your Honor. I was instructed not to. I have no idea what the contents are."

"You did not see this?" the judge asks again.

"No, sir."

"All right," says the judge, folding the letter. He picks up his gavel, bangs it on his bench, and says, "This court is adjourned. All charges are dropped."

Stan is shocked; his attorney is confused. Stan sees Carl Calhoun and Carl's mother, and both of them are yelling at the judge.

The judge bangs the gavel. "Order in this court. Bailiff, be prepared to eject them!" And with that, he exits the courtroom.

At the courtroom door, the boss's men are waiting to shake Stan's hand and escort him to his car.

"The boss says for you to come by when you get out of the Army. You come by if you need a job." Stan shakes their hands, mumbles something about seeing them later, and hurries out.

On the way home, his father tells him, "There's no way you're going to see that guy. He had something on that judge. You know, 'I know that money you took,' or 'I know the girl you're sleeping with.'"

Stan agrees his father could be right. He also agrees that he won't be paying any of them a visit for a job. He is afraid they want him to be one of their enforcers, a guy who beats up people for a living. But he doesn't want that; that's not who he is. He doesn't feel bad about skating on the charges; he just feels damn lucky. Carl Calhoun had attacked his brother and he had fought back.

The kicks and punches had come instinctively, but Stan also knows they had come way too fast. He knows he has a problem.

He decides that he has to see Maureen again—one last time, in hopes he might figure out what happened to them. They'd been so happy once. He has to see her. Has to. Her soft blond hair. He's still angry about her leaving him the way she did, writing him, *Dear Stan, I have to tell you* . . . *blah blah blah* and him threatening to rip up her picture among the platoon members. But he can't not see her.

Yet he knows that she probably doesn't want to see him. She's married, after all. But her husband, he can't be good enough for her, can he? He's thinking of the Stan she once knew before he went to Nam, the Stan she drove out to meet at O'Hare Airport the time he came home from training to see his dying mother. That Stan was good enough for her. He was still a young man who had not killed anyone. He doesn't realize how angry he is when he decides he has to see her. He decides that he must, above all other tasks, retrieve from Maureen his high school letterman jacket; he'd given it to her before leaving for Vietnam. It's a ruse, really, a pretense to show up at her house and make himself known again.

He knocks on the front door, and Mo's mother answers. She is surprised to see him and gives him a big hug and says she is so happy he made it back. She even starts to cry and steps back to look at him. There he is, Stanley Parker, the kid from Calumet high school. Stan last saw her the day she and Mo picked him up

Huey choppers lining up to take Recon and Company A, 1/501st Airborne Infantry, for combat assault into harm's way as Al Dove, at the right edge of the picture, intensely watches incoming choppers.

26

In March 1968, Stan—on a two-day convalescent leave, pictured here with his brother Dub—fell into a pit of needle-sharp punji sticks covered in excrement, a booby trap set by the Viet Cong. One stick punctured his wrist clean through to the other side, and he spent two weeks in the hospital, away from combat. His platoon-mate Charlie Pyle was killed in action while Stan was convalescing.

27

The Recon Platoon assembled at LZ Sally on March 27, 1968, for a combat assault. Left to right: Parker, Lane, Bradshaw, Cromer, Austin, Russo, Soals, Holt, Jewell, and Wongus.

28

Above, a haunting photo of Viet Cong soldiers, developed from a roll of film Stan removed from the pocket of a man he had just killed. Approximately forty thousand Viet Cong and NVA soldiers died in combat during the 1968 Tet Offensive. At right, Stan poses with skulls that he found placed atop each of a cluster of six secluded graves. He was ordered by battalion HQ to collect them as intelligence items to be sent to the rear area for examination. "I, as well as those around me, are trained to kill and have adapted to that characteristic habit very demonstratively," Stan wrote in an unsent letter to Maureen. "I hope that I get out of here alive and when I get back home that I will be able to conduct myself in a sensible, rational, respectable manner and act normal again."

A photo of Stan taken in May 1968, at the end of the Tet Offensive.

Stan in the San Francisco airport on his way home in December 1968 after his twelve-month tour ended. Soldiers back in Vietnam advised him to remove his uniform to avoid being hassled in the airport. But he wore it anyway.

After getting out of the Army, returning home to Indiana, and being unable to reenlist, Stan reunited with Anna Runion and married her in August 1970. They had become the best of friends during the summer of 1964. They have been married ever since.

33

34

After marrying Anna, Stan devoted himself to learning his chosen trade as an ironworker. He followed the ironworking circuit to Wyoming, Montana, Colorado, South Dakota, and Nebraska, bringing Anna and their two sons with him. Stan, the foreman (third from right), kneels on a steel beam 410 feet in the air with part of his crew. It was a steel structure similar to this one from which Stan fell 360 feet and survived in 1977. But Stan missed the military, and in 1976 he found a backdoor way to reassociate with the Army and signed on to become a member of the National Guard's 19th Special Forces Group, splitting his time between training and ironworking. In 1994, he quit ironworking entirely and resumed life as an active-duty Special Forces soldier.

In 1997, after graduating from the U.S. Army's Sergeants Major Academy, Stan began active duty with U.S. Special Operations Command. He deployed to Jordan, Somalia, Kenya, Eritrea, and two tours to Afghanistan.

35

36

Stan during an air mission in Afghanistan around Thanksgiving 2004.

Stan and Tom Brokaw sharing a laugh at Bagram Airfield in Afghanistan, April 2005.

37

38

Stan on the tailgate of a Boeing Vietnam-era CH-47 Chinook, holding his Colt M4A1 carbine and wearing a headset for communication with the helicopter pilot and crew.

Stan checking location on a river in the Hindu Kush mountain region during a ground mission in Afghanistan.

39

Stan with an Afghan boy he rescued from certain death out of a Taliban ambush kill zone on October 29, 2005, deep in the Hindu Kush mountains.

40

Stan and his former Recon platoon-mate Tom Soals returned to Vietnam in April 2014. They are pictured here on a visit to the site of LZ Jane, where the 1968 Tet Offensive commenced for their platoon when it was overrun by soldiers of the NVA's 10th Sapper Battalion.

41

42

Stan looking at images of the war in a museum at the Khe Sanh battlefield.

Stan walking through the rice paddy where Charlie Pyle was killed in action on March 22, 1968.

43

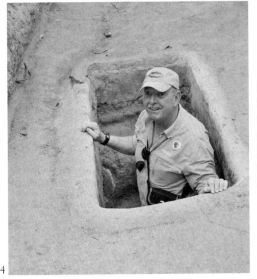

Stan emerging from one of the VC tunnels at Cu Chi, with haunting memories of walking over the very same ground in December 1967 and January 1968 with the VC shooting at Recon from hidden spider holes. Now it's a site for tourists to visit.

44

Stan standing on the spot where he was wounded in action his first time by members of Mr. Sinh's VC cadre and their NVA comrades-in-arms on February 18, 1968.

45

Mr. Sinh and Stan reunited at the site where they tried to kill each other forty-six years earlier on February 18, 1968.

46

at the airport and drove him to the hospital, and he's always been grateful for the kindness she's shown him. He asks her if Mo is home, and she says no, not yet. Mo's at work. She invites him inside. She asks him if he knows that Maureen is married now.

Stan says, yes, he does know. And he leaves it at that. He remembers being in Vietnam and how she'd written that she had started dating a guy name Jack, and how much this had saddened him; he felt like he was suffocating. And when she wrote and told him that she'd broken up with Jack, Stan immediately wrote back and asked if he had any chance with her at all. He even inquired as to whether she'd like to meet him in Japan when he had R&R and she'd said, well, maybe. . . . And then came her letter that she'd gotten married. It all seems like such history now, a long time ago, as he stands waiting in her living room.

Maureen and her husband suddenly walk in the front door. Stan looks at them both, focusing on the husband; he feels himself ready to fight, even though he realizes that he barely escaped jail for assault. Mo does not look happy at all to see him.

The husband steps forward and announces, as if he and Stan are resuming a long-standing conversation about Maureen, "We're married now."

"Married," Stan says, feigning ignorance. "You're kidding?" He suddenly knows that by coming here he's disgraced himself.

Mo's mother is looking nervous and Stan says after a minute that he's only come there to pick up his letterman jacket—the one he gave Mo his senior year. Her mother says she doesn't know where it is, and Stan says, "That's okay, I'll wait."

Maureen disappears into a back room and returns with the jacket.

She walks up to Stan and hands it to him. "It's time for you to leave," she tells him. "This is not some kind of reunion for you after the war."

But the war's the last thing they're going to talk about, and it's the last thing Mo would know how to bring up with Stan, having received all those letters from him when he was overseas, and she tried to answer them. Stan knows that his letters were so filled with longing, loneliness, that there was never really anything she could have written to make him feel better.

"How could you come to my mom's house without my approval?" she asks.

"I was invited by your mom and I was just about to leave."

Her husband says something to Stan, and when it seems Stan is getting angry, Maureen tells him he must go.

He collects himself and he tells her that he's sorry about this unannounced visit. He wonders to himself why he couldn't just have picked up the jacket and left. But no, he had wanted to wait for her. He had to say good-bye. And now he knows he's got a look in his eye—several looks, actually. Anger and sadness. He and the husband start going back and forth again, arguing, and Mo can tell pretty quickly that there's going to be a fight. She tells Stan for the last time to leave.

Stan says fine and stomps out of the house. He gets in the GTX muscle car, throws it into reverse, and smashes the pedal to the floor, peeling out of the driveway, sending smoke up. He comes to a halt in the road, throws the car into first gear, hits the gas, and pops the clutch. The GTX roars so much it sounds like a drag strip out there in the street, and Stan is doing 60 by the time he grabs second gear. He keeps going. He has in his hand her senior school picture, the one he carried all those miles, all those steps, the picture he didn't rip up to keep the guys alive because they said she was their talisman. He looks at it, and he's crying. He throws the picture, wallet sized, out of the window and he thinks it flies away and that he's gone from it forever.

What he doesn't know is that the picture scoots out the window and shoots back inside the car through the driver's-side rear window. It lands on the seat and keeps scooting across the vinyl, then edges into the crack between the back seat and the seat itself and lodges there. It keeps going, sinking down, where he will find it seven years later, in Montana, when he's removing the carpet from the floor of the trunk and cleaning the GTX and there's the picture. There she is, Mo, the very picture that's come back to haunt him, the past always coming back.

Forty-four years later he will email Maureen after finding her on the Internet, tracking her down via Facebook, the search occasioned by questions about his journey through Vietnam and home. He finds she is still scared of him, still wondering if he is still that angry guy who had raced down her street, the man she feared was going to beat up her husband. But about him, Stan had been right: Mo and her husband were not meant to be. They'd long ago divorced. Mo now wondered, these many years later, what she ever saw in him. What she had left from the marriage was a grown son, whom she loved deeply. But beyond that, she had nothing left of Stan Parker, of those days when they were young, in high school, in love, before Vietnam.

On the rebound from this reunion with Mo, Stan falls madly in love with another woman. We'll call her Carly. Stan has a couple of weeks remaining in his Christmas leave before he must return to Fort Bragg. His impending departure makes each hour seem more urgent; he doesn't know when he'll be able to come home again. He meets Carly at a restaurant; she's tall with long brown hair. She's home on break from an expensive state university. He takes her to a party and she's wearing a miniskirt. At midnight, someone lights firecrackers and Stan experiences a flashback, a new sensation: he hears gunshots, not celebration.

He tries shrugging this off and walks with Carly to the dance floor. On the way, a man pinches Carly's bottom. Stan suddenly hits him and he drops to the floor, unconscious. The room turns silent and people are staring at him. He wants to leave and they head for the door. On the way, another guy says something sexual to Carly and Stan hits him too.

She's shocked by his immediate reflexes. *Two down in two minutes*, Stan thinks. *I cannot get arrested again.* He wants to go before the cops show up.

Stan grabs Carly by the hand and they flee to his car. "I've never met anyone like you," she says. "Where did you come from?"

He knows her parents won't approve of him, an ironworker's son. What he loves about her is that she seems to love him, or, put another way, she accepts him.

She is the first person who ever asks him a question about what he did in Vietnam; that she's a woman asking him blows his mind. He doesn't tell her much that's graphic, like about the heads lying on the ground the morning after Tet, or the pile of skulls they found one day that had been churned up out of what looked like a mass grave. The squad sat and held the skulls and rolled them in their hands; they were light, fragile as bees' nests. Higher command had wanted to know if these skulls were American or NVA, and the guys said, "Hell if we know." They moved on and kept walking, thinking that people had once been inside those skulls.

The romance with Carly is so intense it can't last, Stan can feel that. Still, they press on: he asks her if she thinks they can remain a couple after he returns to Fort Bragg. It's January now, he says; he'll be out of the Army in August, eight months off. Will she wait? Then he adds: "You should know I'm thinking of signing up for another tour. I want to go back to Vietnam." This scares the bejesus out of Carly. She's crying, telling him she loves him but she'd worry constantly that he'd be killed. He promises that he won't be going back.

He returns to Bragg to finish his hitch. They talk on the phone; each night he thinks of her. Eventually she stops answering his calls. Eight months later, he receives his discharge from the Army. He's free; he's done his service. At twenty-two years old, he's been shot, blown up, stabbed, and shot down; he's surprised he's still alive. He once again finds his whole life ahead of him. In high school, he'd joined the Army. This time, he doesn't have a next move—except love. Love, he thinks—a woman's acceptance of him—will save him from destruction, or so he believes. He drives to the nice part of town and knocks on Carly's front door. Her mother answers and says, "Carly can't talk right now."

Is she home? Stan wants to know.

"She can't speak to you," Mrs. Mother says. She closes the door, and Stan's heart breaks.

It's fall, 1969. The decade is ending. Something new is coming, but Stan doesn't know what it is. He's sure he must leave Indiana to make a way for himself. He must change if he's going to be happy. He knows this. The boy he thought he was—that boy has fled.

When Dwight Lane comes home to Woodville, Indiana, from the war, he hitchhikes the last few miles to his family's farmhouse. His mom, Verneil, and dad, Earl, are still at work; his mom is a housekeeper and Earl operates the sewage plant at the nearby state mental hospital, and the house is empty. It's snowing when the last car drops him off.

How does a man come home? When you have seen terrible things, shot, killed, maimed, quivered, and quaked at the moment of truth, with the shells coming in, how do you come home from this? Dwight stands at one of those old picture windows, single pane, thick, like the glass of an aquarium, and as he stands close to it, he can feel the winter coolness seeping through from the other side. He looks at the cornfield out the window with the snow falling and the cut-off yellow cornstalks holding a dusting of dry snow on their cut tops, about the diameter of sawed-off leg bones, hundreds of them lined in rows, knee high, their tops mounded with snow. The bones go on and on, row after row.

Dwight is tired and sunburned and the house is so quiet and so empty of anything, but especially the guys. The guys. Where are they? He is sure he is about to crawl out of his skin.

Tim Anderson comes home to Tacoma, Washington, and to a party in his honor hosted by his parents. There's a heavy snow falling outside, a freak storm, and after spending months in Vietnam, the cold weather is disorienting. Tim stays up in his bedroom, refusing to come down. Finally he walks outside and finds a friend standing in the snow, smoking a joint. He tells Tim that as soon as the roads clear, he's heading to California, and one day not long after that the two of them take off in an old mail truck headed to Long Beach, where Tim will stay drunk for most of two years. To make enough to eat, he starts stealing cars from dealerships; he won't steal from people on the street, that's a rule. This is a job, he feels; he's not a criminal. Nothing in his boyhood would have predicted he'd become a car thief, but it seems to him that after Vietnam, all bets are off. One day, he wakes up and realizes that he can no longer remember the war in detail—the things that happened, the things he did. The war seems to have happened to another person altogether. He decides to quit stealing cars and go straight. It's time to start a new life. He wants to go home.

On the day he decides this, he's driving back to Tacoma in the last vehicle he'd stolen. He plans to get home and park the car on a side street and walk away, leaving this old life behind. He hopes the cops find the car and can easily return it to its owner. He wants to make amends. For two years, he's been successful at his trade; now, flashing lights appear in his rear windshield. He's being pulled over. The cop starts to write a ticket for a busted taillight, and when Tim can't provide the correct papers, he's arrested. He spends six months in jail, gets out early for good behavior, and starts working construction. Years later, two things will have happened. He'll have had a successful career as a building foreman overseeing construction of schools, high-rises, and office buildings, and he will wake up in his house in Ocean Park, Washington, in sight of the ocean, wondering about Charlie Pyle. He can hardly remember much of it. Had he dreamed it all? Had he made Pyle up? He will write in a journal, "Being in Vietnam was the most important year of my life. And I remember almost none of it."

Michael Bradshaw comes home to California one afternoon and knocks on his parents' front door and discovers that his mother and father have changed too in his absence. His father opens the door dressed in a bathrobe, his now-long hair pulled back in a ponytail, rock music playing somewhere in the house. His mother walks up smiling and wearing a tie-dyed caftan and invites him inside. Were these the parents who wouldn't let him listen to the Rolling Stones? What has happened? Over time, Bradshaw will be orphaned twice, first by the war from which he's borne as a soldier, then by this homecoming: the place he left behind is not there when he returns, even though his parents are glad and welcoming. Over time, Bradshaw, hardworking, a loving father, devoted husband, will hit the road in an RV and fetch up in parks and campgrounds around California, moving with the seasons, working as a land surveyor, a job that keeps him in the woods and on mountaintops, always scouting, always on the move, always coming home, thinking of the men he once knew in the war.

Returning home, Dwight Lane tries to make sense of Charlie Pyle's death and discovers, as far as he can tell, that there isn't any. *It happened. Charlie died.* This is the best he can come up with.

Dwight had joined the Army to escape Indiana and see the world. Growing up, he often wondered about the scars his father had gotten in World War II, which the old man never talked about. It will be years—on his father's deathbed, in fact—before his father will tell Dwight what he thinks of that war, marching across Europe, the bodies that will spring up in his field of vision years later, back in Indiana, when he's just idling along in his life, trying to be Dwight Lane's father, and sometimes failing, sometimes succeeding.

But if Dwight had been able, as he knelt in the rice paddy with Charlie Pyle in his arms, Dwight would have chosen, with all of his might, at that moment, to slide forward in time and come to a rest at his father's deathbed, and he would have bent close to his father's lips and listened as the old man explained how to understand the death of Charlie Pyle. What would his father have told him? he wonders. *Accept it? Move on? Accept death?* He doesn't know what his father would have said. And he knows that he never will.

The truth is, the platoon loved Pyle in those moments when he was with them alive, and then he was gone. Afterward, after the war, they never look for his family, for his friends. They never look for any sign of him after the war. They remember him, though. They never forget him.

No one looks for Pyle, that is, except for Dwight Lane. Each year, when March 22 rolls around, the anniversary of Pyle's death, Dwight is antsy, irritable, ill at ease. A certain malaise comes over him, as the world does not seem a right place to live. Each year is the same. His friends notice his mood change, coming on strong like the change of seasons, always coinciding with spring, the bloom of the lilac in the middle of Indiana. As an older man, he lives alone in a nice house filled with cigarette smoke and Clive Cussler paperbacks spread on a kitchen table, the house never quiet because of the TV in the next room, a house by the side of the road. There's Dwight, sitting at the kitchen table and looking out at the sunlight of the spring day, every year, until finally, in 1990, he decides it's time and he gets up and walks out to his pickup truck.

He drives into town and parks in front of the florist shop and waits a minute. He walks in, says hello to the clerk at the counter, and fills out the order form for the floral arrangement with a ballpoint pen. He orders something nice that will last awhile and that people can see from a ways off in the graveyard. "How do you want the card to read?" the clerk wants to know, and Dwight says, *"To Charlie: You are not forgotten, and you never will be."*

He writes it on the card and pays for the order. The clerk picks up the phone and dials the florist in Colleyville, Texas, says a few pleasantries, and this ritual will play itself out year after year for twenty-five years, always the same call, nearly the same banter between the florists on each end of the line, and then the clerk hangs up and says, "Will there be anything else, Dwight?"

and he says, "No, I don't believe so." He leaves and gets in his truck and drives back home, the oiled dirt roads empty and rolling through oak forests, his boyhood haunts, the Red Rock River low and forever running in the same direction, away from town. Dwight, on days like these, after posting the order for the flowers, wonders what would have happened to his life had he not gone to Vietnam, had Charlie Pyle not been killed. Would Charlie *not* dying have made any difference in his life, which is like asking whether his life would have been different if there hadn't been so much sadness. What would have happened had he *not* gotten a job after the war working in factories, making batteries and shower cabinets and steel gears for diesel trains and earth-movers, thirty-three years, finally, walking on cement floors, lifting steel, breathing that air, that same air? He wonders why he had to come home so angry at the world. He thinks about what would have happened if so many things had not happened, and he can't know if his life would have been better or worse. His life is what it is, right? The sum total of his experiences.

Each year, the price of flowers creeps up, but who cares? He imagines the bouquet arranged carefully on Charlie's grave; imagines it sitting on the grave in the sun and through the dark of night. He's now on near-total disability from the war—PTSD, bad back, insomnia—and he spends little of his money. After 9/11, there's little incentive to travel, to see the world, because these days you have to take your shoes off in the airport, and it just seems so much hassle to go anywhere. At night, the visions of Charlie and so many other things come back.

Each time Dwight orders flowers, he promises himself, "I'm going to go to Texas, and I'm going to see Charlie's grave, and I'm going to bring flowers myself." But he doesn't know if he'll ever have the courage.

Then, in 2008, Dwight Lane decides it's finally time to visit.

He finds the cemetery in Texas and walks the rows until he locates the simple marker placed there, a bronze plaque cemented into the ground. He remembers a young man who died so young that he can only recall a boy. Nineteen years old. Charlie Pyle, the sweet handsome boy killed by the war, too young. And the world went on without him.

In Vietnam, after the slaughter of Charlie Company by the NVA, Al Dove had taken pictures of the dead and their half-ruined faces and said, "Somebody is going to pay for this," meaning he was going to make someone pay. Years later, he knows this was understandable but foolish thinking. What he did in the war and what happened in the war, no one cares, it seems. People don't talk with him about the war; no one calls him baby killer, rapist, psycho. His service in Vietnam is not an issue with anyone; it's as if he were never there. America, he thinks, doesn't think about Vietnam at all, except when it thinks about Afghanistan or Iraq as these wars slink into "quagmire."

In 1989, twenty years after coming home, something funny happens that brings his war to life again.

Late one night in Southern California in his condo, he can't sleep, so he gets up and turns on the TV and there's the History Channel. He sits down and watches and, by god, he thinks he catches sight of an old buddy, Brian Lewis. It might be some old footage somebody had; Bob Cromer had a movie camera at one time, and for a while it seemed he was always taking movies. But Al doesn't really remember what Cromer did and did not do. And he hasn't seen Lewis in years, can't remember the last time he saw him, in fact. Was it in Bien Hoa, when they were headed home?

The truth is, Al can't remember, but he does know that as he sits on his couch in Southern California, that he's watching

Lewis on the History Channel, back in Vietnam, when they were young. It seems like time travel. Al watches and thinks, *He's still alive. Thank god for that.* Then after this, in 1997, a second weird thing happens. Al's down at the mechanic's garage near his house where he works restoring cars, and he's shooting the breeze with a buddy, and he hears a voice and it's Jerry Austin's. He swears it is. Coming at him through the years, as if it's been launched from another galaxy and had been traveling all this time to intercept him in this garage.

Al looks up and sees this guy walking away from him, just his back, shaped in a white T-shirt. Is that really Austin, could it be? He'd heard Jerry was dead, he can't remember. Tom Soals had called him in 1980 or 1981 and said that Austin had died and that he wanted him to know this, and now Al yells out, "Jerry!" and the guy turns around, and it is him. Not dead. Al sees what's happening before Jerry does, that they're being reunited. Al looks at Jerry, taking it in. He's having trouble placing Al's face, and Al says, "It's me, Jerry! Al Dove. *DOV-UH*," he says, repeating the platoon's nickname for him, and Jerry's face turns white. They walk toward each other, and as they get closer, they hold their arms out and they draw each other in and hold on and each of them is crying. They learn they've been living near each other for at least a decade.

It isn't surprising that Dove thinks Jerry's been dead these many years. On May 21, 1969, after surviving the Tet, and while most everyone else returns to the States, Jerry extends his tour. During a battle, he's wounded so badly that he was tagged as dead and put in a body bag. Several hours later, someone at Grave Registration sees the bag move, opens it, and inside is Jerry Austin, alive. Rumors of his death, however, persist and eventually spread among former members of the platoon.

Seven months and two medical operations later, Jerry is

released from a military hospital at Fort Lewis, Washington, and returns to California. Occasionally he bumps into guys he used to know in Vietnam, and often they tell him they thought he'd died over there. He never gets used to hearing of his own demise, but neither does he feel he's really alive. He's living in a half-world between what had been his existence in Vietnam and the prospect of creating a life in California.

When he'd been discharged from the Army, he'd received no debriefing about life after the war, and he has no way of knowing what to do when he meets people on the street who seem to hate him for having been a soldier. He assaults three police officers when they tell him that all Vietnam veterans are alike: trouble-makers. He's charged with felonious assault.

On the day of his court arraignment, Jerry appears before a judge who happens to have been a World War II veteran, and who had once been in trouble himself twenty-five years earlier for disorderly conduct after his Army discharge. He promises Jerry that if he seeks counseling, he'll reduce the charges to misdemeanors, with three years of probation. He also threatens Jerry with prison time should he break the law again. Jerry eagerly agrees to this second chance, and over time, like Stan Parker, he finds steady, profitable employment as an iron worker. He leaves behind the backpacking and mountain climbing he enjoyed before the war and takes up sport fishing in a boat he names *Geronimo*, the word paratroopers sometimes shout when they jump from aircraft. Hardworking, generous to others, he nonetheless keeps largely to himself, preferring the open water to idle conversation.

He's in the garage today checking his boat's engine repair. On many days, Al has seen the boat steam into the harbor with a man at the wheel and looked at him but never thought it was Jerry Austin. On the hull of the boat were these big letters spelling *Geronimo*. Al had often wondered who in the world would name his boat after a paratrooper's cry. Austin had. All these years he'd thought Jerry was dead.

After years of thinking about Wongus but never calling him, Stan finally reaches him near Christmas 1996, in Connecticut, where he's living with his mother, and Stan says, after all this time, "Francis, how you doing?"

Francis says, "Oh, hi, Parker. It's great to hear from you."

They talk for several minutes and Stan realizes that Wongus doesn't remember him. But in the next second, he seems coherent. It seems that Francis Wongus is high or stoned. Stan wants to reach out to him, take his hand, hold it, and say to him, "Wongus, buddy, 'member that time in February 1968, when we fired up them VC on ambush and they hit us with mortars?" and Francis Wongus says, "Who am I talking to?" His mother picks up the line and says, "Francis can't talk anymore," and she hangs up and Stan is holding the phone to his ear, frozen in place, saying, "Francis."

Stan calls him again a year later. A woman answers the phone, and says "Hullo?" and Stan says, "Is Francis there?" and she gets real quiet and says, "No. Who's this?"

"It's Stan Parker."

"Oh, you," she says. "You should have called him again. After you called last, he was agitated. Why didn't you call him?" and Stan says, "Why? What's happened?" And she says, "Francis is dead, Mr. Parker. He died." Stan picks up from the conversation that either drinking or an overdose killed him. They talk a little while, but none of it explains anything. Stan will never really know what happened to Francis after the war, the places he went. He will never know how he died. Yet Francis's mother made Stan feel that somehow his death was his fault. *Why didn't you call him again and keep him alive?* But Stan knows his death was not his fault. *Why didn't you call him again?* And it's a good question, but what she's saying is: *You were one of the few who understood him. Why didn't you call?*

Stan had called Francis Wongus because he missed him, and he missed the Army. The longing had begun years earlier, shortly after he was discharged on August 7, 1969. Set free, he doesn't know what to do with himself, so he travels around. He visits a friend in Detroit, returns to Gary, Indiana, and turns south to Louisiana, punching the GTX muscle car along country two-lane blacktop, 90, 100, 135 mph. He knows exactly where he's headed eventually—back home, and he knows what job he'll do—he'll be an ironworker, like his dad. He doesn't mind this choice; it's honorable, skilled work. But it's not combat. It's not the Army. He feels the old pull of his experience in Vietnam so much that in October, once he's back in Gary, he tries to reenlist with the 82nd Airborne but, because he's already completed his hitch, Army policy prevents him from signing up again. He enrolls in an ironworker's apprenticeship program and turns his energy, his anxiety, toward making a living in civilian life.

At about this same time, he gets reacquainted with Anna Runion, whose high school picture he had carried in his shirt pocket, beside Mo's and Carol's. Whenever he came home on leave, he'd call Anna, but she always seemed busy working in the personnel office at a local company, Inland Steel.

One day he's driving in the neighborhood when he sees a woman walking to her mailbox. He spins his GTX around and pulls into the drive, ready to introduce himself. She walks toward his car; she seems to recognize him but he can't place her face; she's beautiful. He's mesmerized. She surprises him by saying, "Hello, Stan, I heard you were back from the Army."

Now the pieces fall into place.

"Anna?"

"All one hundred percent of me," she says.

Stan blurts, "How about a date?"

"I would. But I have a boyfriend."

"It doesn't matter," says Stan. "I'll take you out after your date. I'll wait for you anywhere."

Anna considers the prospect. She knows Stanley Parker—knows him from the neighborhood, from high school, from the mobile home park where they once both lived and were best friends. She understands in an essential way Stanley Parker's life, even though she has not seen him for more than three years and doesn't really know what he'd lived through in Vietnam. She knows he's just come home, and that a lot of boys coming home are silent and angry. But Stan seems different. He is smiling and talkative, hungry to enjoy himself and make sure others around him feel fine too. She agrees to the date.

She spends the first several hours of the next evening with her steady boyfriend, then several more after that with Stan, where over dinner they talk for hours. He can't believe the transformation; six years earlier she'd been a pigtailed sophomore, but now . . .

He wonders too how he's changed. He knows the answer, and he can see that she knows too. Yet she talks with him about the war, about his future plans, which soon turns to talking about their plans together. Within a matter of weeks, they're going steady and by April are engaged. In August 1970, they're married. They pack up and head for Wyoming the day after the wedding, where Stan has a job waiting.

Stan refocuses all his energy on home life and learning his trade as an ironworker. But no matter how hard he works at this—and he's a diligent, excellent worker; a caring father and husband—he can't resist: a year after he marries, he secretly tries to reenlist, and again he's told he's ineligible for service. He decides he won't tell Anna. He starts following the ironworking circuit, bringing his family with him. His plan is to make a good living and to be the father to his children that his father was to him.

He finds high-paying work in Wyoming, Montana, Colorado, South Dakota, and Nebraska. By the end of 1976, he and Anna have two sons, Wesley, age three, and Jason, eight months old. In April of that year, shortly after Jason is born, and still hearing the call of military life, Stan learns from his brother Dub that, under a new Army program, he can join Special Forces in the U.S. Army Reserves.

Thinking this is too good to be true, and that the opportunity might somehow be snatched from him, Stan drives four hours to Denver and, without talking with Anna, quickly signs papers to become a member of the Colorado National Guard's 19th Special Forces Group Airborne. He'll have to regularly travel from Wyoming to Colorado, where the 5th Special Forces Battalion of the 19th Group is based, for training, but he'll still live with Anna and the boys and remain steadily employed as an ironworker. At age twenty-eight, after leaving the Army eight years earlier, he's an American soldier again. He couldn't be happier. But now he has to tell Anna.

When he gets home and explains what he's done, she's not thrilled; but neither is she angry. Stan is relieved and grateful. Anna has come to see that his Army experiences have formed Stan into the man he is, the man she loves and admires. A part of him will never really be happy if he isn't facing the prospect of combat, or training for combat. He seems to need something— some force, some prospect of danger—out there, in the world that he can face and try to overcome. This need is a fact of his life, the way other men need golf, or alcohol, or mountain climbing to function. The problem, as they both understand it, is that Stan's lifestyle includes jumping from airplanes, blowing up things, shooting guns, and being shot at. He promises Anna, just as he'd promised his mother years earlier, that he'll be careful, Troop.

Stan completes the U.S. Army's Special Forces Qualification Course at Fort Bragg, a three-month trial involving grueling physical and psychological challenges that students describe as life-changing and mind-bending; 60 percent of them don't finish the course. Newly minted as a Special Forces soldier, he embarks for the world's hot spots, and nearly every year for the next seventeen years, he's absent for several months at a time, deployed in Korea, Honduras, the Philippines, and Thailand, often returning home on Sunday to resume his job as an ironworker on Monday.

After a while injuries start to pile up; while ironworking, he falls off a thirty-five-story steel structure in Wyoming, crashes through several stories of plywood decking, and lands in a safety net; he survives with a broken jaw. During military training, his parachute malfunctions at twelve hundred feet over Idaho during a night jump, and he missiles 95 mph to earth, where he lays with a broken back and cracked ribs for hours before rescue. At home, he gets thrown off a horse and crushes three vertebrae in his back. In his career, he'll make 503 static line parachute jumps, and in the process break numerous other bones, including his pelvis. His capacity for injury, and for surviving it, will remain endless. He suffers each smack of the earth against his head, each crack of a leg on a tree or iron girder, with detachment and curiosity.

Throughout his post-Vietnam life, he rarely talks about the war unless he's with another veteran, and few people ask. One day, though, in 1983, while standing at a gas pump outside Fort

Carson in Colorado, a man notices Stan's billed cap, lettered with "Vietnam Veteran," and he asks if he was really there, fighting. Stan says he was. The man sticks out his hand and says, "Welcome home." It's a quick gesture, facile, even, but the man seems to mean it and its effect on Stan is titanic. No one in civilian life, during the fourteen years he has been home, has ever said anything like this before. That's okay, he thinks. That's okay: he's in the Army again; it's his home now, along with his home with Anna and the boys. He feels he's where he belongs. He cannot wait to get home and tell Anna about this stranger's kind words.

But still, memories of the war are ever-present, persistent. For a while after leaving the Army, he saw a shape in his mind's eye—green, oblong, a machine with a bent tail. At first, he didn't recognize the shape or why he was seeing it. A competent sketch artist, he whiled away time in restaurants drawing on place mats as the shape flickered on the paper, like film stuck in a projector. With each sketch, a detail emerged, until finally, after several weeks, the green shape snapped into focus. What he'd been seeing was the medevac helicopter he was in and which was shot down. He can taste the exhaust, the hot wind, feel the rifle kicking as he fires at the charging enemy soldiers. About this experience, he tells no one except Anna.

Other times, the dreams are nightmares. Anna will wake him and say, "You're having another one?"

"Yep, I sure am."

"Like the other ones?"

"Just like the others."

"In the dream," he tells her, "I'm in a firefight and we're close to being overrun. It's like, if we get overrun, we're done. I'm finished. I'm not going to make it this time. I'm frantic. I mean, there's too many of them."

And then, if he can't fall back to sleep, he often starts thinking about the boys who didn't make it. Sometimes, he thinks about Kass, Pyle, Lintner, and Specialist Marvin Penry.

Penry was a forward observer in Echo Company's mortar platoon. It was Penry's job to crawl close enough to the enemy to radio back accurate coordinates for artillery and mortar strikes. Penry was a good soldier, quiet, steady, he never made a mistake in communicating coordinate information.

One day, Stan bumped into Penry at camp as the platoon was refitting and getting ready to head back on patrol. Penry said he was headed to Hawaii, where he would meet his wife and take some R&R.

"Man, Penry, this is great," said Stan. "You're so lucky. I am happy for you. You get to see your wife and have a good time." He meant it.

Penry, being a nice guy, said, "You know what? I'll give her a kiss for all of you guys."

"Oh, yeah," said Stan, "you give her a big hug."

Penry got on a chopper and Stan waved good-bye as it took off.

Then Stan and the rest of the platoon got word that they had a mission. A rifle company was caught in a bad firefight and they needed help. The chopper crew told them they would be heading into a hot LZ. They would be coming under fire as they landed.

Well, when they landed, the LZ was engulfed in a bad firefight. When it was over, eight paratroopers had been killed and forty-two wounded, including five from Recon.

Stan was surprised when First Sergeant Koontz walked up and said, "Parker, you know what? I think Penry was here."

"What do you mean?"

"He came here because of the firefight. The pilot diverted the chopper to help out."

Stan felt a sense of panic. He started asking around in the platoon: Had anyone seen Penry? Had they? Nobody had seen him.

How could Penry have been here? Stan wondered. Just that morning he'd watched him fly away from this place to another world altogether, to another story altogether that didn't end daily with death or sadness, a story in which Penry got off a plane in Hawaii and sat by a swimming pool with a cool drink, beside his beautiful wife.

When Stan saw First Sergeant Koontz again, Koontz told him straightaway, "I found out that Penry is dead."

Oh, no, thought Stan. *No.*

"Far as I can figure out," said Koontz, "is that Penry heard of the firefight from the chopper crew and he told them, 'Those guys are going to need a forward observer. Put me down.'"

And the chopper had landed and let out Penry, who came under ambush. He jumped into a depression with four other soldiers, a bomb crater, to ride out the flying bullets. The crater had been booby-trapped with a 105mm artillery round, wired to explode remotely. The enemy exploded the trap.

Sergeant Koontz said Penry was probably killed instantly.

"Are you sure?" said Stan.

Koontz said he was.

Stan sat down, looked off at the green hills, and stared. He ran through the sequence of events, as if by retelling them they would make more sense, be more logical, that they would make sense at all. Why would any man get off a chopper to freedom to be put back in this hell? And Stan knew, or he guessed that maybe he knew—love.

But for . . . for what? Love for your fellow soldiers, for the life you had with them, for the constant ache it engendered in your mind, that each minute was precious because each minute might be the final one . . . ?

But Penry had seemed so *happy* about seeing his wife when he'd said good-bye. His getting off the helicopter didn't make sense, at all. How could he do that? How?

None of this—the killing to stay alive, the feeling this would never end—made any sense. Now Penry's wife was in Hawaii and somebody had to find her and tell her that he was dead.

Stan wanted to reach out, stop him, shake him. "Penry!"

As his injuries mount, and his deployments quicken, Stan and Anna decide that, in the interests of his health and welfare, he needs to choose one job or another. By 1994, his deployments are stretching to seven months long and he quits ironworking and resumes life as an active duty soldier. He is assigned to Special Operations Command Central (SOCCENT) and sent to the Middle East. In 1997, after graduating from the U.S. Army Sergeants Major Academy, he begins active duty with U.S. Special Operations Command (USSOCOM) and is selected as the command's Senior Non-Commissioned Officer of the Year. Stan is thrilled with his career; Anna, who quit a successful brokerage job in Colorado to follow Stan to a new home in Florida, is understanding, though her worries mount that any day an unexpected knock at the door will announce Stan's death. Between 1994 and 1997, he deploys to Jordan, Somalia, Kenya, and Eritrea, and in 2004 he goes to Afghanistan, where I meet him one year later as we board a Chinook helicopter headed for the Pakistani border. He's fifty-eight years old and knows that his mandatory retirement date is approaching.

After we meet in Afghanistan, he flies home on leave, where Anna awaits him, happy once more that he is returning safely. As he takes his coach seat near the rear of the plane, dressed in his desert camouflage, a gentleman in a suit walks from the front of the plane and stops at Stan's seat and says, "I'd like to give you my seat in first class."

At first Stan is confused. Then he doesn't believe the guy's offer and says, "No." The U.S. Army had purchased the seat for him and he feels some obligation, being a good soldier, to follow through on expectations, and those were that he would fly home on the Army's dime. Sounds simple, but it's how Stan thinks. Follow orders.

The gentleman leaves and he returns to the front of the plane. Stan thinks, *That was nice.* And then he reflects how different it is from when he came home from Vietnam. Then he hears the captain's voice come over the intercom: "Ladies and gentlemen, we have a slight problem. And we can't take off until we get it fixed." And the captain goes on: "The situation is, we have a first-class passenger who wants to give his seat to a U.S. Army soldier who refuses to switch seats, because the Army bought his ticket for him. We need to encourage him to change seats."

And that's when the people around Stan start clapping for him; they stand and motion to the front of the plane, shooing *Go, Go,* and Stan reluctantly gets up, and then with a great whooshing feeling, takes a step down the aisle. When he gets to the first-class compartment, flight attendants hug him and ask what he needs. The captain comes over and says, "Welcome home, man." Stan sits back in the plush seat, stunned. *Why couldn't this have happened thirty-seven years ago?* he wonders. *Why? Where were you thirty-seven years ago when I came home scared and wondering what I'd done for the past year? Was I crazy? Had I become a crazy person?* And then he starts to wonder if these same people would be clapping for him if they knew, in addition to now serving in Afghanistan, that he is also a Vietnam veteran. The pain is so deep, the insecurity that deep, that these many years later he is still concealing from most people, unless they ask, that he fought in Vietnam.

More than two million Americans served in Vietnam and 58,282 were killed there. Nearly every day, mostly unknowingly, we meet people who fought in Vietnam; or we meet people whose sons and daughters, brothers and sisters, grandparents, mothers and fathers, cousins, distant cousins, neighbors, fought and came home, or fought and died in Vietnam. That sixty-eight-year-old man you see at the buffet line at the Holiday Inn on weekends? He's probably thinking about the war.

The Vietnam Veterans Memorial in Washington, D.C., is one of America's most visited memorials, and it is D.C.'s most visited site. In May 2012, President Obama presided at a ceremony at the memorial, marking the fiftieth anniversary of the U.S. entrance into Vietnam's civil war in 1962. The president told the gathered Vietnam veterans, "Often you were blamed for a war you didn't start. You came home and were sometimes denigrated when you should have been celebrated. It was a national shame, a disgrace that should have never happened."

Before he retired in January 2007, after forty-two years of being affiliated with the U.S. Army, Sergeant Major Stan Parker was informed by Army doctors that he would have to consult with a psychiatrist for an evaluation of his mental health as he exited the service.

Until this time, no one had ever really asked about his well-being. But someone at Special Operations Command, who was processing Stan's request for retirement, noticed his incredibly long record.

"They saw that I had some hairy combat time," says Stan, "and they wanted me to talk with somebody, to see how I felt."

In Vietnam, Stan's job had been to stay alive, and he and the Recon Platoon had accomplished this by killing. Death seemed an entity, a specter, a being, that sprang from the earth; it was always invisible but always present. He would try to explain this distinction to the psychiatrist treating him for PTSD. The best he could manage was by describing how the faces of the dead haunted him, and the sadness he felt that anyone at all had died. He also explained that he felt traumatized by coming home. Over time, he said, he'd found it a bit easier to articulate his feelings.

In the late 1980s, while working on a bachelor's degree, Anna had urged him to enroll in a writing course at a community college. He discovered that writing down some of his experiences made him feel better about them. His teacher, an empathetic young woman whom Stan believed didn't really, at first glance, understand his experience in Vietnam, insisted he write something for class. And then she asked him to read it. Stan was petrified. He showed up in class, holding his paper in hand. She asked to see it. He held it out and she took it, but he wouldn't let go.

Anna was with him and she whispered to him, "Let it go, honey. It's okay."

Stan opened his hand and released the story. He spent a worrisome night at home, wondering what the teacher's response would be when they met again. He feared she would dislike him for the feelings and actions he had described.

She approached him in the hall before class.

"The stains you see on the pages," she said, "are from my tears." As cliché as that might sound, Stan looked down and could see that the paper did look stained. "I had no idea what you'd gone through," said the teacher.

What did you think was happening there? he wanted to ask.

• • •

On May 7, 1999, Stan and his two sons, Wes and Jason, took part in a military air show at MacDill Air Force Base by parachuting out of a C-130 aircraft. Both sons had followed Stan's example of military service and Stan was proud to be jumping with them. Shortly after landing on the ground, Stan received a call from Anna. His father, she told him, had just died of pneumonia.

Stan was stunned. This man to whom he'd always been close was gone. He realized that if he hadn't been in the company of his sons, he likely would have broken down on the spot. Who was he now, he wondered, at this time in his life? Who?

He had been his father's son, he knew that; and now he was an older man, someone he believed his sons respected, just as he had respected his father. But who was he in his private moments—what did that shelf inside himself, where he'd stowed all those memories of the war—what did that place look like?

It wasn't until his retirement, while sitting in the Army psychiatrist's office at USSOCOM near Tampa, that Stan finally began to dig deeply. The doctor had suggested that he write more about his experiences, and now he asked him to read the pages aloud. "That's the next step," he said.

"But I can't." Stan feared that he'd see the lifeless faces again. "You have to."

Stan started reading. He had trouble breathing:

She was a young Vietnamese girl, very obviously a French Colonial descendant and I would guess to be about six or seven years old. Her clothes looked worse than mine. . . . I dropped to one knee as she put her fragile small skinny hand on mine and said, "Hi Airborne, GI number one."

Go on.

As I knelt on one knee looking at her a part of the war I had not seen before or not wanted to see before hit me square between the eyes.

I knew what death was, what hatred was, what frustration was, what fear was, what loneliness was, what hunger was, what war was, and even what love was but all of them through my eyes only.

Now for the first time I saw all this plus more in the eyes of this lovely, dirty-faced, raggedy clad little girl. . . . I wanted to take this poor little girl with me and in doing so hope I could stop the war for her.

Stan described handing her a can of peaches, and that she was then killed by NVA soldiers for accepting his gift.

The night was a long one. I could not get that little girl out of my mind. . . . As the sun was coming up I could hear the noise of something outside the partial building we were set up in. . . . Large rats were eating on the dead pitiful little girl's body across the street.

Without even thinking of what I was doing I raised up my M-16 and started firing at the rats. . . . I do not know how many I shot. My magazine went empty. As I was reaching for more ammo, one of my buddies handed me another full magazine. I fired it up. He handed me another. . . .

I reloaded my weapon, got up, and walked out to the little girl's body. . . . The rats had eaten off her nose, ears, and fingers of one hand. She still held the can of peaches in her left hand. My buddies say I screamed as loud as I could, I do not remember.

When Stan stopped reading his story, the doctor asked for the pages and, slowly, Stan placed them in his hands, just as he would, two years later, reach across the sunlit space in a helicopter in Afghanistan and touch my arm and say to me, "Will you write about us in Vietnam," and another five years after that, I would reach across his kitchen table in his Colorado home and take these pages too and begin this book.

When I meet Stan in Afghanistan, he tells me that he wants to understand what happened to him in Vietnam. I encourage him to organize a reunion of the platoon, and my wife and I decamp for the first of two trips to Huntington Beach, California, where some of his platoon-mates gather and a shared story begins to coalesce out of disparate, and often terrifying and darkly humorous, narratives.

When Stan returns home from the reunion, he continues writing. More memories spool out, many of them about the challenge hc feels years later of living in a world, a civilian one, a world void of war's dangers.

"I guess for me and thousands like me, that's part of the problem," Stan writes, explaining the self-confusion wrought by having been "asked to kill a bad guy at work on Monday of one week and then try[ing] to go out on a civilized date the Monday of the following week with a beautiful young woman, who has no idea what her date, a combat veteran, is all about."

Time can telescope years; a single moment can be so dense that it contains a universe. For the beholder of these perceptions, the effect can be terrifying. Memories strobe back and forth on one's consciousness, whipsawing emotions and thought processes. What Stan decided he needed was to return to Vietnam. By this journey, he hoped to untangle a year of his life so dense that its every minute seemed to have lasted a century. He hoped to come home, finally.

Think of it this way: perhaps the first step he took off the first helicopter in Vietnam, the first push of his boot into its soil, was the first step he took toward home.

En route to Vietnam in April 2014, when we are in the airport lounge in Tokyo, he tells me that he's afraid how he'll react when he meets a Vietnamese person. Will he be scared? Will he want to punch the person? He doesn't think so. But still, he believes that these feelings can come up, and his awareness of them within himself seems brave.

He admits to harboring anger, fear, resentment, even hatred for the Vietnamese people, and his acknowledgment of this also strikes me as an act of bravery. At the same time, he explains he doesn't feel any need to confront an enemy, or, specifically, the former enemy, the soldiers of the NVA and VC.

He wants to see the young man he was, and better know the man he's become.

...solution with myself & can bring Darryl Lintner'...
...eath out of my subconscious where it was burie...
...ntil the last couple yrs. I thought back then that...
...let my own guard down by becoming his friend...
...fter telling myself I did not want to get to know...
...ny new faces. But became his friend telling him...

PART III
HOMECOMING

...o stick with me & he would have a better chance...
...f staying alive. Because of what I told him I felt...
...hat I was responsible for his death & could not...
...ccept the fact that he was killed on my watch. I...
...eally want to talk to Darryl's friend(s) & let them...
...now what a great likeable person he was, how...
...much I enjoyed his friendship. Should I tell them...
...hat Darryl's death was so extremely painful &...
...oubled me be beyond words that I could not...
...neel down beside him that day & tell him how...
...much pain I was in.

...hat decision still haunts me to this day. It is all...
...can do right now to keep the tears out of my...
...yes thinking how ashamed I am of myself & my...
...elfish actions that day. Even tho he & I were...
...he same age he was so young because of his...
...outhful innocence at the time. Maybe I should...
...alk to you before I make the call.

2014

Colorado to Vietnam

Find him now, back in Vietnam.

We are a group of four: Stan Parker; Tom Soals, his former platoon-mate; Anne Stanton, my wife; and me. We've spent the day walking Saigon's streets.

Tom and Stan haven't seen each other in forty-six years. They've come together now because I called them separately and asked them to show me where they had fought, and where parts of them had died, in Vietnam. Both of them possess an abiding love for the men in the platoon and are eager to get reacquainted.

Stan has spent the years disliking the Vietnamese and parts of himself—or, rather, he's been ashamed of himself for a long time about a lot of things (that day he and the platoon started to burn the family's rice outside their hooch, for instance). After surviving Vietnam, he felt in some deep part of himself that there was not another place for him but in the military, in the middle of conflict.

Tom, I think, has spent some of these years wondering how to understand the meaning of his fighting in Vietnam. Often it feels as if it occurred in another lifetime, to another person. Tom's father was a Navy captain and there'd not been much question that his son wouldn't serve, but neither was Tom eager to die and fight in a war many of his peers wanted to avoid. His forfeiture of his college draft deferment, which his father had not opposed, was a brave, considered act and affirmation of his family's legacy, especially, as Tom saw it, while so many others without his advantages were being drafted. He will tell me that this return to Vietnam is overwhelming at times, as it is for Stan too. Stan, however, spent his remaining professional life in military service. Tom worked as a surveyor in Portland, Oregon; a building contractor; an outdoor camping supply employee; and an avid mountaineer, this last providing him with the adrenaline thrills he missed after leaving the Army. If Tom has lived further outside of, or away from, his experiences in Vietnam, Stan has been revisiting them during his long military career. The transformative experiences are potent for both men and never far from their minds. I think that each would still die for the other, though they may not agree on issues that pundits and cable news use to divide and atomize American society.

The truth is, the Vietnam veteran's journey home is entwined with a military and political "event" that tore America in half, the war itself, while the act of homecoming is neither political nor military, but emotional. Ironically, a war that split a country often deepened the bonds between the young men and women fighting its battles.

Our guide for the two-week trip is Bill Ervin, a former Marine who married a Vietnamese woman he met after the war, named Anh Kan. Bill Ervin fought near Khe Sanh, and Anh survived the war but not without witnessing the violence inflicted by American and North Vietnamese Army troops. They are a perfect partnership. Bill Ervin understands what American veterans of Vietnam expect to find when they return to the country. And Anh, a former news anchor on a large Vietnamese network, is affable and diplomatic as Stan and Tom's liaison with the Vietnamese people we meet.

We first visit the War Remnants Museum in Saigon, walking among dozens of wall-sized photographs graphically depicting battlefields covered with the mangled dead, which is to say these photos are bald depictions of what Americans did to the Vietnamese people. Landscapes burned by rolling waves of napalm. Bodies draped across the spindly shards of trees in bombed-out areas. The images smack you as you stand in the smartly lit gallery.

The museum depicts the blood and guts of combat in a way you never see in an American museum about the Vietnam War. It's also true that it'd be possible to mount the same graphic exhibition about combat during World War II. People are killed in all kinds of ways, but it tends to look the same, with blood and limbs everywhere.

During the war, millions of gallons of Agent Orange were sprayed on miles of jungle and countryside in order to deny the enemy sanctuary or cover. The resultant birth defects caused by Agent Orange range from children born missing limbs, to blindness, to severe spinal deformation. . . . In room after room, Stan and Tom stand before enormous photos of children damaged by Agent Orange. Two women, both with deeply bowed spines, sit at a nearby table soliciting donations for Agent Orange victims. The rooms go on and on. There is a related war museum in Hanoi, in the country's north, which is milder in its depiction of war's horrors. Our tour guide informs us that the Saigon museum is designed intentionally to be a more intense experience, as a way to punish the South for fighting the North in the first place. It's as if to say, "See what happens when we fight?" Most of the museum's patrons are Europeans, judging by the accents, and German and French at that. After several hours of wandering the exhibits, past other photos of NVA soldiers celebrating victory in battle, Stan and Tom are ashen faced and exhausted.

Our next stop is Cu Chi, where Stan and the platoon had first rolled up after landing in-country in mid-December 1967. Cu Chi was where they saw Raquel Welch dance onstage and where Stan had come face-to-face with his first NVA soldier, the man with the red star on his pith helmet, whom he was supposed to kill but did not.

We're relieved to be escaping the museum and Saigon's intense traffic of motorbikes. Bill Ervin pilots our van, Anh riding shotgun, through the city's sprawling industrial parks and into greener countryside. The area of Cu Chi has long been a vacation spot for Saigon residents; it's about thirty miles from the city center's opera house, yet heavily wooded. Today, the Vietnamese government has made this former Viet Cong sanctuary into a tourist park.

We pull up in our van and pay an admission fee to walk beyond a fence and enter into what was once part of a battlefield. The Cu Chi bunkers of the enemy army, the underground meeting rooms, and kitchens, as well as the tunnels, are available as a historical amusement and curiosity for paying customers to crawl and walk through. At nearly every corner of a groomed path, mannequins dressed as 1960s North Vietnamese soldiers appear to rear up, having been posed by park personnel in various combat stances. It's spooky and weird, even for me. Stan and Tom shy away from the mannequins whenever they see them up ahead. I can't tell if the Vietnamese government has placed the mannequins around the place to antagonize visiting Americans, but then I think, no. That's just my Americanness speaking.

At certain points, tourists like us—including Germans, French, Italians, Vietnamese—walk down a few hard-packed clay steps and, if they stoop over far enough, enter one of the famed tunnels of the Cu Chi complex. I am immediately claustrophobic, hunched over, essentially walking quickly ahead in a duck-like way, while Stan, at five feet nine, zips through the tunnel but says nothing. He doesn't enjoy it. The air inside is humid and smells like a recently excavated riverbank—not an unpleasant smell, but in a place whose history is filled with so much bloodshed, it's a bad smell.

We duck in and out of the tunnels and continue down the paths and occasionally confront the mannequins set around the park. Gunfire rings out, which makes the sight of the soldier mannequins even more ominous. Stan and Tom seem jumpy at the sound of the gunfire—the shooting grows incessant. Like a firefight. *Bam bam bam*, a metallic sound banging through the silver leaves of humid foliage. We follow the sound of the shooting and up ahead see some light in the tree canopy and come upon an open-air snack bar dotted with wooden tables. You can stand at the snack bar and order a Coke and sandwich and some ice cream and look ahead through a chain-link fence at a gun range.

Stan and Tom just stare at this. The shooting noise is muted by the canopy of woods, but still, it's loud, and I realize that this is likely how the gunfire sounded in these very woods when they were here in December 1967 and January 1968. It had to sound exactly like this because the guns being shot here are the same weapons used by the NVA. And this sound seems to be soaking into Stan's and Tom's consciousness, for they are growing ever quieter. This is a grim place to be.

We can see people, tourists, standing in a dugout, shooting the guns. They've paid a dollar a bullet to fire off a thirty-round clip at a paper bull's-eye target fifty feet away. That's not cheap; it takes about three seconds to fire off a clip.

I think the gun range idea is kind of strange, like operating a guillotine at an exhibit about the French Revolution.

We wander into a large gazebo area, the roof made of high-overhead thatch, and take seats on wooden folding chairs. There's a movie screen up front, and soon we're watching a black-and-white documentary about the Cu Chi area during the war. The Vietnamese call this "the American War," not "the Vietnam War." The footage is grainy, and the subtitled narration has the packaged feel of propaganda, which it is: the movie's narration makes fun of the American invaders who tend to flee from the enemy at the slightest hint of danger.

Suddenly from behind us, someone fires off a pistol—it's actually at the gun range but it seems closer—and Stan, sitting in the front row in his folding chair and watching this movie, jumps up and stiffens and goes into a spasm and then comes back down in his chair all within a matter of a second.

He lands and sits quietly, frozen. I can see his neck turn a little this way and that, as if he's scanning to see who's noticed his flinching at the sound of the gunshot. Mostly he just sits and stares straight ahead as the movie endlessly plays on, telling us more about the history of the area, that "Cu Chi is a 123-square-kilometer park," that the Vietnamese of the nineteenth century picnicked here, and so on, and about how cowardly the Americans were when they were here and how heroic the Vietnamese acted in the war. The movie ends, we all get up, and we're tired. I ask Tom and Stan how they feel. They mumble something; they don't want to answer the question directly. It would be to admit the terribleness of their experience here, that they had been hated by the North Vietnamese, which is an odd thing to state; of course, the Vietnamese had hated them. They'd been at war and killed each other by the thousands and thousands. But it was the hate they felt back home in the States, after the war, that haunts these guys. To realize they've also been hated, with perhaps as much vigor, by the Vietnamese is a shock. Or unpleasant. Or just plain sad to understand.

We walk quietly back to the van and drive back into Saigon, to the hustle and flow, where soon we are ensconced on the street with a friendly bar host who delivers a bucket packed with ice and bottles of Tiger beer sticking up in the ice like brown glass flowers.

Stan begins to cry in the dark humid night. He's wondering, he says, if we will judge him for something that happened earlier that day at Cu Chi, jumping the way he did at the sound of gunfire, when no one else reacted to the sound, including Tom. Of course not, we say, we won't judge you, and we mean it.

Traffic flows past in a momentous stream, just feet away from where we sit on the street's curb. Sometimes I can feel the wind of passing vehicles on my toes in their sandals. It feels odd to have bare feet in Vietnam after hearing Stan tell stories for so long about how violent the place was.

Stan grows quiet. His admission of vulnerability seems to be conjuring something like a confession, for he tells us, breathing in suddenly, that his son has a bone condition that may be connected to Agent Orange. He himself brought a rash back from Vietnam. After seeing a doctor for more than a year, he could never get a diagnosis. He's crying again. He says he "gave" this malady to his son by virtue of his having been exposed to the chemical (and which some studies have also concluded). It's then that Tom Soals tells us that two of his grandchildren were born with birth defects, including blindness and gastrointestinal problems, and died before the age of six. He too thinks this was caused by his exposure to Agent Orange.

I try to grasp the wreckage that Tom, Stan, and the Vietnamese are accounting for and have been living with. Granddaughters blinded by something that happened to Tom more than forty-five years earlier? This seems a trick of time; it *is* a trick of time. How can disease jump like that? And why hasn't Tom gotten sick? He may yet. Many thousands of Vietnam veterans suffer from disorders caused, it's suspected, by exposure to the toxin. The U.S. Department of Veterans Affairs has been reluctant to admit a causal relationship between Agent Orange and these maladies; no one has accepted responsibility for the dioxin's use in Vietnam, which may have resulted in hundreds of thousands of Vietnamese children being born with birth defects.

We can practically reach out and touch the thousands of motorbikes bleating past us. The commotion is, counterintuitively, soothing. As we sit on this street corner in Saigon, Tom and Stan realize that the Vietnamese people, the people of today, couldn't be more gracious. There's a strange disconnect between this warmth on the street and the graphic horror of the war museum. Later in our trip, in Hanoi, we hire a tour guide— twenty-four years old and born well after the war was over. For him, the war is something his grandparents fought in, the French and the Americans. Even the older Vietnamese seem to have forgotten the animosities. The economy in Vietnam is robust; Facebook works fine, if nonetheless subject to censorship; and Bill Clinton is an excellent American, for he opened relations with Vietnam in 1995, which kick-started the Vietnamese economy.

But how are the Vietnamese so cheery on the street? Or how can we walk down the street, we corn-fed Americans, and feel not the slightest sense, hint, or frisson of danger? The truth is, the Vietnamese don't seem to care if we're here. They don't seem to care that Stan and Tom are Vietnam War veterans, and probably came over here and killed somebody in their day. They don't seem to care that these Americans are back. Of course, to the victor go the spoils, and in this case, the spoils are this peace of mind, this sense that they, the Vietnamese, won the war. Nixon pulled out in 1975, the last chopper lifted off, and the North Vietnamese rolled in and the bloodbath began. We Americans turned away.

The Vietnamese have assimilated the pain of this violence—

they've had a thousand years of fighting—better than we Americans. We go to a museum where the truth is hung in black-and-white and Kodachrome color on the walls, and we're in total shock. We sit and drink beer on the street corner in Saigon and try to piece it together. But maybe there's no piecing to be done; maybe, I think, there's no sense to be made of this war. That the pain that many from the platoon have felt, still feel, is just their problem. It's all in their heads. But what nightmare isn't? And does this make the nightmare a fiction? What's to be done?

Who's watching?

Behind us on the street corner, something is watching. An aged woman nearby is selling goldfish. The bright fish sit swimming in water-filled plastic bags that she's placed on a metal cart. The bags jostle and roll, and the suspended fish grow and shrink in size, depending on the movement of the cart. First, one coal-dark eye dilates, then both eyes expand. An entire fish snaps into focus, floating, mouth opening and closing, as if trying to speak. I look at it while it looks past Stan Parker as he sits near the street and cries.

Who let whatever happened to Stan Parker, Tom Soals, and the Recon Platoon *happen*? Who's responsible? Who could've stopped it—whatever it is? Who could have?

And how do you survive something like that?

Time?

Does time heal all wounds?

A week later, we are at the village of Trung Hoa, where Stan was wounded on February 18, 1968.

We're forty miles northeast of Hue and within the thirty square miles of wooded area and rice paddies where Stan and the Recon Platoon did most of their fighting. This is where their journey began and Stan hopes it's where it ends now.

We are driving on a packed clay road, narrow like a cart path, shaded by trees and foliage none of us can name. Bill Ervin is driving and he stops in the middle of the road when Stan says, "Here, right here. I think this is the place."

What place?

The place where it all happened, where a part of Stan Parker died.

And just as soon as Bill Ervin has shut down the van, Stan opens the driver's-side door and steps out. I'm right behind him, and he has maybe two or three steps to take before he's off the side of the road and into the dusty vegetation growing alongside. He passes through this wall of trees, maybe fifteen feet high, and I lose him for a moment.

I step through the trees into sunlight and find Stan standing frozen in place.

He's staring at the ground, or somewhere at a point in the air I can't locate. He seems lost in thought. Whatever it is, it doesn't seem like a happy time for him.

What he's having is, suddenly, a flashback.

Up ahead I see houses and a farm field, the field being maybe fifty yards long and wide. Stan just stands there and doesn't move. He's looking ahead like a man who's afraid to move his head, as if he's got a sliver of glass somewhere in his neck that will kill him if he moves too quickly. I can hear the putter of life in the small village, a hamlet, really—the crack of an ax chopping wood, the close of a screen door somewhere, and Stan says to me, "I'm here."

Barely a croak of his voice.

"I'm here," he says again.

"Where, Stan? Where are you?"

"Where it happened."

He's trembling ever so slightly, and I put my hand on his

shoulder and then remove it. And I stand next to him, not knowing what to do.

"This is where it happened," he says again.

We are standing, he says, almost exactly where he fell in 1968 when he got grenaded by the NVA soldier: They'd grabbed each other, each of them dazed by the previous minutes' firefight.

Stan leads me a few feet to the left and points down at our feet, to a corner in the field, where the two edges of the dike come together, making a foot-high corner. A rice paddy that the farmer has let lie fallow. When Stan was last here forty-six years ago, it had been flooded and he was lying in water covering his face up to his eyes. As he lay there staring at the sky unblinking, the NVA soldier who'd just thrown the grenade at him walked over the edge of the dike and peered down and pointed the barrel of his AK-47 straight at Stan's face.

Stan had played dead and looked at the opening of the barrel, which had seemed incredibly tiny and infinite at the same time. So much of the future would be answered or created by what came out of that barrel. He stared at the barrel, his face a mask, until the NVA soldier decided Stan was dead and, distracted, turned and went off.

Now he can't believe he's back in this rice paddy. How had this happened so quickly? He had simply stepped out of the van and walked down the slight embankment and through the weeds and trees and into the past, and now he's standing here, trembling.

I can hardly believe we're here, either. So easily.

Our journey had begun in Colorado, with Stan looking at maps and identifying the villages, using U.S. Army After-Action Reports (AARs) to identify places where the platoon may have fought. Since Stan had spent his adult life reading maps in the

Army, he was able to find Trung Hoa and LZ Jane without a lot of trouble. Using the AAR as reference, he decided that Trung Hoa was the place where his attack on the machine-gun position of February 18, 1968, had happened. The idea that he might find the rice paddy this quickly had not occurred to him.

Now he grows more animated and starts walking around the small ten-by-ten area where he'd dropped down and fired the antitank rocket across the road; the scrim of trees hadn't been here in 1968. From where Stan had been prone on the ground and fired the rocket, we could hit the van with a quick toss of a stone. Bill Ervin has opened the van's back hatch, and he and Anh are unpacking a picnic basket and preparing lunch. We're going to stop right here and eat in the road. That's how small the village of Trung Hoa is. One hundred people, maybe. Tops.

I can't believe how compact everything is, the distance between the place from which he fired the rocket and the target itself. After hearing Stan Parker talk about this rice paddy so many times, in his retelling, in Colorado, as snow fell outside the kitchen window as we drank coffee, and over the phone, or in text messages, the rice paddy had grown in my mind to immense proportions. I had thought it was maybe one hundred yards long at least. Stan had set off running down the rice paddy, charging the machine-gun position at its end. His entire being was focused on reaching this machine gun. As we look through the trees and listen to Bill and Anh talk about what kind of sandwiches to have for lunch, Stan spots something across the road, about fifty feet away.

"That's where it was," he says.

The machine-gun position.

He's found it, or found a place on which, once upon a time, his entire being had been focused, in a kind of ecstasy. He had taken off running at this place, pretty certain he was going to die. We walk back up the embankment and through the trees and cross the road, which is pleasant underfoot, cool and soft yet packed, and it gives off the sense of having been used for centuries. But, in fact, who knows? It may be just as old as Stan himself. We keep walking. Yet we seem to be walking back through time, and in time, and even, somehow, ahead in time, as Stan re-creates himself here at this moment, reintegrating those parts that had so long sat in pieces around the floor of his life.

"Yep," Stan says. "Here it is."

He reaches up and parts the plants around an object, and we see a concrete obelisk of some sort, a bit taller than a mailbox back in the United States, but what is it? Hard to say. There's writing in Vietnamese on the obelisk. And since Anh is too far away to ask her to translate, we let it go for the moment. Something else catches Stan's eye: a house across the road. Its roof is made of metal, and the walls are poured concrete. It's sturdy, built with care. It sinks in that someone is living here now, that this is a place of pride for someone. Stan realizes that this is the building he'd destroyed by blowing up the machine-gun position, which is now marked by the obelisk. The ammo around the machine gun had exploded, then started cooking off, sending all kinds of shrapnel flying everywhere, flaming pieces of wood, which had whiz-banged through the air and landed on the now-concrete house, and set it on fire. Then, the house had been made of thatch, even the roof, and it crackled and burned rapidly. Stan was lying there in the rice paddy across the road and heard the machine-gun ammo cook as he waited for his buddies to come get him. He was bleeding from the hole on his right side. He was twenty years old and had no idea that he would ever be back in this place, that someday he'd meet me on a helicopter in Afghanistan, and ask me, "Would you write about our journey in Vietnam?"

• • •

Stan calls Anh over to translate what's on the obelisk. It's a black granite column, about twelve inches across. Anh begins: "In honor of the Vietnamese and American soldiers who died here on February 18, 1968."

Anh reads this and Stan and Tom Soals are silent. Stan can't comprehend that the Vietnamese have erected a monument marking this place that he'd thought of so often and that certainly no one in the United States had heard about. How could they even know of this place since he had told so few people of this firefight? He had told so few people anything about the war. That someone in Vietnam, particularly *his former enemy*, had thought to erect this monument gives him a soaring feeling, a sudden feeling of liberation. Who had done this? Who had made the monument? Who had consecrated this place with this gentle and obscure act? Who had been watching?

His enemy had.

He then realizes, of course, that the monument isn't necessarily for him; the people who put it up had lost people in this firefight, and during the longer battle of that day. He's thought of the dead often. Darryl Lintner's death still haunts him.

The death of the little girl too, clutching the can of peaches, has haunted him. He's thought about the NVA soldiers and Viet Cong he's killed, but differently now. They were doing a job and he was doing a job, and, well, he'd been more successful at it than any of those he killed. At the same time, he understood just how random the dying had been. One minute a man was there; the next, he was just bone and mist and, then, nothing. A bloody spot on the ground.

"Come this way," Stan says, "I want to show you where Tinkle and Hinote got shot."

Their wounding is what had precipitated Stan Parker's charge across this rice paddy, toward the machine gun that had shot them—the place where the obelisk now stood. We step through the dry and stiff stalks of plants and weeds, walking along the edge of the rice paddy and go through people's yards, past their houses, with me gesturing and asking if it's okay that we pass through, as they come out of their houses and stand in their doors and look at us and I can see some of them thinking, *There goes another American, looking for the past.*

Do they know what had happened here forty-six years earlier? A middle-aged man says he was too young, but sends us to a house at the end of the road. A figure appears on the road, a short, thin man, with a shock of black hair flecked with strands of silver. He's maybe Stan's age. He walks up to us without saying a word. He's looking at us but not looking at us, and he's having that very universal thought, I think, which is *What am I about to get into here?* when meeting a stranger in a familiar place. Anh says a few words to him in Vietnamese. Stan and Tom are quiet. All of the time we've been in the village, which has been about thirty minutes, Stan has been wondering if he would meet any local Vietnamese who had fought in the war, and who, preferably, had fought in this area during the war. Now with the arrival of this man, Stan's on high alert. He stands off, maybe six feet away, appraising the situation with Tom Soals. I, the reporter, am leaning close to listen as Anh and the man talk back and forth in Vietnamese, a tongue whose music I can't fathom. I'm reminded as I look at Stan that maybe he's standing as he did a long time ago, back in Arkansas, or Texas, on the school yard, when meeting someone new. There's something innocent and vulnerable in the look on his face, something expectant, in the upturned smile on his face. Still, he looks troubled too, or ready to be troubled. We're standing on the road in front of the van and the sun is out, and the air smells fragrant, humid. It's the right kind of day for a picnic, and there's something peaceful and relaxing about this sudden meeting with this gentleman, who introduces himself as Mr. Sinh, as we prepare to have our picnic. I don't know how to describe this except to say that everything that's happening seems like it's supposed to be happening. At the same time, I realize—and Stan and Tom realize—how weird this is to be in this village and meeting Mr. Sinh. The words that come out of Anh's mouth next surprise Stan and Tom: "He says he was here."

"Here, when?" Stan wants to know.

Anh says a few more words in Vietnamese and then begins to speak in English, then stops and returns to Mr. Sinh in Vietnamese, her body language saying, "Are you sure?" And Mr. Sinh nods his head yes, and Anh says, "He was here on February 18, 1968. In the big battle with the American soldiers."

"Now hold on a minute," Stan says. "He's saying he was here fighting against us?" Stan points at the ground, holding the military grid map he's been carrying on this trip, as we plot our moments. "Here?"

"Yes," says Anh.

"Ask him how old he is."

"He says he's sixty-eight."

Stan doesn't swear much, but the look on his face is, *I'll be damned*.

"Ask him if he remembers"—a thought occurs to Stan—"ask him if he knows what that monument is over there."

And Stan points at the obelisk we'd seen earlier.

"Oh, that's to mark the battle, the men who died here. Americans and eight Vietnamese."

Stan still doesn't believe that Mr. Sinh was here. He also looks like he's about to cry. He looks so happy and sad at the same time. He looks like he doesn't know what to think about himself, his life, or anything.

"Ask him if he remembers the shoot-down. Ask him if he remembers a helicopter getting shot down."

Mr. Sinh says, "Yes," vigorously. He adds, "About three in the afternoon."

Stan says, "You're kidding me," because that is, in fact, about the time the helicopter he was in, after picking him up after the grenade attack, was shot down.

"And it was raining then too," says Mr. Sinh.

Stan's getting more excited by the moment.

"Have him show me where," he says, and he hands Anh a pen, who hands it to Mr. Sinh, and now the two men are closer, literally standing closer to each other, and while Stan could have handed Mr. Sinh the pen himself, he didn't. I think I know why. It didn't seem appropriate; some rules still needed to be followed. And it's this rule: that the two men are really finding out if they know each other, if they share something in common, mainly this act of combat, and if they do, they are not strangers, and therefore will instantly share a sense of intimacy that needs not to be created because it's always existed. That's the odd thing about war for men and women: after the fighting, they share a sense of personhood with putative enemies, whom they may never meet again but whom they know in a fundamental way by virtue of either having tried to kill each other.

As Stan looks on, Mr. Sinh opens his hand and lays the palm flat, pointing up at the sky, the hand is small and calloused, the nails bearing garlands of dirt, the badge of someone who works with his hands. I look at the hands and wonder about all the places they've been in the world since February 18, 1968: the objects they've picked up, the things they've done in anger and

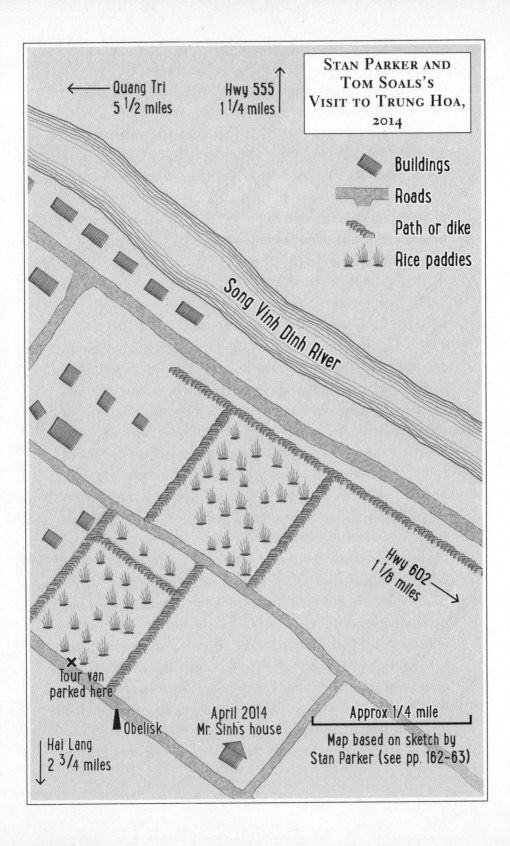

STAN PARKER AND
TOM SOALS'S
VISIT TO TRUNG HOA,
2014

← Quang Tri
5 1/2 miles

Hwy 555 ↑
1 1/4 miles

Buildings

Roads

Path or dike

Rice paddies

Song Vinh Dinh River

Hwy 602
1 1/8 miles →

✕
Tour van
parked here

▲ Obelisk

April 2014
Mr. Sinh's house

↓ Hai Lang
2 3/4 miles

Approx 1/4 mile

Map based on sketch by
Stan Parker (see pp. 162–63)

in friendship. There they are, the hands of the enemy, open now, just before the gaze of Stan Parker. Mr. Sinh begins drawing with ballpoint pen on his opened palm. He starts drawing a map of the village, but mostly of a rice paddy, and a dike, or water source, in the paddy. Before Mr. Sinh gets very far, Stan can already see where the map is going: the palm of his enemy is the center of the map, and the whole world flows from that, beyond the hand's edges, beyond the village of Trung Hoa, the province of Quang Tri, the country of Vietnam, India, Africa, the Atlantic Ocean, the Mississippi, to Colorado, city of Colorado Springs, where Stan Parker's life has come to rest in its final chapters and where he has spent his time laying out days as one more day to figure out what happened to him as a twenty-year-old from Gary, Indiana. And back now to Mr. Sinh's hand, the four square inches of his palm, where he has written in ink the site where Stan Parker's helicopter crashed, all of it right there, literally in the palm of his enemy's hand. It occurs to me that Mr. Sinh is maybe the only person on the planet who remembers this moment that has haunted Stan with the same level of detail that Stan Parker remembers it. Isn't that something? Who else is alive who was here that day? What are the odds that Stan and Tom would've driven into this village and intersected their journey with Mr. Sinh's walk down this quiet road?

Mr. Sinh, we find out, has heard that there were Americans in the village, and he'd left his house to see what was happening. Stan hands him the military map he's been carrying and watches as Mr. Sinh looks at the map, and then readjusts it, so that the top of the map is north. Stan sees Mr. Sinh do this, and it confirms for Stan that Mr. Sinh is a veteran. It further cements his sense of affinity with Mr. Sinh. This simple movement of the map has changed how they relate to each other.

Stan seems to relax, and Mr. Sinh does too; they are now long-lost friends. Stan hugs Mr. Sinh and Mr. Sinh smiles and hugs him back.

Stan and Tom invite Mr. Sinh to have lunch with us, and he accepts the invitation. All through the meal, Stan Parker keeps saying, "My god, I can't believe this. I can't believe we're here together."

"Please ask him what he did in the war," Stan tells Anh. Stan wants to know more. He feels he's onto something here, that the pieces of the puzzle may be falling into place: he knows what happened that day, but he's never been able to figure out all that happened. And who were the other people on the end of the gun? Who was the enemy?

Mr. Sinh explains that he'd been fighting for the Viet Cong in February 1968, and on that day, February 18, he and his cadre of guerrilla fighters had been worried that the Americans would come back in force because the day before, they'd killed a lot of American soldiers in an ambush and they'd braced themselves for a counterattack. Mr. Sinh then says that he was the leader of the VC cadre, and this gets Stan's further attention. He points over at the house, the metal-roofed house that Stan and I had looked at earlier, and says, "That was my command center. My headquarters." And then he adds, "It burned to the ground."

Stan says, "I saw it burn. I set it on fire—I mean . . ." He stops. He wants to back up and start from the beginning.

Mr. Sinh kind of helps him out here, by saying, "That was my machine gun there." He points to the obelisk. "My men were manning it."

"That was the machine gun I charged," says Stan, amazed.

After a moment, Mr. Sinh nods, acknowledging this. This moment completes a circle for Stan, a circle leading home.

He tells Mr. Sinh, "That was the machine gun that shot my

friends, and I took off running and got to about here"—and he points over to the dike in the rice paddy behind us—"and that's where I fired the rocket from."

Mr. Sinh says they thought they had killed the American soldier four or five different times, but he got up and kept charging them. "You are a lucky man." Mr. Sinh smiles.

Anh is quickly translating and keeping up. The information is passing back and forth between Stan and Mr. Sinh, causing a kind of transformation, a transubstantiation, even—the two men communing with each other through the efforts of recounting the tale.

Mr. Sinh explains that when the machine-gun position blew up, he was blown from his command building. Its roof started to burn and he and his men had to abandon it and dissolve into the woods. Hearing this fills in a part of the story for Stan, and he walks over to Mr. Sinh. Before Mr. Sinh can say much of anything, Stan embraces him in a massive hug. He's got a few inches on Mr. Sinh, and he hugs him again, and he's saying, "Oh, man, I can't believe this is happening!"

And, "I'm having so much fun!"

And further, "I'm having more fun here than I ever had in America, coming home."

They are holding each other, a few feet from where they last met forty-six years earlier. Mr. Sinh starts smiling too.

The two of them walk over to the obelisk inscribed with the names of the dead who had died during their fighting.

"I want to tell you something," Mr. Sinh says. "I want to tell that I have often thought of that day."

He pauses, and his face darkens: "I have never forgotten that day."

And here Stan's face goes very still. His eyes are shining. "I was trying to kill you and you were trying to kill me," he says.

"We were enemies," says Mr. Sinh, "but now we are brothers."
They hug each other and will not let go.
They both start to cry.
And then they smile.

EPILOGUE

Coming home now . . . what now of coming home? Stan Parker is walking home after high school wrestling practice when he spots her. Anna. Sitting on her front steps with her skirt drawn under her knees, she says, Hi, Stan, how are you? I am fine. I hear you're joining up. I did. When do you leave, Stan? This summer sometime. Sweetheart, where are you? Stan looks around to the rest of the squad and makes the signal to stop. A fist. Clenched. Filthy. His own.

Stop right now.

The squad drops, waits.

The tree line up yonder is so green. And here it comes, as they expected: gunfire.

Explosions, smoke.

Tim Anderson says, Ev'ry time we come here something happens! Al Dove opens up on the trees with the M-60, and the bamboo spits yellow fire back at the platoon. And right about then Darryl Lintner gets shot. Jerry Austin sees it, so does Paul Sudano. Lintner falls back on his butt and sits still. The guys wait for him to fall over. But he doesn't fall over. His rucksack is holding him up. He sits there, dying.

But in the minds of his friends, Darryl Lintner, age twenty-one, from Perryville, Missouri, is not dying. He will never die. He is falling backward toward the ground, which he will never reach. A man will live forever among the men who love him, who watch over him.

ACKNOWLEDGMENTS
AND SOURCES

Many excellent books have been written about Vietnam, about the reasons the United States entered this war, and whether it should have done so at all. This is not that kind of book. This is a story intensely focused on a group of young men who survived something they often did not understand, but which they knew had changed them. This is a story of their survival and homecoming.

Foremost, I want to thank members of Reconnaissance Platoon, 1/501st, 2nd Brigade, 101st Airborne Division, for sharing the story of their time in Vietnam. These men, like many veterans, have fought their war twice—once on the battlefield and thereafter in memory. Asking them to relive these intimate moments of terror, longing, and hope caused them discomfort, tears, anguish. I deeply appreciate their brave honesty with me and graceful empathy for one another.

In particular, I want to thank Stan and Anna Parker for allowing me into their lives to document a harrowing experience that shaped many things that followed for their family. Since leaving Vietnam in 1968, the war has never been far from Stan's mind, and he generously shared with me his voluminous letters, photographs, and personal writing about his journey as a soldier, husband, father, and civilian. As well, his record keeping, sketching, and map drawing were an invaluable source for the maps, illustrations, and platoon roster in this book. His dogged and fearless search to recollect what happened and how he felt about what was happening animates the journey described in this book, and should inspire, I think, other veterans with that question of their own: "What happened to me in Vietnam?"

Likewise, my deepest gratitude to the Recon Platoon members who invited me into their lives and Vietnam experience and allowed me to witness the complexity of their brotherhood, especially as it deepens as they reflect, now as older men, upon the past. Their courage in this undertaking infuses this story, I hope, with a visceral and emotional urgency. Thank you, Jerry Austin, Tom Soals, Al Dove, Paul Sudano, Michael Bradshaw, Tim Anderson, Dwight Lane, Dennis Tinkle, Tony Beke, Charlie Fowler, Marvin Acker, John Lucas, and Mortar Platoon member Ron Kuvik. Many of these men shared their letters, personal writing, and photographs about the places they fought, the people they met, and one another. Michael Bradshaw's recollections about the death of Charlie Pyle and other platoon-mates added a rich understanding of the platoon's brotherhood; Dwight Lane's own recollection about Pyle and his description to me of sending flowers to Pyle's grave was a revelation about this story's heart, that loss might be assuaged by love, by the honoring of another's memory. Stan Parker and Tom Soals generously offered their time and resources in planning and traveling to Vietnam. Thank you, Stan and Tom.

This book is mainly based on hours of interviews with the men involved in the events described; their personal monographs/ memoirs detailing their thoughts and experiences; letters written to and from Recon soldiers during their tours of duty; U.S. Army After-Action Reports and official records; author travel to

Vietnam and to scenes of battle with Stan Parker and Tom Soals; interviews with the friends and family of Recon members; platoon members' photographs taken in 1967 and 1968; and video and still photography taken by me and by the photographer Tony Demin documenting key areas of interest in Vietnam. During two trips to California, Anne Stanton and I met with members of Recon who'd reunited for multiday interviews, during which separate strands of one story began to entwine. Dialogue in the book recounted to me was done so by people who had participated in the conversations. Portions of the book were reviewed by some Recon members for their clarifications; and Stan Parker reviewed the entire manuscript. In both cases, the suggested corrections were invaluable. Researcher and fact-checker Julie Tate expertly, as ever, retrieved records and facts, and editor Heather Shaw helped with eleventh-hour research and assembly of the book's front and back matter. Thank you, Julie. Thank you, Heather.

I also consulted a number of books about the Tet's wider story in relation to the closely observed events within the Recon Platoon. Some of these books are: *Vietnam: A History* by Stanley Karnow; *Tet! The Turning Point in the Vietnam War* by Don Oberdorfer; *Big Story: How the American Press and Television Reported and Interpreted the Crisis of Tet 1968 in Vietnam and Washington* by Peter Braestrup; *The Cat from Hué: A Vietnam War Story* by John Laurence; *The Tet Offensive: A Concise History* by James H. Willbanks; *The Tet Offensive 1968: Turning Point in Vietnam* by James R. Arnold; *The Tet Offensive: Politics, War, and Public Opinion* by David F. Schmitz; *The Tet Offensive: A Brief History with Documents* by William Thomas Allison; *A Personal Memoir: An Account of the 2d Brigade and 2d Brigade Task Force, 101st Airborne Division, September 1967 through June 1968* by Colonel John H. Cushman; and *The 1968 Tet Offensive Battles of Quang Tri City and Hue* by Erik Villard. Historian Villard also graciously answered questions by phone and email. Further reading is found in the bibliography.

When I began researching, Stan Parker and I sat around his kitchen table in Colorado, as Stan, with boundless energy, pored over recently acquired maps and after-action reports, plotting and replotting his and the platoon's movements. For more than forty years, the events of the Tet Offensive had remained slightly out of focus—crystal clear in some regards; in others, the fighting had taken on the feeling of a fever dream. Watching him fix himself in a place and a time that had meant so much, but had seemed to mean so little to anyone else, was akin to watching someone's rebirth. As Stan's pencil moved over the map in meticulous cursive, a new sense of himself, of where he'd been, and of where he might be going emerged. Stan Parker had long hoped to arrive at a place where he was at peace. Perhaps now this destination is in sight.

Stan Parker, Tom Soals, Anne Stanton, and I are indebted to Mr. Vo Van Sinh in Trung Hoa, Vietnam, for graciously offering his home and his memories as a Viet Cong soldier, when our serendipitous meeting transformed this journey into a true homecoming. As well, Mr. Vo Thanh Tuat, of Danang, recounted his life as an officer in the North Vietnamese Army, beginning with his country's fight against the French at Dien Bien Phu. Facilitating these meetings were the irrepressible Bill Ervin and Nguyen Thi Tuyet Anh of Bamboo Moon Travel in Danang, whose professionalism and bonhomie made our road trip from Saigon to Hanoi a rich and enlightening experience. Mike Sieberg in Saigon and George Burchett in Hanoi helped us see the undertow that the "American War" still presses upon their adopted country. George Burchett recounted his father, author Wilfred Burchett's early excursions with Ho Chi Minh.

ACKNOWLEDGMENTS AND SOURCES

Other people also touched by the war offered their support. I want to thank Anna Parker for speaking with me about her life with Stan Parker, and Maureen Bell Osborn for sharing her insight about Stan Parker after his return from Vietnam, particularly about the day he retrieved his high school varsity jacket. Every soldier needs someone as caring as "Ma" Mickey Rinker, who mailed cookies and news of home from California to dozens of men in Echo Company, who eagerly wrote back. Thank you, Ma, for sharing these letters. Lastly, Thom Nolan shared his memory of his hometown neighbor Darryl Lintner, whose death, like Charlie Pyle's, transformed the platoon.

I'd like to thank the 101st Airborne Division Association for welcoming me at its annual reunion, where I interviewed Ron Kuvic. In the course of writing, I was fortunate to meet Jonathan Shay, whose landmark works *Odysseus in America* and *Achilles in Vietnam* plumb the deep channel that can be a veteran's troubled road home. Over dinner, Jan Scruggs recounted his inspirational work to bring to life the Vietnam Veterans Memorial Wall in Washington, D.C. These meetings affirmed that the war in Vietnam is with us today as one of America's unfinished epic narratives, a period of upheaval still in search of conclusion.

Thank you as well to Phil Caputo, Karl Marlantes, Sebastian Junger, Brian Castner, Brian Turner, David Finkel, Benjamin Busch, Hampton Sides, and Michael Paterniti for their presence at the National Writers Series, where some of the ideas animating this book were discussed. John Laurence offered key comments at an important moment. Some are old friends, others new acquaintances; all are exemplars nonpareil of a writer's task, which might be, to paraphrase T. S. Eliot, "to throw the nerves in patterns on a screen."

To others: Our friends Grant and Paulette Parsons have made life better. John and Christie Bacon provided much appreciated encouragement. Sid Van Slyke and Lloyd Phillips help keep home fires burning, and Marina Call and Cindy Weaver keep the engines running at the National Writers Series. A highly caffeinated thank-you to Jeff and Misha Neidorfler at Morsels, along with their staff, Luke Norris, Ingrid Messing, Tony Pasquino, Dalton Cooper, Connor Steinbauer, and Aleshia Oosterhart; and to Missy and Sean Kickbush and their Brew crew—Patrick Tesner, Jeremiah Burnett, and Corie Wickham—where I wrote parts of this book. Thanks as well to Amy Reynolds and staff at Horizon Books; and to Dave Denison and Jeff Libman at Amical.

Thank you to Sloan Harris and Heather Karpas at ICM Partners for keeping this writer on track. Sloan is the loyal agent and friend every writer and every book needs, and whose support and understanding of story and process have kept this project moving. In film and TV, I am indebted to Ron Bernstein and James Robins Early at ICM Partners, and Ron West at Thruline Entertainment for their continued support of my books and screenwriting. Thank you to Jerry Bruckheimer, Chad Oman, and Melissa Reid for your belief in *Horse Soldiers*. To Mark Gordon, thank you for keeping the story alive.

I owe an immense debt of gratitude to Scribner, my publisher, and to Colin Harrison, its editor in chief. I repeat: Colin is amazing. He read a book proposal about a war few had wanted to remember and believed in the story and my telling of it. Thank you, Colin, for your patience and ideas, which shifted this book's shape, my perception of it, and made both better. I remain grateful. Likewise, I'm very appreciative of Sarah Goldberg's editorial and organizational brilliance. Thank you!

I also want to thank Susan Moldow, Roz Lippel, and publisher Nan Graham for their support and care of my books and writing. I'm very, very lucky to be in their company. I'm also grateful to Brian Belfiglio, Katherine Monaghan, Kara Watson, Ashley

ACKNOWLEDGMENTS AND SOURCES

Gilliam, and Lauren Lavelle in Scribner's publicity department, for their tirelessness in getting books out into the world, where they can be heard and read. Thank you as well to Jeff Umbro of Umbro Media and Jason Bean of JBean Media. Without you, it'd be awfully quiet out there. A huge thank you also to Kathleen Rizzo and Elisa Rivlin for your edit and counsel, and to Erich Hobbing for his fabulous book design.

To my parents, Bonnie and Derald Stanton, and Deb and Tony Demin, my sister and brother-in-law, and their children, Genessa and Wylie, thank you for your support, good cheer, love. Tony, you are a photographer whose pictures are always a complete surprise yet seem inevitable. Thank you for your stunning images of our trip in Vietnam.

To my family. First and last, there is Anne.

She made the journey of this project every step of the way, both across Vietnam and across these pages, managing at the same time two jobs of her own. My gratitude to her is endless, my admiration boundless. Who knew a long-ago pickup truck ride to Montana, during which I tried to impress you by reading James Wright and Yeats poems, would lead us to Vietnam, and to here, to our children, John, Katherine, and William August McCoy Stanton?

To you four: I wish you adventure and the knowledge you are loved unconditionally, and that home is never far. All of you lived this story over many dinner conversations and during many silences of my absences.

I cannot end without saying this: Welcome home, everyone.

BIBLIOGRAPHY AND SUGGESTED READING

BOOKS

Allison, William Thomas. *The Tet Offensive: A Brief History with Documents*. New York: Routledge, 2008.

Anderson, Dale. *The Tet Offensive: Turning Point of the Vietnam War*. Minneapolis: Compass Point Books, 2006.

Anderson, David L. *The Vietnam War*. New York: Palgrave Macmillan, 2005.

Ang Cheng Guan. *The Vietnam War from the Other Side: The Vietnamese Communists' Perspective*. New York: RoutledgeCurzon, 2002.

Appy, Christian G. *American Reckoning: The Vietnam War and Our National Identity*. New York: Viking, 2015.

———. *Patriots: The Vietnam War Remembered from All Sides*. New York: Penguin, 2003.

Arnold, James R. *Tet Offensive 1968: Turning Point in Vietnam*. Westport, CT: Praeger Publishers, 2004.

Bach, Vu, et al. *The 30-Year War, 1945–1975*. Hanoi, Vietnam: Thé Giói Publishers, 2000.

Baritz, Loren. *Backfire: Vietnam—The Myths That Made Us Fight, the Illusions That Helped Us Lose, the Legacy That Haunts Us Today*. New York: Ballantine Books, 1985.

Barrett, David M. *Uncertain Warriors: Lyndon Johnson and His Vietnam Advisors*. Lawrence: University Press of Kansas, 1993.

Berman, Larry. *Lyndon Johnson's War*. New York: W. W. Norton, 1989.

Bonds, Ray, ed. *The Vietnam War: The Illustrated History of the Conflict in Southeast Asia*. New York: Military Press, 1988.

Boutwell, Jerry W. *Stories of War I Tell*. Victoria, BC: Trafford Publishing, 1995.

Braestrup, Peter. *Big Story: How the American Press and Television Reported and Interpreted the Crisis of Tet 1968 in Vietnam and Washington.* Two vols. Boulder, CO: Westview Press, 1977.

Brokaw, Tom. *Boom! Talking About the Sixties.* New York: Random House, 2007.

Brown, Jim. *Impact Zone: The Battle of the DMZ in Vietnam, 1967–1968.* Tuscaloosa: University of Alabama Press, 2004.

Brown, Richard L. *Palace Gate: Under Siege in Hue City: Tet, January 1968.* London: Schiffer Publishing, 1997.

Bryant, Russ, and Susan Bryant. *Screaming Eagles: 101st Airborne Division.* St. Paul: Zenith Press, 2007.

Bui Kim Hong, ed. *President Ho Chi Minh Biography and Career.* Hanoi, Vietnam: Culture and Information Publisher, 2011.

——. *President Ho Chi Minh's Living and Working Place in the Presidential Palace Area.* Hanoi, Vietnam: Thé Giói Publishers, 2011.

Burchett, Wilfred G. *Grasshoppers & Elephants: Why Viet Nam Fell.* New York: Urizen Books, 1977.

——. *Vietnam: Inside Story of the Guerilla War.* New York: International Publishers, 1965.

Burke, Tracey. *The Tet Offensive, January–April 1968.* New York: Wiesel and Wieser, Inc., 1988.

Buzzanco, Robert. *Masters of War: Military Dissent & Politics in the Vietnam Era.* New York: Cambridge University Press, 1996.

Cable, Larry. *Unholy Grail: The US and the Wars in Vietnam, 1965–8.* New York: Routledge, 1991.

Campagna, Anthony S. *The Economic Consequences of the Vietnam War.* Westport, CT: Praeger Publishers, 1991.

Chien Thang. *Highway 9—Khe Sanh Victory 1968.* Hue, Vietnam: Nha Xuat Ban Thuan Hoa, 2010.

Coan, James P. *Con Thien: The Hill of Angels.* Tuscaloosa: University of Alabama Press, 2004.

Currey, Cecil B. *Victory at Any Cost: The Genius of Viet Nam's General Vo Nguyen Giap.* Washington, DC: Brassey's, 1997.

Davidson, Phillip B. *Vietnam at War: The History, 1946–1975.* New York: Oxford University Press, 1988.

Dougan, Clark, and Stephen Weiss. *The American Experience in Vietnam: Reflections on an Era.* Minneapolis: Boston Publishing Company, 2014.

Duiker, William J. *Ho Chi Minh: A Life.* New York: Hyperion, 2000.

——. *Sacred War: Nationalism and Revolution in a Divided Vietnam*. New York: McGraw-Hill, 1995.

Elliott, David W. P. *The Vietnamese War: Revolution and Social Change in the Mekong Delta, 1930–1975*. Two vols. Armonk, NY: M. E. Sharpe, 2003.

Errington, Elizabeth Jane, and B. J. C. McKercher, eds. *The Vietnam War as History*. Westport, CT: Praeger Publishers, 1990.

Falk, Richard A. *Appropriating Tet*. Princeton, NJ: Princeton University Center of International Studies, 1988.

Fall, Bernard B. *Street Without Joy*. Mechanicsburg, PA: Stackpole Books, 1994.

Fenn, Charles. *Ho Chi Minh: A Biographical Introduction*. New York: Charles Scribner's Sons, 1973.

FitzGerald, Frances. *Fire in the Lake: The Vietnamese and the Americans in Vietnam*. New York: Vintage Books, 1972.

Ford, Ronnie E. *Tet 1968: Understanding the Surprise*. London: Frank Cass, 1995.

Foster, Randy E. M. *Vietnam Firebases 1965–73: American and Australian Forces*. Oxford, UK: Osprey Publishing, 2007.

Gadd, Charles. *Line Doggie: Foot Soldier in Vietnam*. Novato, CA: Presidio Press, 1987.

Gaiduk, Ilya V. *The Soviet Union and the Vietnam War*. Chicago: Ivan R. Dee, 1996.

Gardner, Lloyd C. *Pay Any Price: Lyndon Johnson and the Wars for Vietnam*. Chicago: Ivan R. Dee, 1995.

Gettleman, Marvin E., Jane Franklin, Marilyn B. Young, and H. Bruce Franklin, eds. *Vietnam and America: A Documented History*. New York: Grove Press, 1995.

Gilbert, Marc Jason, ed. *Why the North Won the Vietnam War*. New York: Palgrave, 2002.

Gilbert, Marc Jason, and William Head, eds. *The Tet Offensive*. Westport, CT: Praeger Publishers, 1996.

Goscha, Christopher. *Vietnam: A New History*. New York: Basic Books, 2016.

Halberstam, David. *The Best and the Brightest*. New York: Fawcett Publications, 1992.

——. *Ho*. Plymouth, UK: Rowman & Littlefield Publishers, 1971.

Hallin, Daniel C. *The "Uncensored War": The Media and Vietnam*. New York: Oxford University Press, 1986.

Hammel, Eric. *Fire in the Streets: The Battle for Hue, Tet 1968.* Chicago: Contemporary Books, 1991.

——. *Khe Sanh: Siege in the Clouds.* New York: Crown Publishers, 1989.

Hammond, William M. *Reporting Vietnam: Media & Military at War.* Lawrence: University Press of Kansas, 1998.

Ha Thanh Hung. *The Documentary Album of Cu Chi 1960–1975, Album 2.* Ho Chi Minh, Vietnam: Nha Xuat Ban Mui Ca Mau, 2002.

Hearden, Patrick J. *The Tragedy of Vietnam.* 2nd ed. New York: Pearson Longman, 2005.

Herring, George C. *America's Longest War: The United States and Vietnam, 1950–1975.* 4th ed. Boston: McGraw-Hill, 2002.

——. *LBJ and Vietnam: A Different Kind of War.* Austin: University of Texas Press, 1994.

Hess, Gary R. *Vietnam and the United States: Origins and Legacy of War.* Revised ed. New York: Twayne Publishers, 1998.

Hoang Khoi. *The Ho Chi Minh Trail.* Hanoi, Vietnam: Thé Giói Publishers, 2008.

Hoang Minh Thao. *The Vietnamese Military: During the Resistance War against the U.S. for National Salvation and Defense.* Hanoi, Vietnam: Thé Giói Publishers, 2010.

Hoang Ngoc Lung. *The General Offensives of 1968–69.* Washington, DC: U.S. Army Center of Military History, 1981.

Hoang Van Thai. *How South Vietnam Was Liberated.* Hanoi, Vietnam: Thé Giói Publishers, 1996.

Hunt, Michael H. *Lyndon Johnson's War: America's Cold War Crusade in Vietnam, 1945–1968.* New York: Hill & Wang, 1996.

Hunt, Richard A. *Pacification: The American Struggle for Vietnam's Hearts and Minds.* Boulder, CO: Westview Press, 1995.

Isserman, Maurice, and Michael Kazin. *America Divided: The Civil War of the 1960s.* 3rd ed. New York: Oxford University Press, 2008.

Jones, Colonel Robert E. *History of the 101st Airborne Division: Screaming Eagles, The First 50 Years.* Nashville: Turner Publishing, 2005.

Junger, Sebastian. *War.* New York: Hachette Book Group, 2010.

Kaiser, Charles. *1968 in America: Music, Politics, Chaos, Counterculture, and the Shaping of a Generation.* New York: Grove Press, 1988.

Karnow, Stanley. *Vietnam: A History.* New York: Penguin, 1984.

Kaufman, Michael T. *1968.* New York: Roaring Brook Press, 2009.

Kelley, Michael P. *Where We Were in Vietnam: A Comprehensive Guide to the Firebases, Military Installations and Naval Vessels of the Vietnam War, 1945–75*. Ashland, OR: Hellgate Press, 2002.

Knauer, Kelly, ed. *1968: War Abroad, Riots at Home, Fallen Leaders and Lunar Dreams: The Year That Changed the World*. New York: Time Inc. Home Entertainment, 2008.

Kolko, Gabriel. *Anatomy of a War: Vietnam, the United States, and the Modern Historical Experience*. New York: New Press, 1994.

Krepinevich, Andrew F., Jr. *The Army and Vietnam*. Baltimore: Johns Hopkins University Press, 1986.

Kurlansky, Mark. *1968: The Year That Rocked the World*. New York: Random House, 2004.

LaFeber, Walter. *The Deadly Bet: LBJ, Vietnam, and the 1968 Election*. Lanham, MD: Rowman & Littlefield, 2005.

Langguth, A. J. *Our Vietnam: The War, 1954–1975*. New York: Simon & Schuster, 2000.

Lanning, Michael Lee, and Dan Cragg. *Inside the VC and the NVA: The Real Story of North Vietnam's Armed Forces*. College Station: Texas A&M University Press, 2008.

Laurence, John. *The Cat from Hué: A Vietnam War Story*. New York: Public Affairs, 2002.

Lawrence, Mark Atwood. *The Vietnam War: A Concise International History*. New York: Oxford University Press, 2008.

Lewis, Adrian R. *The American Culture of War: The History of U.S. Military Force from World War II to Operation Iraqi Freedom*. New York: Routledge, 2007.

Lewy, Guenter. *America in Vietnam*. New York: Oxford University Press, 1980.

Lind, Michael. *Vietnam: The Necessary War*. New York: Free Press, 1999.

Logevall, Fredrik. *Embers of War: The Fall of an Empire and the Making of America's Vietnam*. New York: Random House, 2013.

——. *The Origins of the Vietnam War*. Essex, UK: Pearson Education Limited, 2001.

Long, Ngo Vinh. *The Tet Offensive and Its Aftermath*. Ithaca, NY: Cornell University Press, 1991.

Macdonald, Peter. *Giap: The Victor in Vietnam*. New York: W. W. Norton, 1993.

Mangold, Tom, and John Penycate. *The Tunnels of Cu Chi*. New York: Presidio Press, 2005.

McGarvey, Patrick J. *Visions of Victory: Selected Vietnamese Communist*

Military Writings, 1964–1968. Stanford, CA: Hoover Institution Press, 1969.

McNamara, Robert S. *In Retrospect: The Tragedy and Lessons of Vietnam.* New York: Times Books, 1995.

McNamara, Robert S., James Blight, and Robert K. Brigham. *Argument Without End: In Search of Answers to the Vietnam Tragedy.* New York: Public Affairs, 1999.

Military History Institute of Vietnam. *Victory in Vietnam: The Official History of the People's Army of Vietnam, 1954–1975.* Translated by Merle L. Pribbenow. Foreword by William J. Duiker. Lawrence: University Press of Kansas, 2002.

Moss, George Donelson. *Vietnam: An American Ordeal.* 4th ed. Upper Saddle River, NJ: Prentice Hall, 2002.

Murphy, Edward F. *Semper Fi Vietnam: From Da Nang to the DMZ, Marine Corps Campaigns, 1965–1975.* Novato, CA: Presidio Press, 1997.

Nelson, Craig. *The Age of Radiance: The Epic Rise and Dramatic Fall of the Atomic Era.* New York: Scribner, 2014.

Nguyen, Lien-Hang T. *Hanoi's War: An International History of the War for Peace in Vietnam.* Chapel Hill: University of North Carolina Press, 2012.

Nguyen, Viet Thanh. *Nothing Ever Dies: Vietnam and the Memory of War.* Cambridge, MA: Harvard University Press, 2016.

Nha Ca. *Mourning Headband for Hue: An Account of the Battle for Hue, Vietnam 1968.* Bloomington: Indiana University Press, 2014.

Nolan, Keith W. *The Battle for Hue: Tet 1968.* Novato, CA: Presidio Press, 1983.

———. *The Battle for Saigon: Tet 1968.* Novato, CA: Presidio Press, 1996.

Oberdorfer, Don. *Tet! The Turning Point in the Vietnam War.* New York: Da Capo Press, 1984.

Olson, James S., and Randy Roberts. *Where the Domino Fell: America and Vietnam, 1945–2004.* 4th ed. Maplecrest, NY: Brandywine Press, 2004.

O'Nan, Stewart, ed. *The Vietnam Reader: The Definitive Collection of American Fiction and Nonfiction on the War.* New York: Anchor Books, 1998.

Page, Tim, and John Pimlott. *Nam: The Vietnam Experience 1965–75.* New York: Barnes & Noble, 1995.

Pearson, Willard. *Vietnam Studies—The War in the Northern Provinces, 1966–1968.* Washington, DC: Department of the Army, 1975.

BIBLIOGRAPHY AND SUGGESTED READING

The Pentagon Papers: The Defense Department History of United States Decisionmaking on Vietnam. Gravel Edition. Five vols. Boston: Beacon Press, 1971–72.

Perlstein, Rick. *Nixonland: The Rise of a President and the Fracturing of America.* New York: Scribner, 2008.

Phillips, Rufus. *Why Vietnam Matters: An Eyewitness Account of Lessons Not Learned.* Annapolis, MD: Naval Institute Press, 2008.

Pike, Douglas. *PAVN: People's Army of North Vietnam.* Novato, CA: Presidio Press, 1986.

Pisor, Robert. *The End of the Line: The Siege of Khe Sanh.* New York: W. W. Norton, 2002.

Prados, John. *The Blood Road: The Ho Chi Minh Trail and the Vietnam War.* New York: John Wiley & Sons, 1999.

———. *Vietnam: The History of an Unwinnable War, 1945–1975.* Lawrence: University of Kansas Press, 2009.

Prados, John, and Ray W. Stubbe. *Valley of Decision: The Siege of Khe Sanh.* Boston: Houghton Mifflin, 1991.

Rapport, Leonard, and Arthur Norwood Jr. *Rendezvous with Destiny: History of the 101st Airborne Division.* Old Saybrook, CT: Konecky & Konecky, 1948.

Rawson, Andrew. *Tet Offensive 1968: Battle Story.* Gloucestershire, UK: Spellmount, 2013.

Reporting Vietnam: Part One, American Journalism 1959–1969. New York: Library of America, 1998.

Riboud, Marc, text by Philippe Devillers. *North Vietnam: Face of North Vietnam.* New York: Holt, Rinehart &Winston, 1970.

Robbins, James S. *This Time We Win: Revisiting the Tet Offensive.* New York: Encounter Books, 2012.

Rottman, Gordon L. *Khe Sanh 1967–68: Marines Battle for Vietnam's Vital Hilltop Base.* London: Osprey Publishing, 2005.

———. *North Vietnamese Army Soldiers 1958–75.* Oxford, UK: Osprey Publishing, 2009.

———. *Viet Cong and NVA Tunnels and Fortifications of the Vietnam War.* Oxford, UK: Osprey Publishing, 2006.

———. *Viet Cong Fighter.* Oxford, UK: Osprey Publishing, 2007.

Schell, Jonathan. *The Military Half: An Account of Destruction in Quang Ngai and Quang Tin.* New York: Alfred A. Knopf, 1968.

Schmitz, David F. *The Tet Offensive: Politics, War, and Public Opinion.* Lanham, MD: Rowman & Littlefield, 2005.

Shaplen, Robert. *The Road from War: Vietnam 1965–1970*. New York: Harper & Row, 1970.

Sharp, U. S. Grant. *Strategy for Defeat: Vietnam in Retrospect*. Novato, CA: Presidio Press, 1978.

Shay, Jonathan. *Achilles in Vietnam: Combat Trauma and the Undoing of Character*. New York: Scribner, 1994.

———. *Odysseus in America: Combat Trauma and the Trials of Homecoming*. New York: Scribner, 2002.

Sheehan, Neil. *A Bright Shining Lie: John Paul Vann and America in Vietnam*. New York: Vintage Books, 1989.

Shore, Moyer S. *The Battle of Khe Sanh*. Washington, DC: Marine Corps History and Museums Division, 1969.

Shulimson, Jack, Leonard A. Blaisol, Charles R. Smith, and David A. Dawson. *U.S. Marines in Vietnam: The Defining Year, 1968*. Washington, DC: Marine Corps History and Museums Division, 1997.

Shulzinger, Robert D. *A Time for War: The United States and Vietnam, 1945–1975*. New York: Oxford University Press, 1997.

Silverman, Mike. *Vietnam: The Real War: A Photographic History by the Associated Press*. New York: Abrams, 2013.

Steinman, Ron. *The Soldiers' Story: Vietnam in Their Own Words, An Illustrated Edition*. New York: Wellfleet Press, 2015.

Summers, Harry G., Jr. *On Strategy: A Critical Analysis of the Vietnam War*. Novato, CA: Presidio Press, 1982.

Taylor, Sandra C. *Vietnamese Women at War: Fighting for Ho Chi Minh and the Revolution*. Lawrence: University Press of Kansas, 1999.

Thanh Co. *Quangtri Citadel*. Hue, Vietnam: Nha Xuat Ban Thuan Hoa, 2010.

Tran Dinh Dung. *The Document Album of Cu Chi 1960–1975*. Ho Chi Minh, Vietnam: Nha Xuat Ban Mui Ca Mau, 2002.

Truong Nhu Tang with David Chanoff and Doan Van Toai. *A Viet Cong Memoir: An Inside Account of the Vietnam War and Its Aftermath*. New York: Vintage Books, 1986.

Tucker, Spencer C., ed. *The Encyclopedia of the Vietnam War: A Political, Social & Military History*. New York: Oxford University Press, 1998.

Turley, William S. *The Second Indochina War: A Short Political and Military History, 1954–1975*. Boulder, CO: Westview Press, 1986.

Turner, Karen Gottschang, with Phan Thanh Hao. *Even the Women Must Fight: Memories of War from North Vietnam*. New York: John Wiley & Sons, 1998.

Turner, Kathleen J. *Lyndon Johnson's Dual War: Vietnam and the Press.* Chicago: University of Chicago Press, 1985.

The Vietnam Wars: 50 Years Ago—Two Countries Torn Apart. New York: Life Books, 2014.

Villard, Erik. *The 1968 TET Offensive Battles of Quang Tri City and Hue.* Washington, DC: U.S. Army Center of Military History, 2016.

Warr, Nicholas. *Phase Line Green: The Battle for Hue, 1968.* Annapolis, MD: Naval Institute Press, 1997.

Warren, James A. *Giap: The General Who Defeated America in Vietnam.* New York: Palgrave MacMillan, 2013.

Werner, Jayne S., and Luu Doan Huynh, eds. *The Vietnam War: Vietnamese and American Perspectives.* Armonk, NY: M. E. Sharpe, 1992.

Westheider, James E. *The Vietnam War: Daily Life Through History.* Westport, CT: Greenwood Press, 2007.

Westmoreland, William C. *A Soldier Reports.* New York: Da Capo Press, 1989.

Willbanks, James H. *The Tet Offensive: A Concise History.* New York: Columbia University Press, 2007.

———, ed. *Vietnam War: The Essential Reference Guide.* Santa Barbara, CA: ABC-CLIO, 2013.

———. *Vietnam War Almanac: An In-Depth Guide to the Most Controversial Conflict in American History.* New York: Skyhorse Publishing, 2009.

Wirtz, James J. *The Tet Offensive: Intelligence Failure in War.* Ithaca, NY: Cornell University Press, 1991.

Worth, Richard. *Tet Offensive.* Philadelphia: Chelsea House Publications, 2002.

Young, Marilyn B. *The Vietnam Wars: 1945–1990.* New York: HarperCollins, 1991.

Young, Marilyn B., and Robert Buzzanco, eds. *A Companion to the Vietnam War.* Oxford, UK: Blackwell Publishing, 2002.

Zhai, Qiang. *China & the Vietnam Wars, 1950–1975.* Chapel Hill: University of North Carolina Press, 2000.

Zumwalt, James G. *Bare Feet, Iron Will: Stories from the Other Side of Vietnam's Battlefields.* Jacksonville, FL: Fortis Publishing, 2010.

JOURNALS, MAGAZINES, AND NEWSPAPERS

The 101st Airborne 1968 Vietnam Yearbook. Oklahoma City: Paseo Press, 1985.

Culbert, David. "Television's Visual Impact on Decision-Making in the USA, 1968: The Tet Offensive and Chicago's Democratic National Convention." *Journal of Contemporary History* 33, no. 3, July 1998.

Geyelin, Philip. "It's Not Just 'Vietnam Syndrome.'" *Washington Post*, December 15, 1987.

Guan, Ang Cheng. "Decision-Making Leading to the Tet Offensive (1968)—The Vietnamese Perspective." *Journal of Contemporary History* 33, no. 3, July 1998.

———. "Khe Sanh—From the Perspective of the North Vietnamese Communists." *War in History* 8, no. 1, 2001.

Haberman, Clyde. "Agent Orange's Long Legacy, for Vietnam and Veterans." *New York Times*, May 11, 2014.

Hanson, Victor Davis. "The Meaning of Tet." *American Heritage* 52, no. 3, May 2001.

Journal of Contemporary History 33, no. 3, July 1998.

Ornsein, Charles, Hannah Fresques, and Mike Hixenbaugh. "The Children of Agent Orange." *ProPublica* and *Virginian Pilot*, December 16, 2016.

Pach, Chester J., Jr. "TV's 1968: War, Politics, and Violence on the Network Evening News." *South Central Review* 16, no. 4, Winter 1999–Spring 2000.

The Tet Offensive: The History and Legacy of the Most Famous Military Campaign of the Vietnam War. Charles River Editors.

"Tet Offensive: Turning Point in Vietnam War." *New York Times*, January 31, 1988.

Vietnam, 28, no. 5, February 2016

Vietnam, 29, no. 5, February 2017.

Woods, Randall Bennett. "LBJ, Politics, and 1968." *South Central Review* 16, no. 4, Winter 1999–Spring 2000.

BIBLIOGRAPHY AND SUGGESTED READING

UNPUBLISHED MATERIALS

Acker, Marvin. Correspondence, 1967–68.

Austin, Jerry. Correspondence, 1967–68.

Beke, Anthony. "Stressor Statement," August 10, 2009.

Beke, Joseph. Correspondence concerning Anthony Beke, July 28, 2009.

Bradshaw, Michael, "Another Year."

———. "Burning the Shit."

———. "Charles R. Pyle."

———. "E Co-Recon, 1st Bn/501st Inf. Airborne, 101st Airborne Div. Rep. of Vietnam, Dec. 1967 to Dec. 1968: Notations Regarding the Death of Unit Members During the First Year 'In Country.' "

———. "My Bestest Good Ol' Buddy Ever."

———. "My Nickname, Mad Monk."

———. "Why, Please?"

Cushman, Lieutenant General John (ret.). "Forty Years Ago This Week Index, Second Brigade Task Force of 101st ABN Division."

———. "Personal Memoir, September 1967–June 1968."

———. "Recon Plt, 1st (Abn) 501st, 2nd Brigade, 10-1st Abn Div, December 1967 thru 1968. Combined chronological listing of information retrieved from Commanders (1/501) Situation Reports, 1/501 After-Action Reports (AARs), and remarks from Personal Memoir account 2nd Bde, 101st Abn Div Sep 67–June 68."

Fowler, Charlie. Correspondence, 1967–68.

Parker, Stan. Correspondence, 1966–68, personal memoir.

Various sources; letters sent to and received by R. F. "Mickey" Rinker, Napa, CA; December 1967–January 1969.

GOVERNMENT DOCUMENTS

Combat After-Action Reports, November 30, 1967–January 4, 1969.

Commander's Situation Reports, November 30, 1967–January 4, 1969.

Daily Staff Journal or Duty Officer's Log, November 30, 1967–January 4, 1969.

Intelligence Summaries, November 30, 1967–January 4, 1969.

Operational Report/Lessons Learned, August 1967–October 1968.

Operation Orders, November 30, 1967–January 4, 1969.

Operations Summaries, November 30, 1967–January 4, 1969.

Van Som Pham and Van Duong Le. "Viet Cong 'Tet' Offensive 1968, Part 1," Bibliogov Project.

———. "Viet Cong 'Tet' Offensive 1968, Part 2," Bibliogov Project.

———. "Viet Cong 'Tet' Offensive 1968, Part 3," Bibliogov Project.

WEB SOURCES

Bradshaw, Melissa. "A Life Lived," www.newspaper.twinfallspubliclibrary.org.

Bradshaw, Michael. "LZ Jane," www.angelfire.com/rebellion/101abndiv vietvets/page24storybradshaw1.html.

———. "The Old Unit," www.angelfire/rebellion/101abndivvietvets /page28storybradshaw3.html.

———. "There Have Been Days," http://lzsally.com/library/stories/days .php.

———. "The Truth of It All," www.angelfire.com/rebellion/101abndivviet vets/page232BradshawTruth.html.

Kuvik, Ron. "Reciprocity," www.angelfire/rebellion/101abndivvietvets/ page27storykuvik.html.

"My Lai Massacre," www.history.com/topics/vietnam-war/my-lai-massacre, 2009.

"Saigon Execution: Murder of a Vietcong by Saigon Police Chief, 1968," www.rarehistoricalphotos.com/Saigon-execution-1968.

Smith, Ray. "U.S. vs NVA Casualties," rjsmith.com

ABOUT THE AUTHOR

Doug Stanton is the author of the *New York Times* bestsellers *In Harm's Way: The Sinking of the USS* Indianapolis *and the Extraordinary Story of Its Survivors* and *Horse Soldiers: The Extraordinary Story of a Band of U.S. Soldiers Who Rode to Victory in Afghanistan*, which is the basis for a Jerry Bruckheimer–produced movie by the same name, starring Chris Hemsworth and Michael Shannon, to be released by Warner Bros. in 2018. Stanton is a founder of the National Writers Series, a year-round book festival, and lives in his hometown of Traverse City, Michigan, with his wife, Anne Stanton, and their three children, John, Katherine, and Will. He attended Hampshire College and the University of Iowa Writers' Workshop. His writing has appeared in the *New York Times*, the *New York Times Book Review*, *Time*, the *Washington Post*, *Men's Journal*, the *Daily Beast*, and *Newsweek*, and in *Esquire* and *Outside*, where he has been a contributing editor.